M000080630

For my oldest — and loveliest Arthurian friend — with gratitude and affection.

Dor

King Arthur in Popular Culture

For Sally Slocum

King Arthur in Popular Culture

Edited by Elizabeth S. Sklar *and*
Donald L. Hoffman

FOREWORD BY ALAN LUPACK

McFarland & Company, Inc., Publishers
Jefferson, North Carolina, and London

Library of Congress Cataloguing-in-Publication Data

King Arthur in popular culture / edited by Elizabeth S. Sklar and
Donald L. Hoffman ; foreword by Alan Lupack.
    p.   cm.
    Includes bibliographical references and index.
    ISBN 0-7864-1257-7 (softcover : 50# alkaline paper) ∞
    1. Arthur, King—Influence. 2. Popular culture—United
States—History—20th century. 3. Popular culture—Great
Britain—History—20th century. 4. Arthurian romances—
Adaptations—History and criticism. I. Sklar, Elizabeth Sherr.
II. Hoffman, Donald L., 1940–
DA152.5.A7K57   2002
942.01'4—dc21   2002000872

British Library cataloguing data are available

©2002 Elizabeth S. Sklar and Donald L. Hoffman.
All rights reserved

*No part of this book may be reproduced or transmitted in any form
or by any means, electronic or mechanical, including photocopying
or recording, or by any information storage and retrieval system,
without permission in writing from the publisher.*

On the covers—front: a spinner from a Prince Valiant
board game (photograph by Elizabeth S. Sklar); back:
Lancelot and Merlin nesting dolls (photograph by
Lloyd Smith, City of Edinburgh Council)

Manufactured in the United States of America

McFarland & Company, Inc., Publishers
  Box 611, Jefferson, North Carolina 28640
  www.mcfarlandpub.com

Contents

Music

Fun and Games

The Internet

Esoterica

Foreword

ALAN LUPACK

Some years ago at a meeting of the Popular Culture Association, I met Sally Slocum at a session in which someone was giving a paper about the Arthurian legend in popular culture. We began speaking about other papers on the topic at the conference and lamented the fact that there was no group specifically for the study of Arthuriana as there was for the study of detective fiction, science fiction, films, and any number of other elements of popular culture. Sally decided to do something about that and went on to organize and to chair for many years the Arthurian Legend section of the Popular Culture Association, a position in which she was succeeded by one of the editors of this volume, Elizabeth Sklar.

Though traditionally only the best of Arthurian literature, art, and music has been deemed worthy of scholarly attention, the work presented in the Arthurian section of the Popular Culture Association and other forums has demonstrated the importance of looking at popular manifestations of the Matter of Britain—even for the understanding of the "great" Arthurian works. To take an example from the nineteenth century: it becomes immediately evident how popular Tennyson's *Idylls of the King* and his other Arthurian poems were when one considers how present they were in Victorian and early twentieth-century society, not only through the numerous editions of the poems but through the artifacts that brought them into people's everyday lives. A series of twelve Minton tiles depicting scenes from the *Idylls,* for instance, appeared in fireplaces, in furniture, in flower boxes, and in trivets. It says a lot about the impact of the *Idylls* and about Victorian attitudes towards women that a housewife might lift her teapot and see an image of Guinevere grovelling before Arthur because she has been unfaithful. Arthurian images based on Tennyson's poems could

1

also be found on buttons, in children's coloring and picture books, and in a range of art and illustration. All of these manifestations suggest the depth to which the legends have penetrated the popular-cultural idiom.

Tennyson's "Sir Galahad," which presented an idealized view of the Grail knight, became so popular that it was memorized and repeated. The image of Galahad by George Frederick Watts, believed to depict that ideal, was used as an inspirational model when the Arthurian legends were taken up by those interested in providing wholesome examples for the young. First in America and then in England, Arthurian youth groups were formed to help boys and girls deal with the trials of adolescence. Initially inspired by great writers and artists, these groups soon became a popular phenomenon, spreading throughout America and influencing the development of the Boy Scouts. This movement caused hundreds of thousands of youngsters to read about and imitate the knights and ladies of Camelot. Every chapter of one such youth group, the Knights of King Arthur, was advised to provide the boys with a copy of Watts' painting. Perhaps it is the influence of these clubs that explains why the Grail, the unique object that could be obtained only by the chosen few, has now become a cliché. Every sport has its Holy Grail, news magazines abound with Grails, and computer magazines are full of them—the Grail of laptop batteries, the Grail of PDAs, the Grail of voice and data integration, Java as a corporate Holy Grail, and even the "Holy e-Grail" of "getting enough bandwidth."

The pervasiveness of Arthurian material in twentieth-century culture is a matter of much interest, and the study of such a pervasive motif surely reveals much about our society. New Arthurian films are regularly released; TV shows like *Highway to Heaven*, *MacGyver*, and many others have used Arthurian themes; Arthurian characters, especially Merlin and Morgan, appear in hundreds of comic books; Arthurian allusions permeate popular music; product and business names are drawn from the legends, undoubtedly because advertisers and marketers believe the names have a resonance that will sell; toys and games, from the early Parker Brothers *Camelot* boardgame to the recent Ken and Barbie Arthur and Guinevere dolls, capitalize on the Matter of Britain; popular fiction from fantasy to romance is continually turning to Arthurian material. These numerous manifestations make it clear that the study of popular Arthuriana is important because it is a study of our culture on many levels. Not only does it help us to appreciate the place and significance of great works of art, literature, and music; but it also helps us to understand our society, our values, and our dreams.

Thus it was an inspired notion that Sally Slocum had when she began the Arthurian Legend section of the Popular Culture Association. What more fitting tribute to her could there be than the essays in this volume, which demonstrate in their variety and creativity that the work she began is being carried on by a host of scholars?

Preface

Countless literary redactions, adaptations, and versions of the Arthurian legend have been produced since the early twelfth century, when Geoffrey of Monmouth gave us the first coherent narrative account of King Arthur's career in his *History of the Kings of Britain*. Despite a somewhat checkered history over the centuries, and despite its aristocratic and theological genesis, the Matter of Arthur has irrevocably embedded itself in modern British and American culture. Twentieth-century America, in particular, proved a rich breeding-ground for the Arthurian mythos, not only in film and high- or mid-culture fiction (novels, short stories, fantasy fiction, science fiction), but in such areas of popular and mass culture as television, gaming, advertising, material goods, comic books, musical theater, pop music, and an assortment of esoteric genres. Nor does the widespread appeal of the legend seem to be diminishing with the advent of a new millennium. The internet fairly bristles with Arthuriana, ranging from academic and scholarly sites to those created by informed amateurs, wistful enthusiasts, and members of the lunatic fringe. Arthurian figures and icons—Merlin, Camelot, Excalibur, the Grail—have become household words, product names, and journalistic throwaways, even for individuals who have no familiarity whatsoever with the Arthurian narrative in any of its permutations.

The origins, history, and trajectory of the Arthurian legend are well-documented and need little discussion here. More relevant to our immediate concerns, perhaps, is the curious phenomenon of this legend's durability and the facility with which it has migrated over the course of time and place. While a truly satisfying explanation for the unparalleled elasticity of the Matter of Arthur has yet to be offered, a reasonable approximation may have been made (inadvertently, perhaps) by a colleague of ours, Martin Schichtman, who once precipitated a near riot amongst a sizeable group of otherwise sedate and ordinarily well-behaved medievalists at a major academic conference by declaring, in a manner that brooked no contradiction, "The Grail is an empty signifier."

Whatever Schichtman's agenda may have been on that memorable occasion, the concept turns out to be a fairly powerful one when applied to the Arthurian legend as a whole. Like the Grail, holy or unholy, the Matter of Arthur may be seen as an empty receptacle, waiting to be filled with whatever substance may speak to the individual or cultural moment. It has proved, for example, a particularly rich medium for ideological display. Geoffrey's Arthurian narrative was, among other things, a coded critique of the notoriously incompetent King Stephen; Chrétien and other high medieval romancers found the Matter of Arthur a convenient vehicle for ideologies endorsing hereditary aristocracy, while the French authors of the early thirteenth-century Vulgate Arthurian cycle found the legend equally convenient as a platform for religious doctrine. Similarly, Malory's fifteenth-century *Morte D'Arthur*, the fountainhead for almost all post-medieval adaptations of the legend, bespoke the despair of an age plagued with regnal failure and social chaos. The first Henry Tudor capitalized on dubious genealogical associations with Arthur to valorize his claim to the English throne. And so it has gone throughout the centuries. Tennyson, Twain, T.H. White, Thomas Berger, Donald Barthelme, Marion Zimmer Bradley, to cite but a handful of the more visible contributors to the modern Matter of Arthur: all have invoked the legend to limn the temper of their times.

More than a handy vessel for official ideologies and cultural credos, however, the Matter of Arthur speaks with equal eloquence to the less codifiable facets of human nature: to our wishes, anxieties, desires, and above all to our innate sense of play. Its elite genesis notwithstanding, the Arthurian legend in its modern manifestations casually transcends boundaries of class, status, gender, and age. It speaks to an impressive range of individuals, from Don Hoffman's African-American student whose Ghanaian grandmother regaled her family with tales about Palomides, Malory's Saracen knight, to the Middle American consumer, business entrepreneur, or filmgoer, to the kid down the block who mows your lawn and the household couch-potato or technological wizard. The essays in this volume demonstrate the extent to which the Arthurian legend permeates the very fabric of contemporary culture, surfacing in a remarkable variety of surprising venues and disparate registers.

In some respects, our enterprise is hardly a novel one. Post-medieval

Arthuriana, the study of which was launched by pathfinders William A. Nitze in 1940 and Nathan Comfort Starr in 1954, has been the subject of many excellent books and essays over the past several decades. The seminal work of Beverly Taylor and Elisabeth Brewer, *The Return of King Arthur* (1983), and Raymond H. Thompson's *The Return from Avalon: A Study of the Arthurian Legend in Modern Fiction* (1985) were soon followed by a number of equally important contributions to this field, including Muriel Whitaker's *The Legends of King Arthur in Art* (1990), Debra Mancoff's *The Arthurian Revival in Victorian Art* (1990) and her two subsequent essay collections (1992 and 1998), Alan Lupack's meticulously-researched editions of hitherto largely unknown nineteenth- and twentieth-century Arthurian texts, and Sally K. Slocum's 1992 *Popular Arthurian Traditions*. Kevin J. Harty's groundbreaking work on Arthurian film, including *Cinema Arthuriana* (1991) and *King Arthur on Film* (1999), has created a new and highly productive subgenre of academic Arthurian studies. The most recent entries, *King Arthur in America* and *Arthurian Literature by Women*, both by Alan Lupack and Barbara Tepa Lupack, and Christine Poulson's *The Quest for the Grail: Arthurian Legend in British Art 1840–1920*, all published in 1999, attest to the continuing vitality of scholarship in this area.

This, then, is the roster of our predecessors, to whom we are indebted professionally and, in many cases, personally as well. With some notable exceptions, however, such as Harty, Lupack, and Tepa Lupack, most scholars of modern Arthuriana have tended to feel more comfortable remaining in relatively close proximity to the cultural products with which they are most familiar—to the types of text they are professionally trained to deal with, for example, such as fiction, poetry, the visual arts—and in the safety zone of historically circumscribed chronology: "modern" is frequently figured as broadly post-medieval, with considerable emphasis on nineteenth-century cultural artifacts. To date, relatively few Arthurians have ventured into the sometimes murky corners and cultural byways that not only constitute perhaps the most eloquent testimonial to the extraordinary dissemination of this legendary material, but also, in our view, construct a significant index to cultural temper as well. The essays assembled here explore this territory. Our authors have "taken the adventure" into some of the unmapped zones of our culture at large, wandering in their quests for contemporary Arthuriana from the den to the marketplace, and thence through a variety of cultural playspaces to the hinterlands of the exotic. In sum, what we aspire to offer in this volume is a collaborative reading of the marginalia to the master-text of Arthurian legend.

Works Cited

Barthelme, Donald. *The King*. New York: Penguin, 1990.

Berger, Thomas. *Arthur Rex: A Legendary Novel*. New York: Delacorte, 1978.

Bradley, Marion Zimmer. *The Mists of Avalon*. New York: Ballantine, 1982.

Chrétien de Troyes. *The Complete Romances of Chrétien de Troyes*. Tr. David Staines. Cambridge, MA: Harvard University Press, 1977.

Geoffrey of Monmouth. *History of the Kings of Britain*. Tr. Lewis Thorpe. Harmondsworth, UK: Penguin, 1966.

Harty, Kevin J. *Cinema Arthuriana: Essays on Arthurian Film*. New York: Garland, 1991.

_____. *King Arthur on Film: New Essays on Arthurian Cinema*. Jefferson, NC: McFarland, 1999.

Lupack, Alan. *"Arthur, the Greatest King": An Anthology of Modern Arthurian Poems*. New York: Garland, 1988.

_____. *Arthurian Drama: An Anthology*. New York: Garland, 1991.

_____. *Modern Arthurian Literature: An anthology of English and American Literature from the Renaissance to the Present*. New York: Garland, 1992.

_____, and Barbara Tepa Lupack. *Arthurian Literature by Women*. New York: Garland, 1991.

_____. *King Arthur in America*. Woodbridge, Suffolk, UK; Rochester, NY: Garland, 1999.

Malory, Sir Thomas. *Complete Works*. 2nd ed. Ed. Eugène Vinaver. New York: Oxford UP, 1971.

Mancoff, Debra. *The Arthurian Revival in Victorian Art*. New York: Garland, 1990.

_____. *King Arthur's Modern Return*. New York: Garland, 1998.

_____. *The Return of King Arthur: The Legend Through Victorian Eyes*. New York: Abrams, 1995.

Nitze, William Albert. *Arthurian Romance and Modern Poetry and Music*. Chicago: Univ. of Chicago Press, 1940.

Poulson, Christine. *The Quest for the Grail: Arthurian Legend in British Art 1840–1920*. Manchester: Manchester University Press, 1999.

Slocum, Sally K. *Popular Arthurian Traditions*. Bowling Green, OH: Bowling Green State University, 1992.

Starr, Nathan Comfort. *King Arthur Today: The Arthurian Legend in English and American Literature, 1901–1953*. Gainesville: University of Florida Press, 1954.

Taylor, Beverly, and Elisabeth Brewer. *The Return of King Arthur: British and American Arthurian Literature Since 1800*. Cambridge, Cambridgeshire, UK: Totowa, NJ: Barnes and Noble, 1983.

Tennyson, Alfred, Lord. *Idylls of the King in Twelve Books*. Intro. J.H. Fowler. London: Macmillan; New York: St. Martin's, 1969.

Thompson, Raymond H. *The Return from Avalon: A Study of the Arthurian Legend in Modern Fiction*. Westport, CT: Greenwood, 1985.

Twain, Mark. *A Connecticut Yankee in King Arthur's Court*. Harmondsworth, UK; Baltimore, MD: Penguin, 1971.

Whitaker, Muriel. *The Legends of King Arthur in Art*. Arthurian Studies 22. Cambridge: D.S. Brewer, 1990.

White, T.H. *The Once and Future King*. New York: Berkeley Medallion, 1966.

Marketing Arthur: The Commodification of Arthurian Legend

Elizabeth S. Sklar

The candle clock came along during the reign of King Arthur.
—"It's Time for a Short History of Clocks,"
in *Meijer House & Home* (advertising flyer ca. 1991)[1]

If prizes were awarded to legends for durability, the matter of Arthur would win hands down. From its first "official" recording in Geoffrey of Monmouth's *Historia Regum Britanniae* (c.1139) to the present (if we discount a 300-year sabbatical along the way), the matter of Arthur has spoken to and for countless generations in a wide variety of cultures.[2] The Arthurian legend's inherent generic melange of historical verisimilitude, romantic idealism and tragic realism, along with its generous and infinitely expandable cast of characters, endows it with extraordinary adaptability. Equally multivalent is King Arthur himself, whose "history" was already mythified by the time Geoffrey of Monmouth undertook to embellish it into a coherent narrative, and who, in much medieval Arthurian fiction, was less a central figure than a starting point, the hub from which events radiated and around which the narrative circulated. The promise of Arthur's return, as once and future king, legitimizes—perhaps demands—the legend's perpetual retelling. Thus, despite its British origins, and despite the fact that, in some sense, King Arthur is an insular culture hero, the legend disdains national boundaries. A receptive vessel waiting to be filled by the aspirations, anxieties and desires of any individual or group that chooses to appropriate it, the Arthurian legend has proved sufficiently manipulable to simultaneously accommodate and mirror a vast array of differing ideologies, cultural preoccupations, and value systems, from twelfth-century French courtly society, to late medieval Lancastrian England, to the Victorians and beyond.

We are no exception. Our own culture-at-large has enthusiastically received the Arthurian legacy and appropriated it with surprising gusto: from fiction, films, television, rock music, advertising, and the gaming community, evidence abounds that the Arthurian legend is part of our cultural currency. In the final decade of the twentieth century, for example, the Detroit Institute of Arts celebrated "King Arthur's Birthday," a TV revival of "Get Smart" set its climactic episode in a Knights of the Round Table exhibit, and Indiana Jones and his quirky dad set off in quest of the Holy Grail. "Far Side" creator Gary Larson has drawn on Arthurian motifs more than once, as have other cartoonists, and the Starship Excalibur will ring a bell with any Trekkie worth his or her salt. Even discount chain Meijer Thrifty Acres is sufficiently certain of its customers' cultural literacy to purvey the bemusing bit of non-information cited in my epigraph. In short, no longer the exclusive property of the educated or academic elite, the Arthurian legend and its icons are as securely entrenched in the public domain as McDonald's golden arches.

The most telling index of the extent to which we have appropriated the legend—and the most self-revealing, perhaps—is the commodification of Arthur, his entry into the marketplace as both vehicle and product. Arthurian icons have been appropriated by private enterprise and invoked by advertisers. Arthurian narrative is packaged and sold in a variety of products, from Merlin music boxes and Arthurian Tarot cards to comic books and computer games. What follows is a description of the ways in which Arthurian legend inhabits the marketplace, and a reflection upon some possible implications of the commodification of Arthur.

ii

Marketplace Arthuriana may be divided loosely into two broad categories: promotional Arthuriana and Arthurian products. Promotional Arthuriana is a kind of catch-all category, designating any use of or allusion to the legend or its central images as a vehicle or "hook" to direct potential customers' attention to otherwise unrelated products or services. This category is dominated by what we might call "onomastic" Arthuriana, that is, the invocation of major Arthurian icons in the *naming* of establishments, services, companies, and such palpably non-medieval products as communication services, motorcycles, and machine tools. My own collection of onomastic Arthuriana, which consists largely but not exclusively of Detroit-area businesses, includes establishments such as the Excalibur Restaurant and three Round Table restaurants, the King Arthur Lounge, Merlin Industries, Merlin Liquor, Merlin Pharmacy, Excalibur North car sales, Merlin Magic Muffler (a branch of a Chicago-based operation), Excalibur Shoes, Camelot Travel (a national franchise), and (my favorite in this category) Merlin's The Restaurant Coney Island. Residential communities, too, avail themselves of Arthurian associations: we have Camelot Apartments, Camelot Hall Convalescent Center, Camelot Villa Mobile Home Community (complete with Camelot Boulevard and Ivanhoe Street), and a suburban subdivision known as Excalibur Homes.

Among the services promoting themselves through Arthurian association are Camelot Cleaners, Camelot Chimney Company, Camelot Inn Catering, Camelot International (a housing rental agency), Camelot Photography, Camelot Realty, Excalibur Barber Shop, and Excalibur Hair Styling. In the world of high technology, AT&T pushes its MERLIN Plus Communications System and the University of Michigan's on-line holdings catalogue calls itself "Mirlyn." Products that invoke Arthurian icons in their naming include the Excalibur motorcycle, Excalibor Van, Excalibur low carbon alloy bar, Varitron's Merlin Express (an "amazing new portable lettering system"), Excalibur down coats, Excalibur Cutting Tools, Excalibar Tools (apparently unrelated to the previous product, if orthography is anything to go by), and, of course, King Arthur Flour.[3]

Although onomastic Arthuriana comprises the majority of the items I am classifying as promotional Arthuriana, the Arthurian legend is also invoked from time to time by advertising as well. One of the classiest examples of Arthurian advertising is a sumptuous six-page spread promoting Royal Viking Cruise Line. "On Easter Island," reads the text of the first page, "the unblinking statues know of this place. So do the shopkeepers of Hong Kong and the starlets in the south of France.... It is every place you could want to be, and the best of every place." The sequel, a double-page display of a mysterious seascape, tantalizes further: "A million tales in a hundred tongues might describe this place. But in the end, it is perhaps best captured in a single word." The advertisement climaxes in a centerfold shot of a cruise liner, the looming caption of which reveals that single word: CAMELOT. Less reverential is a full-page advertisement for the New Orleans Hilton, which transports King Arthur, Merlin, and a few hapless knights in full plate armor to a contemporary board room. These are not happy campers: the knights are slumped in varying poses of dejection, an abashed-looking Merlin meets no one's eyes, and King Arthur is obviously in a state of high dudgeon. Levelling an accusatory forefinger in Merlin's general direction, the king complains, "I distinctly said I wanted a *round* table." The burden of this witty advertisement—the knights, visors down, are surely meant to be taken for medieval counterparts of the faceless yes-men of American business myth—is that the Hilton's "meeting wizards" get "the details right" (unlike certain obsolete enchanters we could name). Occasionally, Arthurian images turn up as promotional embellishments, the pictorial equivalent of the passing reference in verbal texts, as on the box-top illustration for Celestial Seasonings Mint Magic Tea. Although the Arthurian references here are neither direct nor primary— the central figure is a generic magician, accompanied by an equally generic and utterly non–Arthurian unicorn—the magician's flowing robes, long white beard, and tall pointed hat evoke canonical post–Victorian representations of Merlin; and the golden tea cup that hovers below the enchanter's down-turned palm (surrounded as it is by a palpable aura) might easily be read as a domesticated Grail.

Whether they take the form of onomastics, advertisements, or incidental passing allusions, whether reverential or parodic in tone, promotional Arthuriana share a single motivation: to cause money to change hands. With the pragmatism so valued in American culture myth, entrepreneurs and promotors literally capitalize on Arthurian associations. Yet the text assembled here is not just another saga of capitalist exploitation. Patterns emerge from the collective evidence that may suggest both how this appropriation functions and what it reveals about us as consumers— consumers not of products or services but of the Arthurian legend itself; for, like any manipulative tactic, the use of Arthurian images for promotional purposes reveals as much about those who consent to be manipulated as it does about those who pull the strings. One feature common to all promotional uses of Arthurian legend is the fact that they are essentially non-narrative in nature. They neither imply nor assume knowledge of Arthurian fictive history, but instead count almost exclusively on the associations evoked by the individual icons. A related feature is that while visual imagery is occasionally employed, these are primarily *verbal* icons, textual allusions relying for effect on word magic rather than on visual associations. Moreover, the lexicon of Arthurian onomastics and advertising is surprisingly limited. Despite the potential wealth of Arthurian-derived personal and place names available for appropriation, only a select few are actually employed. No establishment, service, or product, for example, invokes Lancelot or Guinevere (for obvious reasons, I suppose); and well-known Arthurian loci such as Avalon or Glastonbury are commemorated only in the occasional street name. Appropriately, given his traditional status as a background figure, King Arthur himself appears infrequently. Evidently, only Excalibur, Camelot, the Round Table, and Merlin seem to have acquired sufficient cultural resonance to qualify as effective marketing vehicles.

In keeping with their non-narrativized, language-like behavior, commodified Arthurian images tend to function tropologically, as simile, metaphor, or metonymy, and like any of the traditional tropes, these key Arthurian images derive their effect through their evocative ability, their power to tap the connotative potential of the Arthurian imago. These are not, however, interchangeable signifiers; each icon has its characteristic markers, acquired cumulatively through contextual redundancy in the marketplace. Some are more or less predictable from their traditional literary associations; others are not. The Round Table, for example, simultaneously the most traditional and the most reductive of this iconic quartet, draws on King Arthur's literary reputation for hosting fabulous feasts; ignoring the important socio-political aspects of the Round Table, it is associated exclusively with restaurants, thus signifying camaraderie, sociability, and (presumably) fine dining. Merlin proves a more flexible vehicle, and more receptive to contemporary realities, while still obeying the constraints of his traditional character. To him are assigned sundry potions (Merlin Liquor, Merlin Pharmacy, Mint Magic Tea), mechanical repairs (Merlin Magic Muffler, Merlin Industries—a welding and joining concern) and the modern magic of leading-edge technology (Merlin Express Lettering System, AT&T Merlin Plus, and the Mirlyn on-line library system). Merlin thus signifies the quick fix, the cure for what ails you.

But if the Round Table and Merlin prove a comfortable fit with tradition, Excalibur and Camelot have been reinterpreted to encode more culture-specific values and desires. Excalibur, traditionally a symbol of prowess, of manhood, of potency, and of structural stability, is now most commonly associated with processes, products, and services that require precision work, such as industrial tools, hair styling, and motor vehicles. Thus Excalibur has come to signify high quality, top performance, and overall excellence—a class act, as it were. Mazda, for example, honors its most productive dealers with the Mazda Excalibur for "sales excellence," "achievement," and "outstanding sales leadership." The slogan for Excalibur ELT Golf Balls says it all: "Quality. Craftsmanship. Commitment."

Of the four major Arthurian icons under consideration here, Camelot has been the most dramatically reinterpreted. One might reasonably expect

Camelot to signify glamor, romance, and elegance—as it evidently does in the hands of the Royal Viking promotors—an escape into luxury. But this is not the case. In the vocabulary of promotional Arthuriana, Camelot speaks largely to personal well-being: to cleanliness (Camelot Cleaners, Camelot Chimney Sweeps), to health (Camelot Hall Convalescent Center and the now-defunct Camelot Family Medical Center), to nurturing (Camelot Inn) and to good, albeit modest, living (Camelot Apartments, Camelot Villa Mobile Home Community).

In effect we have domesticated Camelot, and with it the Arthurian legend as a whole. Granted, the commercial viability of the legend still depends in part on its promise to fulfill the desire for glamor, for romance, and for status, as evidenced by the euphemistic nature of much onomastic Arthuriana: the Round Table Restaurant serves "charburgers" and other typical diner fare; Camelot Hall Convalescent Center is a sad institution of last resort, while Camelot Apartments, like the similarly-dubbed mobile-home communities, provides utilitarian, low-income housing. But the composite text of marketplace Arthuriana speaks more to pragmatism than to fantasy. Our quest is modest: as consumers, at least, we seek not an escape from the work-a-day world, but merely an enhancement of it. The fleeting wish to be queen (or king) for a day submits to a collective yearning for comfort, for ease, for nurturance, for things that don't break down, and for instant remediation when they do.

iii

Although some advertising Arthuriana suggests a target audience that includes the idle rich (Royal Viking Lines) and the aspiring board president (Hilton), the primary target for promotional Arthuriana appears to be Middle America, particularly those of relatively modest status and earning power. The majority of the Detroit-area establishments invoking Arthurian legend, for example, are situated in predominantly blue-collar neighborhoods; interestingly, onomastic Arthuriana generally do not survive in transitional areas or those in which gentrification has already occurred. These demographics seem to reflect nation-wide trends; thematized Arthurian establishments, like King's Gate Adult Community, a mobile home park in Florida, or the Excalibur Hotel and Casino in Las Vegas (of which more shortly) attract a similar segment of the population. One further point here: despite the traditionally androcentric nature of Arthurian narrative, the target audience for promotional Arthuriana, in keeping with the general domestication of Arthurian icons, is essentially ungendered.[4]

The demographic target for Arthurian *products*, however, is another matter altogether. Leaving aside the occasional artifact probably aimed toward the same consumer as promotional Arthuriana—a "musical replica of King Arthur's castle" that plays the theme from *Camelot* or the inescapable pewter Merlins that proliferate in mall Gift Shoppes, for example—Arthurian products target a mixed bag of elite populations, from the New Age devotees who read the invisible world from the Arthurian Tarot,[5] to whoever cared to shell out $675 a few years ago for the International Arthurian Society's replica of Excalibur. The primary target population here, though, consists in those who buy comic books, graphic novels, and games of all descriptions (board, role-playing, and computer): adolescent and post-adolescent males—a distinctive contrast with the non-gendered, diffuse, and more mature consumer targeted by promotional Arthuriana.[6]

Arthurian products differ from promotional Arthuriana in a number of other significant respects as well. Where promotional Arthuriana deploy the matter of Arthur as a vehicle, to mediate between the consumer and whatever is being sold, Arthurian products—like fiction and film—in some sense sell the Arthurian legend itself. Additionally, where promotional Arthuriana function allusively or tropologically, Arthurian products are narrativized: they either offer reinterpretations of the legend or encourage creative, improvisatory reinterpretation, thus giving back as much as they take by participating in the ongoing re-creation of the matter of Arthur. Rejecting both the domestication of Arthurian icons and the appeal to pragmatism that characterize promotional Arthuriana, Arthurian products are predicated on the exotic, transporting the audience or participant from mundane reality into other worlds, be they historical, fictional, or some fantastical mixture of the two.

Predictably, these escape worlds are above all macho worlds, adverting to neo-medieval androcentric, patriarchal norms that conveniently disambiguate current shifts in gender-role definition. Women in both comic books and role-playing games are marginalized at best. In Arthurian comic books, women—when present at all—play passive roles, functioning more as background decoration than as players in the narrative action; the rare empowered female figure (of whom Morgan le Fey is the paradigm) is manipulative and subversive, an object of fear and loathing infinitely threating to the patriarchal structure.[7] Although Arthurian gaming, in accordance with the slowly growing female penetration of this primarily male bastion, is somewhat less staunchly patriarchal than the comic book genre, it still marginalizes female characters even as it reluctantly admits them. *Pendragon*, probably the least androcentric of these games, lists some fifty-three

"Women's Names"; the list of male character names, however, totals nearly two-hundred-thirty. Dividing female character types into three categories— ordinary women, women who have names, and extraordinary women—the rules admit only the last-named as player characters, even then noting that "extraordinary women still have suppressed roles when compared with the adventuring knights." There is some doubt as to the propriety of women characters in fighting (i.e., major) roles: "Your gamemaster might allow women knights in *his* ... game (italics mine). Always assume they are not allowed, then check with your gamemaster." A similar caveat appears in the *Prince Valient* rule book, which includes a brief section on Female Adventurers, but cautions that "Female Adventurers ... must be played differently from men ... for the purpose of consistency with current historical knowledge." Where "Male Adventurers have all the privileges of going where they want and doing what they want ... Female Adventurers must be more subtle ... or else be ready to deal with distrust and dislike from ordinary people." The coda to this caveat is revealing: "Most female Adventurers will be used to such distrust, and will know how to compensate."

Another notable difference between promotional Arthuriana and Arthurian products lies in their attitudes towards the Arthurian legend itself. Where promotional Arthuriana, by its very nature, tends to be exploitative and glib, the major Arthurian products treat the legend seriously, even reverentially. Nowhere is this more obvious than in Arthurian board and role-playing games, which, like the wargaming from which they derive, place a premium on historical accuracy and (in this case) literary authenticity. *Knights of Camelot*, a fantasy boardgame (TSR, 1980), for example, promotes itself as "Drawing extensively from the works of Sir Thomas Malory"; player chits include all the major and many of the minor figures, both male and female, from the *Morte D'Arthur*, and for those who prove themselves sufficiently worthy, the game culminates in the Grail Quest. *King Arthur and the Knights of the Round Table* (Wotan, 1986) includes in its rule book a well-informed (if orthographically dubious and sometimes grammatically questionable) discussion of the historicity of King Arthur, with reference to Malory, to the Old French Vulgate Arthurian cycle, and to the history of sub–Roman Britain; the latter, maintains the author (clearly a convert to the new purism that has infected Arthurian enthusiasts, of late), brings us "closer to the reality" of Arthurian legend than do the versions by later medieval authors like Malory. Reservations about the historicity of Malory's Arthuriad notwithstanding, the rule book opens with a summary of the *Morte D'Arthur* and contains an appendix on the Major Knights of the Round Table, all derived from Malory.

The most scholarly of the lot is *Pendragon* (Chaosium, 1985); "based on the pioneering works of Chrétien de Troyes, the French Vulgate texts, and Malory's *Le Morte d'Arthur*," this game is a veritable treasure-trove of information both historical and literary. Sidebars in the Player's Book include disquisitions on heraldry, the rules of precedence for both feasting and daily social interaction in late medieval society, the knighting ceremony, feudal politics, medieval musical instruments and weaponry, chivalry, and courtly love (*fine amour*). There are, as well, generous quotations from Malory, from Andreas Capellanus, and (in the Game Master's Book) from the *Mabinogion*. The bibliography of the Game Master's Book consists of texts that might serve in any college-level course in Arthurian legend: *The Anglo-Saxon Chronicle*, Matarasso's translation of the OF *Queste del Saint Graal*, the romances of Chrétien de Troyes, Geoffrey of Monmouth's *Historia*, both Patrick Ford's and Lady Guest's translations of the *Mabinogion*, and a brief evaluative discussion of three different editions of Malory's *Morte D'Arthur*.[8] Although it may be invoked to greater or lesser degrees, this valuing of authenticity seems to hold genre-wide. *Excalibur* (Wotan, 1988), which centers not on Arthurian narrative but on the economic, military, and political aspects of feudalism, casts its players in the role of "major Knights of the Round Table," and the rule book is liberally sprinkled with apposite quotations from Malory. Even the introductory-level *Prince Valiant* (Chaosium, 1989), less preoccupied with authenticity than its models since it is aimed towards a younger audience and intertextual with a comic strip, includes Malory in its List of Arthurian Sources and provides a short-list of traditional Arthurian characters such as Merlin, Mordred, Tristan, and Morgan le Fey.

Although computer gaming is premised on a different kind of textuality from role-playing games—as Christy Marx notes in her introduction to *Conquests of Camelot*, the player "will certainly encounter ideas ... never found associated with a King Arthur story anywhere else"—Arthurian computer games place as much emphasis on authenticity as their non-technological counterparts. Despite her disclaimer, for example, Marx devotes the first three pages of the instruction manual to the historicity of Arthur and the nature of the Grail; the latter discussion adduces Chrétien and Malory as well as anthropological theory concerning the origins of the Grail. Similarly, the script and documentation to Virgin's *Spirit of Excalibur*, the objective of which is to locate and defeat Morgan le Fey, are deeply indebted to both the chronicle tradition and to Malory. Set in the sixth century, shortly after King Arthur's death, and referencing such historical events as the Battle of Badon and the Saxon invasions, the game casts the player in the role of Constantine, Arthur's "historical" successor. The fictive world, however, is populated by characters from Malory's *Morte D'Arthur*; the glossary includes names and descriptions of both major and minor Malorian figures as player characters, and a supplement adds textual and contextual depth by describing figures who played major roles in Malory's Arthuriad but who are no longer living at the time when play begins. A five-page discussion of the English sub–Roman period, and an eight-page survey of the "Myths of Arthur," which references Malory, Tennyson, T.H. White, Mary Stewart, M.Z. Bradley, and Parke Godwin, rounds off this impressively-researched documentation. Although the sequel is set in tenth-century Muslim Spain, it still retains Arthurian authenticity with surprising references to arcane traditional figures such as Sir Ironside, Sir Brandiles, and the little-known but important Malorian arch-villain Breuse Sans Pitie.

Arthurian games, with their insistence on strict adherence to received tradition on the one hand, and their encouragement of creative reinvention on the other, allow gamers to simulate an authorial process undoubtedly very like that followed by their medieval forbears who chose to adapt the Arthurian legend to their own particular ends and cultural imperatives. Arthurian comic books and graphic novels, although they target the same general audience, are simultaneously more product-like and more "literary" than the games, in that, like Arthurian films and fantasy fiction, they offer up ready-made rereadings of Arthurian narrative. Understandably, reverence, sound scholarship, and high seriousness are not the keynotes of all Arthurian comics. Answerable to a very different set of generic conventions, of which irreverence must be counted high on the list, comic book treatments of Arthurian legend are remarkably various in both tone and stance, ranging from the respectful to the frivolous to the downright exploitative. To the last description belong *Excalibur Comics*, which to my knowledge have nothing whatsoever to do with matters Arthurian beyond the title, and *Arthur Sex*, a nasty little venture into Arthurian pornography. At the other end of the spectrum are serious graphic reinterpretations of the legend, such as Matt Wagner's elegant *Mage* or Mike Barr's witty and well-informed *Camelot 3000*, a "maxi series" consisting of ten issues later assembled into book form. Barr's preface, with its scholarly grounding and its emphasis on Malory, along with the comprehensive treatment of the legendary materials in the series proper, suggest a closer affinity to Arthurian gaming than to more traditional comic book adventures in Arthurland.

Also indebted to the historical emphasis of Arthurian gaming are two early 1990s "maxi series" comics, *Camelot Eternal* and *Merlin*. Both adhere to what I have called the "new purism," eschewing glamorized medievalism for more somber settings and representation that suggest the Dark Ages time frame currently considered the "authentic" period of Arthurian legend. Both draw some or most of their matter from the chronicle tradition, as represented by Geoffrey of Monmouth, rather than from the fictional traditions of medieval romance: *Camelot Eternal* features a version of Arthur's combat with the Giant of Mont St. Michel, while *Merlin* opens in the reign of King Vortigern, during the Saxon invasions of Britain, which is where the Arthurian portion of Geoffrey's *Historia* begins. *Merlin* further authenticates itself through the use of archaic diction and syntax. The black and white graphics in both series, whether a matter of deliberate choice or the product of financial exigency, enhances the ambiance of high seriousness here.

Occupying the middle ground between the merely exploitative comics and those that aspire to make a serious contribution to the on-going re-creation of Arthurian legend are the traditional comic-book series—*Iron Man*, *Swamp Thing*, and *Spider Woman*—which have made episodic use of the matter of Arthur. Fanciful, self-indulgent, and literally *ex tempore*, they bypass "the world of clocks and calendars" to either zap their protagonists back to Camelot through "existential wormholes," or import Arthurian characters into the present, as in the now-classic 1978 issue of *Spider Woman*, in which Morgan le Fey manages to project her "astral self" through the space-time continuum to inhabit Spider Woman's body—an uncomfortable situation for everyone concerned. It is a given that these are playful productions; serious reinterpretation and authenticity are hardly at issue here. *Iron Man* #150 is not much more than a costume drama in Arthurian setting for yet another showdown between the protagonist and his nemesis, Dr. Doom, while *Swamp Thing* #87 is a whimsical exercise in demystification: King Arthur is portrayed as a crank whose behavior reels between the crabby and the downright tyrannical as a result of the "voices in his head which only the Grail will cure." The Grail Quest itself is branded a "stupid, miserable quest," and the Grail knight is one Sir Justin, a veteran time-traveller with no roots whatsoever in Arthurian tradition.

It should be noted that frivolity and authenticity are not necessarily mutually exclusive categories in this genre; the X-rated *Arthur Sex* rivals Barr's *Camelot 3000* in terms of the sophistication of its literary allusions, referencing such Malorean arcana as "The Fair Maid of Astolat" (Lord Escalot) and "The Knight of the Cart" (the villain Maleagant); further, it quite correctly situates Camelot in Winchester, and works in a sly allusion to the Grail legend as well in the person of "Percevelda," a lady of scant attire and scantier scruples. But the very irony here points up an important feature of Arthurian comics in general: differences in tone, stance, and attitude notwithstanding, comic book treatments of the legend share with gaming the assumption of consumer familiarity with the general outlines of Arthurian narrative and with some of the major events of Arthurian fictive history such as the Grail quest and the fall of Camelot; they assume as well recognition of major Arthurian figures and their traditional roles: Merlin's function as advisor to King Arthur and protector of the kingdom, for example, or the adversarial roles played by Morgan le Fey and Mordred. Thus, one way or another, these are all "in-jokes" that depend for comic, parodic, or satiric effect on the audience's possession of a common body of knowledge—in this case, at least a rudimentary familiarity with Arthurian narrative.[9]

iv

In a class by itself is the Excalibur Hotel/Casino in Las Vegas, in which commodified Arthuriana achieves virtual apotheosis. An Arthurian product that partakes of all the features of promotional Arthuriana, it reads like a compendium of strategies for transforming the matter of Arthur into hard cash. Engaging in onomastic overkill—one may eat at the Round Table Buffet, Lance-a-lotta Pasta, the Camelot Dining Room, or Sir Galahad's Prime Rib—the establishment literalizes its own advertising slogan, "There has been nothing like it since Camelot," luring customers into a world of "Knights, sorcerers, castles, battlements, drawbridges, moats, jugglers, mimes, jousting and sword fighting." Like Arthurian gamers—but lacking the creative permissions of gaming—guests may indulge in role-playing as they shop in the "medieval village," or attend the "medieval feast" that accompanies King Arthur's Tournament (M.C.'d by Merlin himself). It is a comic book come to life, Arthur in Disneyland. Only here may one actually purchase the entire package of Arthurian promises—romance and glamor combined with nurturance, convenience, and well-being, family fun at a price that would please any pragmatist. Boasting "the Best Vacation Value in History," the Excalibur Hotel is the ultimate in the marketing of Arthur.

It is tempting, of course, to read our commodification of Arthur as symptomatic of the legend's inevitable decline in a society whose imaginative capacity has been vitiated by its obsession with material gain, to argue that the commercial exploitation of things Arthurian cheapens, degrades, and devalues the high ideals that the legend purportedly encodes—a form, perhaps, of cultural whoremongering. My read, however, is quite the opposite: that the commodification of Arthur both bespeaks and contributes to the health of the legend in its contemporary American environment, and insures its perpetuation for some time to come.

In the first place, the very fact that Arthur sells at all testifies to the legend's viability as cultural currency: it is neither permissible nor profitable to play fast and loose with someone else's property. We don't see El Cid or Odysseus invoked to market used cars, mufflers, luxury cruises, or herbal teas, nor are we invited to dine in elegance at the Roncevalles Restaurant or to spend a luxurious yet affordable weekend getaway at Heorot Hall Hotel. The allusive or associative nature of promotional Arthuriana also bespeaks cultural embedding. The key images invoked by advertisers and entrepreneurs are productive only because they require minimal decoding, importing immediately-available clusters of connotation. To function effectively, allusion depends on a culturally-shared frame of reference. The marketability of Arthur, as vehicle or as product, suggests that the Arthurian legend constitutes just such a frame of reference, that the matter of Arthur comprises an integral part of our cultural lexicon, and one that is not likely to become obsolete in the foreseeable future.

I would suggest, in fact, that the marketplace contributes more vitally to the survival and perpetuation of the Arthurian legend than does the academy, for it reaches an infinitely larger and generally more complicitous audience. Visual representations of Arthurian icons or narrative, whether in advertising illustration, establishment logos, or graphic texts, keep the Arthurian image before our eyes. Odds for perpetuation are enhanced by the self-referential nature of the genres in question, which virtually guarantees replication, and by the fact that today's idealistic adolescents are tomorrow's entrepreneurs and consumers. Nor, in the end, are the medieval roots or the essential idealism of the legend entirely compromised by Mammon. Through its generic valuing of authenticity, Arthurian gaming counters the reductionist thrust of promotional Arthuriana by insisting on textual fidelity and adherence to the "facts" of medieval history. And, for all its apparent cynicism in exploiting the matter of Arthur for financial gain, promotional Arthuriana imports and perpetuates the idealistic elements of the legend by speaking to both the culturally-encoded aspirations and the fundamental human needs of its audience. In sum, as long as Arthur sells, his legend is alive and well.

Notes

1. This essay originally appeared in *The Platte Valley Review* (21:1, 1993, pp. 61–82), a special issue on "Reading the Middle Ages" edited by Rebecca Umland. The current editor of *The PVR* has graciously granted permission to reprint this article in its present, slightly revised, form.

2. We have, in addition to the well-known Arthurian traditions of France, England, Wales, and Germany, Arthurian texts from Italy, Iceland, Spain, Portugal, the Netherlands, Scandinavia, and (according to one informant, a recent immigrant) Poland as well. On the devaluing of Arthurian legend in England from the Jacobean period to the antiquarian revival of the late eighteenth century, see James D. Merriman, *The Flower of Kings* (Lawrence, KA: Kansas UP, 1973).

3. See the following essay, Zia Isola's "Defending the Domestic: Arthurian Tropes and the American Dream," for a detailed discussion of King Arthur Flour.

4. Amongst the items available to me, only the Mazda Excalibur Award promotional display, with its unabashedly phallic representation of the sword in the stone, avails itself of the macho potential inherent in the legend. Under the circumstances, Mazda's slogan, "It Just Feels Right," does not seem in the best of taste.

5. See Emily Auger, "Arthurian Legend in Tarot," in the final section of this volume.

6. Jason Tondro and Peter Corless provide broad overviews of Arthurian comic books and Arthurian gaming in their respective essays here.

7. On popular representations of Morgan, see my "Thoroughly Modern Morgan: Morgan le Fey in Twentieth-Century Popular Arthuriana" in *Popular Arthurian Traditions*, ed. Sally Slocum (Bowling Green: The Popular Press, 1992). A notable exception to the general gynophobic tendencies of comic book Arthuriana is *Camelot 3000*, in which Guenivere (a.k.a. Joan Acton) is a futuristic air force commander, and Sir Tristan is reincarnated as a woman, a state he/she objects to only because of the difficulties it causes in her/his relationship with Isolde. A more recent entry into the politically-correct arena is the *Lady Pendragon* series, a mixed bag of post-feminist gesture and bodice-ripper graphics.

8. The scholarly nature of Arthurian gaming in general is best represented in Phyllis Ann Karr's *The King Arthur Companion* (Reston, VA: Reston Publishing, 1983), an invaluable resource book for any Arthurian enthusiast.

9. In-jokes, in fact, occasionally occur within the texts as well. Iron Man, alias Tony Wells, observes during his first night at Camelot, that "Any historian would probably kill to trade places with me," and when Swamp Thing quite properly challenges Merlin's inauthentic linguistic choices ("If this is the early Middle Ages, then why do you speak in Modern English?"), Merlin coolly replies, "We use it as our secret battle language."

Games Cited

Advanced Dungeons & Dragons Deities & Demigods Cyclopedia. James M. Ward with Robert J. Kuntz. Ed. Lawrence Shick. Lake Geneva, WI: TSR Games, 1980.
Conquests of Camelot. Christy Marx et al. Coarsegold, CA: Sierra, 1990.
Excalibur. London: Wotan Games, 1988.

"The Grey Knight" (*Pendragon* scenario). Larry DiTillio. Albany, CA: Chaosium, 1986.

King Arthur and the Knights of the Round Table. Matthew Hill et al. London: Wotan Games, 1986.

Knights of Camelot Fantasy Boardgame. Lake Geneva WI: TSR Hobbies Inc., 1980.

Pendragon. Greg Stafford et al. Albany, CA: Chaosium, 1985.

Prince Valiant: The Story-Telling Game. Greg Stafford et al. Albany, CA: Chaosium, 1989.

Spirit of Excalibur. Irvine, CA: Virgin Mastertronic International, Inc., 1990.

Vengeance of Excalibur. Irvine, CA: Virgin Games, 1991.

Comics Cited

Arthur Sex: The Erotic Adventures of King Arthur, vols. 1 and 2. Westlake Village, CA: Aircel, 1991.

Camelot 3000. Mike W. Barr and Brian Bolland. New York, NY: DC Comics Inc./Warner Books, 1988.

Camelot Eternal; 6 issues. Plymouth, MI: Caliber Press, 1990 et seq.

Handbook of the Marvel Universe, #9. New York, NY: Marvel Comics Group, 1985.

Iron Man #150. New York, NY: Marvel Comics Group, Sept. 1981.

Mage. Matt Wagner. Norfolk, VA: Starblaze, 1987.

Merlin, 6 issues. R. A. Jones et al. Newbury Park, CA: Adventure Comics/Malibu Graphics, 1991 et seq.

Spider Woman 1:5. New York, NY: Marvel Comics, August 1978.

Swamp Thing #87. New York, NY: DC Comics, June 1989.

Defending the Domestic: Arthurian Tropes and the American Dream

ZIA ISOLA

I. From Legend to Logo

> *"It was devised by Merlin to embody a very subtle meaning. For in its name it mirrors the roundness of the earth, the concentric spheres of the planets and of the elements in the firmament; and in these heavenly spheres we see the stars and many things besides whence it follows that the Round Table is a true epitome of the universe."*
>
> Queste del Saint Grail

A mounted knight carries a banner aloft as his horse canters lightly from the center of a golden disk, its front hooves crossing over at the perimeter into an outer ring of deeper gold. The knight is dressed in a suit of mail, covered by a white tunic upon which is figured a large red cross. His posture is erect, his face alert and benevolent; the aspect and bearing of both horse and rider betoken vigilance, rectitude, virtue. The device on the knight's banner replicates the design of his tunic, red cross on white field invoking a history of chivalry that evokes the order of Knights Templar, is exalted in the figure of Galahad, and culminates (but does not end) with Spenser's Red Crosse Knight. Written in an inverse arch beneath the prancing hooves of the knight's horse is the slogan "Naturally pure and wholesome." Arching above horse and rider in bold calligraphic script is the product name: *King Arthur Flour*.

If not a properly "literary" rendition of Arthurian legend, the King

Arthur Flour logo with its attendant semiotics certainly invokes the same genre of virtues and idealism as Arthurian literature always has. The perfect roundness of the company logo—like the fabled Round Table—suggests the simultaneous establishment and enclosure of wholeness, entirety, and (perhaps) uncorrupt separateness. The marketing success of King Arthur Flour, like other North American companies that recall Arthurian names and icons, depends upon a ready recognition on the part of consumers of the idealizing and purifying ambitions of Arthur's legendary realm, which is of course to say, the idealizing and purifying ambitions of the literary production that adheres to an elusive fragment of cultural memory that can never be successfully substantiated. The historical identity of Arthur is a perennial topic of debate in academic circles, and no doubt will remain so. On the subject of the moral and ethical identity of Arthur, however, there is much agreement, at least insofar as it may be said that Arthurian knighthood embodies, as Caxton avers in his preface to Malory, "prowesse, hardynesse, humanyte, love, curtosye, and veray gentylnesse."[1] Arthur's Camelot is thus conceived as source and haven of such virtues, a walled city filled with noble folk in an otherwise brutish land; at the heart of this city, like a hub from which issue rays of the strongest light of nobility, is the Round Table and its members who model and defend the purity of Arthur's vision.

The King Arthur Flour knight—namesake and iconic representative of that regal paragon of chivalry—is implicitly then both an emblem of interior purity and defender of the boundaries that enclose and protect that same pure interior. This is the legacy of Arthur, son of the mighty Uther Pendragon and the fair Igraine; Arthur, who effortlessly pulled Excalibur from the great stone on New Year's Day; Arthur, who in battle fought fiercely but fairly, granting quarter to vanquished enemies; Arthur, who beat back the Saxon darkness and united "Walys, Yrland, and Scotland, and moo reames than I will now reherce,"[2] and who, having gained the obeisance of such great lords, then brought them to feast in a fine castle in the city of Camelot, seated in sumptuous equality at the great table. Given any thought, a sack of flour might seem the least congruous place to employ such a powerful archetypal image, yet the King Arthur Flour knight is oddly comfortable in this context, as in fact Arthurian tropes in general seem to be in many facets of North American retail marketing.

Were it not so common to see Arthurian material thus deployed, one might think it highly unlikely that such an eclectic and esoteric legend—amalgamated as it is of Celtic, Roman and Christian mythology—would find such acceptance in the popular imaginings and pocketbook responses of modern American consumers. Indeed, the popularity of Arthur in the United States goes beyond acceptance; consumer response to Arthurian tropes and images might more properly be defined as recognition and identification. A central aim of this essay is to examine that phenomenon and to speculate on some possible reasons for the unlikely but undeniable persistence of Arthur's popularity in the marketing world. What I would like to add to prior readings is the suggestion that the popularity of associating Arthurian legend with American domestic life persists not in spite of but, rather, *because of* the very elements which such marketing elides, that is, the aura of magic and supernatural potency, the presence of unfriendly and subversive elements, and even the darkest aspects of the legend—the incest, adultery and betrayal which contribute to the eventual ruin of the very figure we want to think of as unassailable and eternal.

One of the earliest of American consumer products to use Arthurian brand naming, King Arthur Flour (established 1790 in Boston, Massachusetts),[3] if precocious, is now by no means unusual in its affiliation with the Matter of Britain. King Arthur Flour, Round Table Pizza, Avalon Wood Stoves, Camelot Music, Camelot Vineyards and (perhaps most sensationally) Excalibur Hotel and Casino are but a few of the most familiar contemporary American products bearing Arthurian names, though of course this list does not even begin to scratch the surface of restaurants, repair shops, new age paraphernalia and other genres of consumer goods that are inspired by, named for, or referential of what is arguably the most portable and elastic chivalric myth of the middle ages, nor does it address the wealth of books, films and games that invoke imagery of King Arthur and his Camelot.

Mine is not the first scholarship to remark on the enduring popularity of Arthurian themes in the American retail market. In her 1993 essay, "Marketing Arthur" (*Platte Valley Review* Vol. 21 and reprinted in this volume), Elizabeth Sklar surveys the broad field of American marketplace Arthuriana, and though she bases a good deal of her argument on Detroit area businesses which employ Arthurian references, the insights she offers extrapolate neatly to the national market. Indeed, the recent introduction by Toyota Motor Company of the new "Avalon" as the company's flagship model indicates the degree to which marketers recognize the viability and popularity of a referent which is able to cut across regional, class, gender and even (especially) product genres. As Sklar has rightly noted, the tropological elements of Arthurian legend are expandable, adaptable and ever appealing to U.S. consumer markets.

More recently, Alan Lupack and Barbara Tepa Lupack's co-authored book *Arthur in America* (1999) features a number of essays examining the American appetite for all things Arthurian, from literary adaptations of Arthurian themes to national advertising blitzes that reincarnate Arthur, Guinivere, Lancelot and other members of the court as commodified cultural icons. The authors observe that consumer culture in the United States has succeeded in adapting "the Matter of Britain to American concerns" and this adaptation is "the ultimate democratization" which "makes the legends accessible to everyone and which promotes the ideals of the Arthurian realm as attainable by anyone who cultivates the right values" (Lupack and Lupack 326).

Perusing the products and advertising that engage Arthurian tropes, one may in fact discover a range of values, many of which speak directly to conventional chivalric virtues such as integrity, loyalty, and bravery. Other values and qualities—such as dedication to high standards of craftsmanship, luxury, comfort, wholesomeness and freshness, are at best derivative and contrived, extracted only partially from "original" sources such as Geoffrey of Monmouth, Chrétien de Troyes, or Thomas Malory, then vigorously developed by marketers to extol the presence of such values in their products and services. Because Arthur is such a durable and malleable cultural icon, Arthuriana has provided the American imagination with an infinite source of tropes and images, readily adaptable to a variety of uses, from marketing campaigns to political ideology to digitized video games.

Somewhere in this expansion of "Arthurian" values to cover the vast American marketplace, an ideological and tropological melding takes place (as is often the case with successful advertising) such that the ideals of American life and various product claims have become almost indistinguishable; meanwhile, consumers are exhorted to "live the legend." So prevalent are references to Arthur, Lancelot, Merlin and the feats of the members of the Table Round in the marketing of American consumer goods, and so synonymous do their claims seem with a certain quality of life, that the relationship between Arthurian legend and the American Dream is rarely questioned. In reality, however, there is a significant disjuncture between Legend and Dream. The domestic aspirations of the American Dream that are featured in such advertising equate utopia with a composite of suburban housing, heterosexual marriage, children born in wedlock and kitchens filled with the aroma of baked goods, quite unlike "home life" in Arthurian narratives. In fact, these aspects of American domesticity sharply contrast with and are least represented (if at all) in medieval Arthurian literature, which more often than not focuses on the adventures of a solitary male figure, adventuring far from the comforts of home court.

Despite the foundational degree to which Arthur's court is conceived by contemporary American marketing departments as a matrix of domestic virtue, Arthurian narratives are in fact filled with tales of magic, subterfuge, bastard children and bloody violence. Arguably, these dark and at times nightmarish episodes and characters comprise an oppositional dialectic against which the legend of Arthur is established. Arthur is not merely defined in contrast to these elements, he is, rather, constituted in great measure by them: Arthur is himself a bastard son (conceived through Merlin's subterfuge and Uther's lust); though he espouses Christian-based morals and celebrates Christian holidays, he is counseled by the enigmatic Merlin—a pagan wizard—and aided by other supernatural beings such as the Lady of the Lake. Finally, in no version of the legend does Arthur raise a family, though in some he does sire the bastard Mordred, who (in following the Vulgate Mort Artu, Malory identifies as Arthur's son and nephew) is conceived unwittingly by Arthur with his half-sister, Morgause. When the greater context is taken into account, then, Arthurian legend is unlikely material for "family fare." Though we may theorize types of "purity" (ethnic, national, religious) for Arthur's kingdom and his knights, there is little evidence in medieval literary sources of the type of purity American Arthuriana fashions, and even less evidence of a model for the sort of wholesome family life of which America dreams.

Upon reflection, it is remarkable that Arthurian tropes enjoy the popularity they do in the American retail marketplace, a market that largely directs its efforts toward middle-income Protestant families—families, which, moreover, exist within a purportedly democratic political system, not a monarchy. Indeed, as Lupack and Tepa Lupack have pointed out, the relationship of American political values to chivalric culture is apparently quite paradoxical, insofar as American democracy professes not to be about monarchy, aristocracy, or inherited rank, but rather prides itself on plurality, elected representation, and advancement according to individual merit. Yet in spite of these sites of disjuncture, Arthurian material appears to be even more popular in the United States than in the United Kingdom, where it has served a long and distinguished tenure as proto-nationalistic narrative and cultural model.

A possible explanation of this seeming paradox may have to do with congruencies in American political ideology and the ideals that are commonly associated with Arthur's Camelot. Ever the good host, Arthur is amenable to inscriptions and overlays upon his chivalric signifiers, and likewise the political ideology of his legend is graciously accommodating. So, for example, the Round Table comes to represent democracy, the Grail

Quest is analogous to Westward Expansion,[4] Arthur's unification of the warring tribes of Britain comes to symbolize the (purportedly) unified identity of America's racially and culturally diverse population, and King Arthur himself becomes Gary Cooper as Old West sheriff in the Hollywood movie *High Noon*—one man who could (and did) make a difference because he was willing to stand up for truth, justice, and moral goodness. One of the most remarkable instances of the facility with which Arthur may be adapted to American civic ideals is the association of the Kennedy administration with the realm of Camelot. Shortly after her husband's assassination, the ever media-savvy Jacqueline Kennedy suggested the connection to Theodore H. White, the historian/reporter who introduced the Camelot connection to the American public.[5] It was not much of a stretch however; the idealism of the youthful Kennedy administration dovetailed neatly with the legend of a boy-king who unified a realm and professed virtue as a creed. Congruence with America's political ideology may, after all, make sense, perhaps because Arthur's utopian dream aims for a de-hierarchized body politic, and is therefore not unlike the American dream of a democratic utopia. Both speak to high-minded ideals of inclusion, unification and righteousness, both exercise utopian fantasies based on visions of harmony, abundance and secure borders.

II. What's Food Got to Do with It?

> "He wolde never ete
> Upon such a dere day, er hym devised were
> Of sum aventurus thyng, an uncouthe tale
> Of sum mayn mervayle that he myght trawe,
> Of alderes, of armes, of other aventurus"
> SGGK Fitt I, 91–95

Even if one can discover affiliations between two seemingly disparate political systems, it remains less apparent what a legendary medieval king, a sorcerer and a lot of hyper-masculine knights in armor have to do with the part of the American Dream that includes the nuclear family, truth in advertising, baked goods and suburban mini-malls. In particular, it is surprising that food products would find a champion in Arthur, since the enterprise of eating or drinking is at best fraught (as it is for Gawain when confronted with the adventure of the Green Knight at Arthur's Pentecostal feast) and occasionally disastrous (as it is for Tristan and Iseult when they quaff Brangaene's enchanted wine). Even for the Fisher King, sustained as he is by a miraculous and blessed type of food, the dinner hour is a less than comforting undertaking, as poor Perceval will attest. Yet it is often in the marketing of food, feasting, and drinking that one is best able to witness the full scale implementation of American Arthuriana. While it is readily apparent why a fantasy video or role-playing game would want to invoke the magical and unlocatable landscape of Arthur's Britain, understandable why a cutlery company or machine shop might choose the name Excalibur to signify its keen-edged craftsmanship, and reasonable that a luxury hotel might want to summon associations with the sumptuousness of court life, it is less clear what sort of logic would pair food products with chivalric imagery.[6]

Of particular interest are two North American companies, King Arthur Flour, which I have already mentioned, and Round Table Pizza. Both companies routinely affiliate Arthurian tropes with product qualities such as freshness, wholesomeness and purity, and include in their corporate statements claims to principle that resonate with Arthurian codes of virtue. In this, of course, they are not unique; as previously discussed, Arthurian tropes are regularly called upon to signify product quality, reliability and even corporate integrity. King Arthur Flour and Round Table Pizza, however, tilt the association to very specific modes of virtue, using phrases that refer to chivalric registers of honesty and purity in order to invoke modes of "wholesomeness" corresponding to a particular type of suburban lifestyle. Therefore Round Table, "the last honest pizza," touts its "fresh, never frozen" ingredients, and King Arthur Flour promotes its flour as "naturally pure and wholesome." Both companies use explicitly chivalric images for their logos: King Arthur Flour has its own standard-bearing knight, as discussed in the opening of this essay, while Round Table Pizza represents itself with a logo of three brightly colored shields. As two of the most successful and long-lived "Arthurian" companies, King Arthur Flour and Round Table Pizza are exemplary (founded in 1790 and 1959 respectively), though in general it is safe to say that within the realm of product naming and promotion, the fantasized world of Arthur's Britain and the quotidian (if equally fantasized) world of suburban America are deeply imbricated.

Even so, how is it that a flour company and a pizza parlor have so successfully identified their products with the values of Arthur's court? Speaking as a consumer, when I think of King Arthur, Camelot, or other Arthurian tropes, I never automatically associate things like purity, wholesomeness or fresh ingredients. Even when I think of Arthur's famous banquets, an entirely different range of qualities come to mind, influenced mostly, I suppose, by watching B movies and going to weekend theme fairs. A medieval banquet is therefore composed of oversized turkey legs, corn on the cob, and boar heads roasted on a spit. Never mind the historical inaccuracy of these associations; the point is, when I think of a medieval banquet, I do not think of pizza and home-baked bread. Nevertheless, when I see King Arthur Flour and Round Table Pizza, I feel a comfortable nostalgia and friendly response to the product logos.

Interestingly, these two companies capitalize on some of the most masculine icons from Arthurian legend: The Round Table, around which assembled—according to Malory—no less than 150 of the bravest, strongest, and most famous knights in the civilized world, and King Arthur himself, paragon and role model for all knightly virtues. Gender bias notwithstanding, the products of these two companies seem to be most about the inner sanctum of American family life (food preparation, communal eating) and further, seem least of all to be targeting a macho-minded consumer base. In fact, it would appear that the primary demographic target for these products is a woman (especially in the case of King Arthur Flour)— most likely a married woman with children. This consumer base is distinguished from the markets for things like Arthurian cinema and television, which seem to address themselves to both genders, or Arthurian board, video and role-playing games, which direct themselves to specifically male fantasies and masculine role-playing (Sklar 71).

The apparent ease with which the Arthurian chivalric myth is able to incorporate such modifications, and the equal ease with which American consumers are able to accept the inscription of suburban aspirations upon a medieval world would seem to indicate some deep and time-tested affinity between the two. But I do not think that is because we are inherently chivalric about our eating habits. And though we may certainly have succeeded in democratizing Arthur even as we have romanticized modern life, essential elements make correspondence possible between the imagined and the real, the past and the present, without modification or manipulation by promotion specialists. The central common denominator in all three venues—the legend of Arthur's kingdom, the American domestic dream, and the implicit promises of companies such as Round Table Pizza and King Arthur Flour—is a fantasy of fulfillment. American retail advertising capitalizes on the recognition of this most common and therefore virtually universal fantasy, easily superimposing the contours of one dream (archaic, archetypal) upon those of another (more modern but equally archetypal, equally fantastic).

III. Where Have All the Horrors Gone?

> *"And whan sir Mordred saw kynge Arthur he ran untyll hym with hys swerde drawyn in hys honde, and there kyng Arthur smote sir Mordred undir the shylde, with a foyne of hys speare, thorowoute the body more than a fadom. And whan sir Mordred felte that he had hys dethys wounde he threste hymselff with the myght that he had upp to the burre of kyng Arthurs speare, an dryght so he smote hys fadir, kynge Arthure, with hys swerde holdynge in both hys hondys, uppon the syde of the hede, that the swerde perced the helmet and the tay of the brayne. And therewith Mordred daysshed downe starke dede to the erthe."*
>
> Malory, *Morte Darthur* XXI, iv–xiii

Commercial co-optation, while perhaps extending the shelf-life of certain aspects of the legend, has at the same time undoubtedly compromised the complex richness of the opposing tensions that make Arthurian narratives so intriguing in the first place. The wholesome qualities of Round Table Pizza and King Arthur Flour are radical (if gentle) reinscriptions upon the palimpsest of Arthur's shield, inscriptions which redefine both form and substance of "Arthurian" chivalric virtues. Particularly in the case of Round Table Pizza, in fact, there is virtually nothing tropologically related to Arthurian legend save the company name. The three shields of the Round Table Logo—which might have but do not feature heraldic insignia of dragons or lions—collectively convey a new object of quest: according to the official company website (http://www.roundtablepizza.com) the bars of the shields are meant to signify the letters F-U-N. In addition to such reinterpretation of the particulars of virtue, American domestication of Arthurian legend has also apparently resulted in a processed version, a version that is sanitized, purified and made wholesomely palatable by the elision of the fantastic, marvelous and morally ambiguous elements of the legend.

Indeed, Arthur's Camelot stands for virtuous living and fellowship, and the Grail Quest can be read as a search for the ultimate object of consumption. But just outside the city walls (and sometimes within) dwell the necessary Others that give Arthur's world its dialectical definition. Where in contemporary American marketing is the thoroughly *un*christian Merlin who draws his power from dark unnamable sources? Where the ruthless Pendragon who is as full of blood lust as he is of generative force? Where the decidedly not domestic, rarely maternal (and not well behaved) women such as Morgan le Fay, Guinevere, Iseult or Nimue? Where the treacherous Mordred? Where the grisly Green Knight, who under the inducements of Morgan's magic so strangely interrupts Arthur's feast on Pentecost? Where the Questing Beast, the Wasteland, the suffering Fisher King or the great and tragic Lancelot, riven by his divided loyalties to king and queen? And what is the legend of Arthur without these elements?

I would like to return to my earlier question of what King Arthur and company have to do with American domestic life and family values—or, perhaps more usefully, what does Arthurian chivalry have to do with women, children and questions of purity?

When thinking of such knightly preoccupations as *fin amors*, jousting tournaments, or crusades against infidels, the connection seems oblique, except insofar as a knight might participate in all these activities in order to win a lady's hand. Yet even this connection is strained, since the conventions of courtly love—whether one wishes to read them as adulterous or chaste—do not exactly promote values attendant to modern conceptions of family life. When one considers further, however, the codes of chivalry and the sworn vows to which a knight was duty-bound—namely to defend (in this order) holy church, widows and orphans—the connection becomes clearer. A knight's first duty is defense—defense of institutions (the church, the crown), defense of helpless subjects (women and children chief among these), defense of territories (Christendom, the royal realm, the castle). And so borders, boundaries and limits of all kinds would seem to be a knight's rightful, natural, and even obligatory place.

Nor is it surprising that Round Table restaurant—"home of the last honest pizza" and bastion of family fun—should identify itself with a logo composed of heraldic shields, suggesting, again, superior defensive power in the protection of interiors from outside assault. Thus the corporate logos of both companies, by invoking the semiotics of chivalry, advance consumer confidence in the integrity of corporate mission and product quality while implicitly securing the boundaries of domestic enterprise (domestic should be read as suggesting both "home" and nation). So knight and shield circulate at the perimeters of our anxieties over the preservation of one of our most fundamental aspirations, that is, the American Dream of a happy, safe and well-fed family, a family, moreover, that is sustained by products ensuing from domestic American labor. The energy and cultural prowess we summon to defend this dream speaks on the one hand to the value we as a society place on the safety of our families, and one need not look to comparisons between small feudal fiefdoms and the American pioneer family to legitimate our desire to protect home and hearth. On the other hand, that this *particular* chivalric legend is drawn upon is telling, given that, even in its most glorious moments, Arthur's Camelot was perpetually threatened and in the end undone by malignant powers, both human and supernatural.

It is precisely these troublesome elements that make this particular representation of chivalric defense so appealing and so durable, allowing us to imagine ourselves, even in our most mundane moments (eating pizza after soccer or making a batch of oatmeal cookies) to be engaged in an ancient contest against the forces of darkness. The perpetual recurrence of the Once and Future King speaks to our aspirations for a safe and just and well governed universe—yes—but the continual reassertion of this icon is also symptomatic of tensions and anxieties over our most cherished and unstable institution—domestic family life.

If we are somehow arrogating aristocratic and heroic virtues to our quotidian experience by enlisting tropes from Arthur's masculinized economy of virtue, we are also acknowledging the extreme fragility of the very conventions which seem, because of that conventionality, perennial and unassailable. In drawing upon Arthurian ideals and idealized knights to defend our own American utopias, our chivalric imaginings parallel not only our aspirations but our fears.[7] Just so, the most basic conventions and institutions of the American Dream—family life, safety, freedom from tyranny—are ever at risk, especially in a world that includes daily reports of divorce, food poisoning and consumer fraud, not to mention the more horrific accounts of child abuse, uncontainable toxic waste and random school shootings. The "Dark Ages," it would seem, remain with us yet.

On feast days in Camelot, Arthur, in the glowing comfort of his torch-lit hall, is ever unwilling to eat until he has witnessed a marvel, as if to suggest that by such placement the unruly elements of "aventure"[8] might be located and contained by being "brought to light." In similar fashion, the American Dream, at its most domestic and comfort-filled moments repeatedly returns to the margins of its imagined security in order to perform a gesture of containment, offering a semiotic shield against elements that threaten to disturb the most basic acts of sustenance. In the mundane conflict between the utopian world we imagine and the very real threats to that world, we summon in our acts of consumption (both retail and alimentary), a chivalric champion: Arthur, king of the most famous of imagined communities, knight of honor, defender of all domestic boundaries.

Notes

1. Vinaver, xv.
2. Vinaver, 11.

3. A reply from the King Arthur Flour Company regarding my query about the date of establishment: "The company was founded in 1790... Originally it was known as 'Henry Wood & Son.' In 1890 the company adopted the name "Sands, Taylor & Wood." The year 1896 referred to on our Web site is the year that the Arthurian legend inspired a family of brand names. George Wood—no relation to Henry—attended a musical production called "The Knights of the Round Table." He came away convinced that the legendary virtues of strength, purity, honesty and loyalty to ideals were precisely the values he wished his flour to represent. Finally, in 1999 the name was changed to "The King Arthur Flour Company, Inc." to reflect how we are most widely recognized." Ana Villaverde, Marketing Specialist, King Arthur Flour Company, email to the author, 30 November 2000.

4. Note that at the ultimate reaches of this expansion the United States even has its own Avalon: at the western edge of the North American continent, on Catalina Island, 40 miles off the coast of Southern California, is the small resort town named after Arthur's mythical resting place.

5. Others have noted this connection; see Lupack and Tepa [Lupack, 276–277 and Knight 28–31].

6. The banquet hall does come to mind, but in the case of foods which are not the sort of exotic fare a royal banquet might include, the association seems more ironic than apropos.

7. One may well note the architectural logic of many suburban housing developments, which are enclosed by high, fortress-like walls, explicitly echoing the design of a walled medieval city.

8. Vinaver, glossary: "a(d)venture, sb. chance; risk; danger; enterprise; chance occurrence; remarkable experience."

Works Cited

Knight, Stephen. *Arthurian Literature and Society*. New York: St. Martin's, 1983.

Lupack, Alan, and Barbara Tepa Lupack. *King Arthur in America*. Cambridge: D.S. Brewer, 1999.

Malory, Sir Thomas. *The Works of Sir Thomas Malory*. 3 vols. Eugene Vinaver, Ed. 2nd ed.; Oxford: Clarendon Press, 1967.

Queste del Saint Graal. Trans. Pauline Maud Matarasso. Baltimore: Penguin, 1970.

Sir Gawain and the Green Knight. R.A. Waldron, Ed. Evanston: Northwestern University Press, 1970.

Sklar, Elizabeth S. "Marketing Arthur : The Commodification of Arthurian Legend." *Platte Valley Review* 21.1 (Winter 1993): 61–82.

Tintagel: The Best of English Twinkie

JAMES NOBLE

Having told her that I was in England visiting sites associated with the Arthurian legend, I was not surprised when the manager of the Chalice Well property in Glastonbury asked me where I was headed next. I was, however, more than a little taken aback by the vehemence with which she responded to my reply. "Tintagel!" she exploded, "then I'm afraid you are about to experience the very worst of English Twinkie!" Having lived all my life in Canada, a country where politeness is a virtue more highly prized than cleanliness, I refrained from remarking than I could not imagine anything much more "twinkified" than Glastonbury had become since my last visit there ten years before.[1]

During the course of the three preceding evenings I had sat in the bar of the *George and Pilgrim Inn* nursing a pint of lager and eavesdropping on some of the more animated conversations taking place around me. For one group of middle-aged American tourists in particular, each evening in the pub had produced excited talk about experiences of Glastonbury that had entailed meditating at the site of Arthur's tomb in the ruins of Glastonbury Abbey and under Joseph of Arimathea's thorn tree on Wearyall Hill; of channeling Merlin on the summit of Glastonbury Tor; of firewalking and dowsing; or of sitting for a tarot, rune, or crystal reading by one of the local practitioners of these esoteric arts. This is not to disparage any of these activities or those who practice them, but to suggest that, since my last visit to the town, the age-old story of King Arthur had clearly become part of a New Age culture that Glastonbury had seen fit to embrace and promote for commercial gain. Since one of the purposes of my trip was to determine the extent to which the Arthurian sites in England had been affected in the past decade by what can only be described as a steadily increasing interest in things Arthurian, particularly in the realm of popular culture, the prospect of "twinkie" at Tintagel intrigued me more than my informant in Glastonbury could possibly have realized.

I arrived in the legendary birthplace of King Arthur to discover a small village arranged along both sides of a single street that terminates on a bluff overlooking the ruins of Tintagel Castle. On the edge of the bluff stands *King Arthur's Castle Hotel*, at one end of which a sign entices visitors into the *Excali-Bar*. Not far from the hotel, on a crescent named *Knight's Close*, is a modern housing development called *Camelot Flats and Bungalow*. What might be described as the "business section" of Tintagel consists of the equivalent of a couple of city blocks; lining the two sides of the street are a series of shops, museums, restaurants, and hotels, at least half of which bear names such as *Merlin's Cave*, *Excalibur Restaurant and Tea Room*, *Merlin's Gifts*, *King Arthur Bookshop*, *King Arthur's Arms*, *Pendragon Gallery & Gifts*, and *King Arthur's Cafe*.

Clearly, the economy of the village relies heavily on its association with the medieval legend of King Arthur and does everything it can to promote that connection. Without even a trace of irony or apology, the shops in the village cater to tourists by furnishing them with inexpensive souvenirs of their visit to King Arthur's birthplace. Plastic replicas of Arthur's sword Excalibur are readily available in vivid shades of orange, red, and green; ceramic statues of Merlin are ubiquitous and range in size from the small shelf model to the large piece suitable for coffee table or mantle. Aprons, tea towels, place mats, nightshirts, T-shirts, and sweatshirts emblazoned with some reminder of the Arthurian story are to be had in a wide range of colours and sizes. To my mind, however, perhaps the saddest and most telling signifiers of the extent to which Tintagel is prepared to exploit its Arthurian connections are two signs posted outside the *King Arthur's Arms* hotel. One sign invites tourists to visit *Guinevere's Lounge* and "try some tasty food, from an Excaliburger to a Steak." The second sign, located at the entrance to the hotel pub, advertises the specialty of the house—a selection of jacket potatoes called *Famous Spuds*. The *King Arthur Spud* features a tuna and sweet corn filling, the *Sir Galahad* cheese and ham, the *Sir Lancelot* sausage and beans. Or for the tourist committed to experiencing the Arthurian legend at its fullest, the *Round Table Spud* offers a choice of three different fillings.

Arriving in Tintagel at the very beginning of the tourist season, I experienced the village ready for the onslaught of summer visitors but not yet overrun by them. I was given some sense of what the place must be like in high season, however, by the owner of the hotel at which I was staying. He informed me that on any given day in July or August there could be as many as thirty-five tour-buses and three or four hundred cars parked along both sides of the village's single street and in the large "downtown" parking lot, which, not surprisingly perhaps, bears the name *King Arthur's Car and Coach Park*.

The principal tourist attraction in Tintagel is, of course, the ruins of the castle in which Arthur is purported to have been born. Interestingly, however, it is the one spot in the whole village where fact and fiction seem not to have become conflated. A sign posted at the entrance to the castle ruins informs visitors that the site is *The legendary birthplace of King Arthur*. But the sign goes on to read as follows:

> High on the cliff edge ahead of you are the remains of the medieval castle built by Richard, Earl of Cornwall, between 1233–36.
> The castle was built at least 500 years after a real or fictitious "Arthur" fought the Saxons away to the East in the 6th century. An "Arthur" may never have come to Tintagel, but it is probable that at about that time Tintagel was the stronghold of the kings of Cornwall.

This disclaimer notwithstanding, I suspect that most visitors to the site believe themselves to be at King Arthur's birthplace. And indeed it is hard, even for someone as cynical as I can be in such circumstances, to stand on Tintagel Head amid the castle ruins and not to entertain the fantasy that one is indeed standing on the spot where the Arthurian legend had its beginnings. For there is about the place that indefinable sense of mystery that rests at the heart of the legend, that intangible something that succeeds in hooking some of us initially, and that ultimately succeeds in keeping us hooked to the story of Arthur and his knights.

Hooking the gullible is clearly what Tintagel's other principal tourist attraction is all about. Located at the opposite end of the village is a large stone building called *King Arthur's Hall of Chivalry*. The Hall was the brainchild of millionaire Frederick Thomas Glasscock, a partner in the British custard firm of Monkhouse and Glasscock, who retired to Tintagel in the late 1920s.[2] Legend has it that he one day saw a display of Monkhouse and Glasscock jellies and custard powders in the window of a local grocer's shop, a display that also included replicas of Excalibur and the Round Table. The window display so excited Glasscock's imagination that he set about to create in Tintagel a new Arthurian Order. Circa 1930, to house what he called *The Fellowship of the Order of Knights of the Round Table*, Glasscock built a stone hall, which he named after King Arthur. Children could join Glasscock's Arthurian Fellowship as *Searchers*; for a small fee, teenagers could become *Pilgrims*. To qualify as a *Knight*, one had to be proposed and seconded by members of the Fellowship and to undergo a probationary training that lasted for twelve months. For a small fee, newly dubbed knights were presented with a book on the Fellowship and other pieces of relevant literature.

So successful was Glasscock in marketing his new Arthurian Order that in 1933, on the Feast of Pentecost, a day synonymous in the Arthurian legend with new beginnings, Glasscock opened a second and much larger hall on the site. This second hall, called *The Great Hall of Chivalry*, was an impressive undertaking, some 5000 square feet in size and constructed of granite. The building contains seventy-two stained glass windows of varying sizes: the smaller ones around the lower periphery of the hall feature the heraldic devices of Arthur's knights, whereas the large windows at both ends and high on the sidewalls depict episodes from the legend and the moral principles for which Glasscock believed the original Arthurian Order to have stood and for which his new Order should likewise stand. Given my family name, I was particularly struck by one of these windows, which bears the Tennysonian dictum "Better not to be at all than not to be Noble!"

The hall contains three Round Tables, the largest of which is constructed of granite and sits in front of the dais housing *The Great Granite Throne*. On a ledge above and behind the throne hovers a large uncut stone supporting an anvil in which a sword is embedded. It is from the Great Granite Throne that Glasscock apparently presided over meetings of the Fellowship in his capacity as King Arthur. The strong sense of theatre that would seem to have characterized these meetings is evoked by Ronald Youlton in his recollection of the knighting ceremony:

> The new knight would be suitably attired for the ceremony while those already knighted wore robes of blue or red according to their rank, whether knights of the sword or sceptre. The principles of the Order were read from a scroll, prayers were said, oaths made. The ceremony started in semi-darkness until the sword Excalibur was drawn from the scabbard with great flourish and Glasscock (in the role of King Arthur) struck the new knight on the shoulder, giving him his name: Sir Galahad, perhaps, Sir Lancelot or Sir Bedivere.

Soon after the opening of the Great Hall in 1933, Glasscock made a trip to the United States to promote his new business venture. His efforts proved so successful that, upon his return to Tintagel, he was required to hire secretaries to keep up with all the correspondence arriving from overseas. Sadly, Glasscock died only a year later aboard the Queen Mary while making a second recruiting expedition to America. Without its Arthur, the *Fellowship of the Order of the Knights of the Round Table* did not survive for long, and the building constructed to house the Order soon became a meeting place for the local Masonic lodge.

Interestingly, however, the Fellowship conceived by Glasscock was revived in 1993 by the new owners of the building and (at the time of my visit at any rate)is actively recruiting members at a cost of £40 a year. It is to these prospective members that one of the two signs at the entrance to the building seems intended to appeal. It is a sign that reads:

> ARTHURIAN EXPERIENCE
> These are the only buildings in the world dedicated to the ideals and legend of King Arthur.
> These Halls are the headquarters of the fellowship of the Knights of the Round Table of King Arthur.
> The fellowship attracts Arthurian scholars and romantics of all ages from all round the world.
> It is here, in King Arthur's Hall, that the classic legend is told by Robert Powell, highlighted by laser, music and sound. Then, in the Great Hall of Chivalry you see the wonderful stained glass windows, the great granite throne and, of course, the round table.
> ——————————
> Our shop carries a comprehensive range of cards, books, prints, jewellery and gifts—do feel free to come in and walk around.
> AS SEEN ON NATIONAL LOTTERY LIVE HERE FEBRUARY 95

The announcement that this is the only building in the world dedicated to the *ideals* of the Arthurian legend, that it is the headquarters of a fellowship of knights, and that this fellowship attracts Arthurian scholars and romantics from all around the world is surely meant to suggest that King Arthur's Great Hall of Chivalry is something other than a mere tourist trap. Indeed, the sign implies that the experience of hearing Robert Powell's multimedia rendition of the "classic" Arthurian story and of seeing the "wonderful" stained glass windows, the great granite throne, and the Round Table(s) is for the Arthurian pilgrim who visits the site everything that Canterbury must have been for the medieval Christian.

Significantly, however, it is at this point in the sign that the unapologetic combination of romantic idealism and unabashed commercialism that characterizes the Tintagel experience in general is to be discerned, for those not interested in becoming knights of the Fellowship are invited to enter the building anyway for the purpose of inspecting the merchandise for sale in the shop. Although its significance puzzled me when I first saw it, the sign's allusion to the National Lottery draw held at the site in February of 1995 now strikes me as yet another marketing ploy designed to tempt the tourist into "taking a chance" on the Great Hall by sampling some, if not all, of what it has to offer.

Although the sign on the other side of the pathway likewise advertises the lottery and a shop containing "something to suit everyone," it says nothing about the fact that the building houses a fellowship of Arthurian knights. This sign reads:

> The Legend of Arthur
>
> Stretching back behind this house are the two vast halls built in the 1920's as a tribute to the Arthurian ideals.
>
> In the first hall, Robert Powell tells the classic story of King Arthur and the knights of the Round Table, with laser light, music and sound—a remarkable experience.
>
> The great Hall of Chivalry, 5000 sq. ft. of granite, contains thrones, Round Table, Sword in the Stone, and the superb 72 Pre-Raphaelite stained glass windows of Veronica Whall.
>
> Try out the Great Granite Throne and see the beautiful colours of the windows, yes, cameras are allowed. This is a place for romantics of all ages.
>
> FEEL FREE TO WALK AROUND OUR SHOP. THERE IS SOMETHING TO SUIT EVERYONE.
>
> AS SEEN ON *NATIONAL* LOTTERY LIVE HERE FEBRUARY 95.

Whereas it, too, advertises a multi-media retelling of the Arthurian story by Robert Powell and an opportunity to explore the architecture and contents of the Great Hall, it is significant, I believe, that this particular sign offers the visitor a more directly *participatory* experience of the site than does the sign on the opposite side of the pathway. It assures prospective visitors that the "remarkable" experience of listening to and watching the Powell narrative unfold will be followed by the opportunity to "*try out* the Great Granite throne," to "*see* the beautiful colours of the windows" and to *take pictures* of all the site has to offer. The verbs employed on this sign advertise a physical, hands-on experience for the uninitiated, whereas the wording of the sign on the opposite side of the pathway seems intended to appeal to those already acquainted with the Arthurian story.

As both signs suggest, the shop through which one must pass to get to the Great Hall is designed to accommodate a wide variety of tastes and interests. The merchandise for sale is highly eclectic and ranges from inexpensive plastic shields, swords, and helmets, mass-produced in Asian sweatshops far from Tintagel, to relatively expensive one-of-a-kind paintings and handcrafted articles in ceramic, wood, and stone produced by Cornish artists and artisans. Most of the expensive items in the shop have no immediate or obvious connection to the Arthurian legend, whereas virtually all of the inexpensive items do.

Those who pay to pass beyond the shop are not permitted to enter the Great Hall until they have experienced the laser, music, and sound show staged at half-hour intervals in Glasscock's original construction, the King Arthur Hall. Once visitors have been seated, the room is plunged into total darkness for about a minute. As a red laser light on the ceiling begins to pulsate, the voice of Merlin invites us to travel with him back through "the mists of time" to the days of King Arthur. For the benefit of the imaginatively challenged, a vaporizer fills the room with a fine mist as Merlin begins to speak. Suddenly, a bright white light pierces the mist and illuminates a painted panel on one of the walls. As Merlin explains, the panel in question tells the story of King Arthur's birth at Tintagel. As the account concludes, the room is again plunged into darkness. Within a few seconds, however, the white light flashes on another panel depicting the acquisition of Excalibur. Cumulatively, the ten panels painted by artist William Hatherell and arranged around three sides of the room succeed in affording the visitor a visual and auditory version of the Arthurian story as recounted by the fifteenth century English writer Sir Thomas Malory.

Interestingly, however, the Arthur of this multimedia narrative is not only a highly sanitized version of his medieval original, but also the product of a late twentieth-century misogyny that, ironically enough, is quintessentially medieval in that it attributes the ultimate downfall of Arthur and his Round Table to the wiles of a woman. Significantly, however, the Eve to our Adam is not, as she is in Malory, Arthur's unfaithful wife Guinevere; instead, she is Arthur's evil sister Morgan le Fay. The Arthur of the Tintagel narrative is not, as he is in Malory, a womanizer who fathers Mordred by committing incest with the promiscuous Morgause. Instead, he is a happily married man who is tricked into sleeping with his sister when Morgan resorts to her magical powers and disguises Morgause to look like Guinevere. Needless to say, the laser and sound show says nothing about Arthur's attempt to rid himself of Mordred by killing all the children in the land born on Mordred's birthday, nor does it say anything about the fact that Arthur's death at the hands of Mordred is the consequence of a peevish impetuosity that Malory's Arthur had been warned to curb if he wished to survive the encounter with his son. The Tintagel narrative informs us that Arthur falls at Camblan because of a curse visited upon him by Morgan at the time of his birth; it is as a result of this curse that Excalibur and its life-preserving scabbard fail Arthur at the moment he most needs both instruments. In Malory, of course, the scabbard has long since disappeared by this point, and there is no suggestion whatever of a natal curse on Arthur or anybody else.

Although Malory's Morgan bears no love for her brother and attempts on more than one occasion to kill him, Malory's Arthur is not the hapless victim of Morgan's treachery that the Tintagel laser and sound show makes him out to be. Clearly, Malory's Arthur is a figure the owners of King Arthur's Hall of Chivalry either do not wish or cannot afford to promote. Whether the sanitized Arthur of Tintagel's laser, music, and sound show is the offspring of a moral or a commercial ideology I did not have the opportunity to determine; in either eventuality, however, I would venture to guess that his medieval counterpart proved to be endowed with a complexity that made him much too human and with a humanity that rendered him far too complex for the commercial marketplace of modern day Tintagel.

Notes

1. This paper was originally presented at the annual meeting of the Popular Culture Association in San Antonio, TX, in 1997. Tintagel as described in the paper is as I found it in late April of 1995.

2. All information in this paper relating to Glasscock's Great Hall of Chivalry is taken from Brenda Duxbury and Michael Williams, *King Arthur Country in Cornwall* (Bossiney Books, 1979), pp. 22–32.

Arthur, Popular Culture, and World War II

DONALD L. HOFFMAN

When Arthur first appears in the context of a coherent history (Geoffrey of Monmouth's *History of the Kings of Britain*), he is the leader of the Britons against the invading hordes of Saxons. About half a century later, the Saxon priest Lawman translated Geoffrey's Latin prose into alliterative English couplets. While retaining Arthur's role as a British war hero in the narrative, the translation concludes with a poignant reminder of the author's position as a member of the Saxon race, which centuries ago may have defeated the British, but was now oppressed by the new Norman invaders. Lawman has no trouble translating the relevance of Arthur to call on him as the protector of the island, revising Merlin's famous prophecy of the promised hero to pray that in these perilous times "an Arthoure shulde yet come *Anglen* to fulste." While he may introduce that distinguishing *an*, it seems clear that for Lawman Arthur is now the champion of the English, protector of the island against all invading forces. Nearly eight hundred years later, Arthur's defense of the island against Germanic invaders took on an uncanny relevance as the islanders were forced to protect themselves from the Nazis. The structural parallelism would seem almost to demand a popular explosion of Arthurian propaganda in World War II.[1]

There are, however, surprisingly few attempts to situate Arthur in this perilous time. Only four authors, one sort of unwittingly,[2] seem to have attempted with varying success to envision an Arthur in the midst of this contemporary war. Only these novelists, John Erskine, T.H. White, Dennis Anderson, and Donald Barthelme,[3] significantly implicate Arthur in the Great War that is, has been, or is yet to come.

45

In the period between the two wars, John Erskine, a professor of literature at Columbia and music at Julliard, wrote two novels on Arthurian themes, books that were quite popular, although they did not quite match the appeal of his tales promising to reveal the private lives of historical notables, such as Adam and Eve and Helen of Troy. His Arthurian novels, *Galahad: Enough of His Life to Explain His Reputation* and *Tristan and Isolde: Restoring Palamede*, nevertheless sold well. The titles themselves serve to introduce the reader to Erskine's slightly quizzical, urbane approach to the narratives. His clearly antiheroic attitude, however, is not intended to diminish the legends, but to domesticate[4] them, to read them from a contemporary Jazz Age perspective and to find characters not unlike ourselves with passions and disappointments, goals and failures, that are more often ordinary than spectacular and become heroic only by accident and in hindsight. Heroes, like everyone else, Erskine seems to suggest, are only trying to muddle through.

In the process of muddling through, however, Erskine's medieval characters frequently find themselves in extremely contemporary situations. In *Tristan and Isolde*, for example, he shifts the focus from the famous lovers to one of the most intriguing minor characters in Arthurian literature, the Saracen Palomides. In doing so, he introduces the modern problem of the alienated hero, and is able to reflect some of the concerns of the Harlem Renaissance of which, as a professor at Columbia, he was virtually in the geographical heart. Refracted through the art and sensibility of a professor of medieval literature, however, Palomides' blackness may well seem more a theoretical concept than a lived reality, but as a hero of color his Palomides also calls into question the often assumed univocal, universal meaning of the Holy Grail.

While Palomides introduces the silenced issue of race into the Arthurian legend, Erskine's earlier novel, *Galahad* (1926), addresses an issue that will erupt in the years before the war. *Galahad* infuses the traditional plot of Galahad's birth and his eventual undertaking of the Quest with a structure and theme derived from Freud and Ibsen, who are both concerned with bringing buried secrets to light. For Erskine's Galahad, the secret is the mystery of his conception and the greater mystery of his father's love for Guinevere. The revelation of Lancelot's love for Guinevere is particularly explosive in this revision because Galahad himself has already fallen in love with her. He feels doubly and deeply betrayed by the woman who has tried to mould him into the agent of her vision, a vision of a new, ennobled Camelot greater than that imagined by Arthur or maintained by Lancelot, her disappointing husband and her disillusioned lover.

It is Guinevere who imagines a quest that "leaves the ladies" out, a possibility that Galahad cannot at first imagine. She goes on to explain her vision at greater length.

> "If I had a son, I'd wish for him first a strong and healthy body. That means strong passions, Galahad—strong everything the body makes you think of. I'd want him to be excited over all forms of beauty—not merely interested, but roused. I'd want this excitement in him to be so terrific and so untiring that all of his life, from one end to the other, would be like going to a fire. Ordinary men, of course, are afraid of it, or they haven't the strength to keep it up. Some of them are really glad to be weak, in order to be safe. But the kind of man I'm talking about—the excitement, unfortunately, might lead him every which way—he might try to go to all the fires at once. Choose one dream, Galahad, and be faithful to that, but don't say the things you decided not to do were necessarily bad; don't make your choice easier by pretending yours was the only good life possible. I hope you will love everything that can be loved, even though you give up most of it—keep the bodily delight in the world, yet discipline yourself."
>
> "It sounds difficult," said Galahad, "even if I knew what to choose. You didn't say what."
>
> "I don't know what," said Guinevere. "But I'm sure we ought to leave the world more exciting than we found it. More beautiful, with more in it to respond to."
>
> "And more to deny ourselves of," said Galahad [218–219].

Guinevere may seem quite benign but her ecstatic vision is the stuff of the aesthetic fascism associated with the Futurists, like Marinetti in Italy, as well as anglophone Imagist and Symbolist poets like Ezra Pound, the early T.S. Eliot, and even W.B. Yeats. Like D'Annunzio's Francesca da Rimini she wants to live in the ecstatic moment when she is all flame and to worship men and women who are all beautiful and strong and heroic, like the sculptures at Rockefeller Center (coincidentally owned by Erksine's employer, Columbia University). There is no inherent evil in Guinevere's vision, except for its exclusivity, but the worship of beauty can too easily shift into a scorn for the unbeautiful and eventually a willingness, even a mission, to eradicate them. As the later poetry of Ezra Pound demonstrates, there is not a great distance between finding an individual or a behavior unattractive to finding an entire race unattractive, either physically or morally, and, therefore, expendable.

Guinevere attempts to define a kind of multivalent exclusivity, encouraging Galahad to "love everything that can be loved," but also warning him not to pretend that the life he embraces "was the only good life possible." She also encourages him to maintain a balance between bodily delight and discipline. There is a beauty to her plan, but it is a plan that ignores the agent. Like Muriel Sparks's Miss Jean Brodie, who misreads poor, stupid Mary MacGregor and sends her off to die accidentally fighting for the wrong side in the Spanish Civil War, Guinevere misunderstands not the intelligence but the disillusion of her pupil. And, like Jean Brodie, Guinevere fails to understand that the student is in love with the teacher. When he learns of her relationship with his father, he feels betrayed, and although he adopts her vision, he drains the joy from her ecstatic dream. He does, indeed, leave out the ladies, but also leaves out the openness of her vision, as well as the beauty and charity of it. He chooses, instead, as Erskine well knew and assumed his readers would know, to reject the quest for beauty and to embrace *The Quest for the Holy Grail* with all its cloistered and radical asceticism.

Probably neither Erskine nor his Galahad had a particularly subtle understanding of the thirteenth-century narrative. Erskine, after all, lived in a disillusioned era in which few could appreciate, at least not without a fierce partisanship, the beauty of the *Grail*'s theology. Erskine would surely have read the text as the antithesis of Guinevere's vision. He would have seen the original quest as the *summa* of what was wrong with the Catholic Middle Ages, which he would have seen as an era of repression and fanatical Crusades, an era that acknowledged multicultural values only to find arguments to annihilate them. Erskine, then, reads the *Quest* with its ruthlessly single-minded vision as something close to the fairer twin of contemporary Fascism.

It is not likely that in 1926 Erskine fully understood the horrors of the wars to come. His *Galahad* is, however, neatly situated between aesthetics and politics. The trendy fascism of the twenties and thirties is voiced by Guinevere, but Galahad, more truly perhaps that he was aware, begins to put into action the frightening implications of a ruthless vision of absolute purity. The poetic visionary Guinevere is consumed in the flames of ecstasy; Galahad puts this vision into action and his flames will consume the world, as what he imagines crosses the line from the Imaginary to the Maginot and beyond.

About ten years after the publication of Erskine's *Galahad*, T.H. White began work on his own Arthurian corpus, *The Once and Future King* and the poignant and didactic *Book of Merlyn*, which, written between 1936 and 1942 (*Merlyn* 137), was not published until 1977. What in Erskine had been a fearful premonition of a totalizing ideology had for White become the threat of an imminent invasion. The introduction to *The Book of Merlyn* leaves no doubt about the context.

> We now find King Arthur of England, sitting in his campaign tent on
> the eve of battle. Tomorrow, he will face his bastard son Mordred and
> that youth's army of Nazi-like Thrashers on the battlefield [xxi].

The implicit analogy between Arthur protecting his island from the continental invaders and the British defending themselves from a German invasion has now become explicit and White has aligned himself with ancient Lawman calling upon an Arthur to help the English.

The trauma of the world-historical context provides a somber background to White's often witty and magical novel. White may have been aware of his American predecessor, Erskine, from whom he could have derived his contemporary spin on the ancient legend. Erskine could have given him an approach to the legend that freed him from the literary baggage of both Malory and Tennyson and allowed him to deal with more ordinary heroes, an Arthur somewhat bemused by his destiny and a Lancelot who becomes something of an accidental lover. Above all, Erskine may have provided White with a Guinevere who is implicated in creating Camelot, not merely in destroying it. And it is interesting that it is precisely the subjects of Erskine's novels, Galahad and Tristan, who are pretty much left out of White's revisioning of Malory, which largely avoids the narratives of *The Quest of the Holy Grail* and (except for Morgan le Fay) the plot and characters of *The Book of Sir Tristram of Lyonesse*.

The closest thing to an ideological debate in Erskine's novel is the conversation between Galahad and Guinevere which contrasts an aesthetic fascism with a more aggressively totalizing one. In T. H. White, the great debate is between the values of ants versus the values of the eagles. Introduced in *The Once and Future King* in "The Sword in the Stone," the debate is continued in *The Book of Merlyn*. The diligent ants, ranked under the banner EVERYTHING NOT FORBIDDEN IS COMPULSORY, provide White with a model of an endlessly tedious, laborious Fascist society. "Their life," White writes, "was not questionable: it was dictated" (128). Passive as they are, they show no resistance or even comprehension when the numbing tune that accompanies their labors changes from "*Mammy, mammy, mammy*" to "*Antland, Antland Over All*," a not particularly subtle allusion to the contemporary threatening anthem, "*Deutschland, Deutschland Über Alles*." White is particularly devastating when he describes how the ants react to their indoctrination.

> A strange feature was that the ordinary ants were not excited by the
> songs, nor interested by the lectures. They accepted them as matters
> of course. They were rituals to them, like the Mammy songs or the

> conversations about their Beloved Leader. They did not look at these
> things as good or bad, exciting, rational, or terrible. They did not look
> at them at all, but accepted them as Done [129–130].

Recalling the great tradition of English aphorism (and perhaps the contemporary critic of British politics, George Orwell), White jettisons theoretical baggage to cut to the chilling reality of the oppression of the
proletariat enabled more by apathy than by force and the unassailable
impression that what Is has always Been.

Opposed to the nightmare society of the ants, which seems inflected
by Orwell as well as reflections of the Nibelungen and the modern world
fearfully filmed in Fritz Lang's *Metropolis*, White presents the airy anarchy
of the geese. They are far superior to the ants in their music alone with
such cheerful ditties as,

> We wander the sky with many a Cronk
> And land in the pasture fields with a Plonk.
> Hink-hank, Hink-hink, Honk-honk [173].

This contrast of the ants and the geese establishes the models of utopia
and dystopia that inspire Arthur's notions in *The Once and Future King* of
what to strive for and what to avoid. By the end of his reign, however, his
son Mordred learns from the ants how to anticipate the Nazis. In *The Book
of Merlyn*, the neat opposition is somewhat qualified through an analysis
of capitalism which Merlyn believes has no basis in nature, but which,
rather like the cerebellum, is a creation unique to man. His solution is to
outlaw *public* property and he concludes, fifty years and more before it
became a buzz word, by inventing *globalism*.

> ...You must abolish such things as tariff barriers, passports and immi-
> gration laws, converting mankind into a federation of individuals. [...]
> but the main thing is that we must make it possible for a man living
> at Stonehenge to pack up his traps overnight and to seek his fortune
> without hindrance in Timbuktu... [101]

Merlyn's vision here is a compound of brilliance, beauty, silliness, magic,
and muddle. A lot, it seems, has been learned from the geese, and, while
there is certainly much to fear from nations, Merlyn overlooks the tenac-
ity of nationalism, and his praise of an incipient globalism seems to ignore
the dangers of a radically unchecked multinationalism. On the least profound level, White's Merlyn seems to imply that World War II was fought
to make the world safe for NAFTA.[5] As Merlyn counters Nazism (and

Communism) with Capitalism, one may wish for a more subtle analysis of the forces of civilization and for a less sentimental encomium to the virtues of private property. Nevertheless, the muddle of White's analysis seems astonishingly relevant to contemporary issues, and, in contrast to contemporary discussions, astonishingly clear-sighted and free of cant. If he cannot quite reconcile the anarchy of the geese with the coercive forces of the not-so-very free market, he is inspired by a noble hope for an optimistic globalism that raises the standard of living and the number of Rolls-Royces rolling through the undeveloped nations. Unlike the AFL and CIO, he sees no danger of the civilized world falling generally to the level of the hypothetical coolie and his bowl of rice. He does, in fact, allow for the possibility of this occurring but blames the Western coolie rather than the Eastern laborer. He believes with a grand optimism, often belied by his own somewhat caustic view of human nature, that the industrious laborer will be operating in a neutral economic landscape. He sees only the goose-like potential of nearly anarchic globalism, while ignoring the "*antifying*" potential of the multinational corporate ideology. In opposing Capitalism to Totalitarianism, he overlooks the degree to which a totalizing capitalism can include contradictions within itself, can even become a totalitarian system capable of accommodating a remarkable degree of anarchy.

Erskine and White as prophet and participant view the issues of the war in significantly different ways. Erskine in a relatively sanguine and optimistic decade sees only the somewhat theoretical problems of what at the time was a relatively trendy mixture of Futurism and Fascism. Thinking backward to the Middle Ages, he sees the Jazz Age urge to a new and beautiful (and implicitly white) future as opening itself to the Galahad option of a rigid program, ascetic and unforgiving. In an age of academic complacency and positivist assumptions, he was, however, almost entirely unaware of how completely a Galahadian pogrom could be implemented with a terrifying rigor. White, on the other hand, writing in the midst of the war was painfully aware of the Nazi threat to Civilization As We Know It, particularly As We Know It in Britain. Unfortunately, he ignored, or was possibly unaware of, the deepest horrors of the Mordredlike invaders, and settled on an analysis that was both insightful and peripheral. In his emphasis on economics, he avoids confronting the problem that had been raised by Erskine, that an aesthetic vision of the Good and the Beautiful can so violently and horribly be perverted into a need to eradicate the less good and the less beautiful. And neither dealt with the danger of reified Universals in a corrupt Particular political context.

A far less sophisticated view of twentieth-century politics is presented in the first novel to resurrect Arthur as a hero of the Second World War, Dennis Lee Anderson's *Arthur, King*. The novel opens during the London Blitz while Jenny and Edith are relaxing in Merlin's Pub. The next scene gives us Arthur lying in the mud on Salisbury Plain, where he has apparently been lying for several hundred years, for he wakes up to find his country still at war and groggily takes his place on the side of the righteous in World War II. As Norris Lacy points out, the novel, perhaps surprisingly, is the only one that takes advantage of Arthur's position as leader of the "English" against invading Germanic tribes. This move does, of course, involve an unexamined acceptance of the Layamon shift to Arthur as an English (rather than British) hero, and ignores the irony of the fact that the "English" were precisely those Arthur was originally fighting against. Indeed, a truly British Arthur would have found little difference between the plucky English and the beastly Germans that the novel requires. This issue does not trouble Anderson, who, as with most authors of war propaganda, does not question who the good guys and the bad guys are. The noble English are good, are us, and are invaded by the despicable Huns, who are bad, who are obviously not us, and the heroic Arthur returns as a humble airman to save the day one more time. The *rex quondam* fulfills his promise as *rex futurus*, even if he maintains sufficient humility to try not to wrest the crown from George VI, who is barely mentioned in the novel, or challenge the leadership of Winston Churchill, the *dux bellorum*, who figures somewhat more prominently.

Having identified the good guys (the English with Arthur helping them) and the bad guys (the Germans, with, predictably, Mordred helping them), the novel presents few surprises and few interesting variations on the Arthurian tradition. The author, identified as a "former paratrooper," is at his best in accurate and enthusiastic depictions of aerial warfare. His skill at plotting and character, however, while entirely adequate for a mass market paperback, do not strive for, nor achieve, much beyond that relatively basic level of competence.

Anderson does deserve credit for placing Arthur in the twentieth-century conflict where he would seem most adequately to fulfill his ancient promise. Although it is an almost inevitable consequence of that concept, he perhaps deserves credit as well for creating Mordred as a sort of *diabolous quondam et futurus* to return again as Arthur's nemesis. There is, however, no analysis, political, economic, or ideological, in the novel, which merely serves chauvinistically to cheer the "right" side and hiss the "wrong" side. All the English are virtuous, all the Huns are vicious, and that is all we need to know. Neither the novel nor the situation it presents excite much thought. The world is fraught and on the brink, but it is not complicated or particularly interesting.

A far more complicated view of the world reveals itself in the post-war, indeed postmodern, novelist Donald Barthelme. Although both Anderson and Barthelme[6] did not publish their World War II novels until the 90s, Anderson's novel reeks of the simplicity of war propaganda from a half century earlier. Barthelme's World War II novel, *The King*, on the other hand, presents a complex examination of twentieth-century absurdity and corruption. While in the end this posthumous novel may not have come up to Barthelme's exacting standards, it is a minimalist comic masterpiece, even—if the term is not entirely oxymoronic—a minimalist epic. Unlike Erskine and White, Barthelme does not entirely avoid a kind of pseudo-medieval language. Indeed, he begins with a parody of Malory that quickly shifts to more serious issues. The first chapter focuses on Lancelot, who is, as always, the object of the gaze, but he is presented wholly from the point of view of engaged anonymous speakers. The section captures Malory's frequent neglect to identify speakers or to clarify context. But Barthelme's minimalist erasures take Malory's neglect of details to an unusual extent.

"See there! It's Launcelot!"
"Riding, riding—."
"How swiftly he goes!"
"As if enchafed by a fiend!"
"The splendid muscles of his horse move rhythmically under drenchèd skin of same!"
"By Jesu, he is in a vast hurry!"
"But now he pulls up the horse and sits for a moment, lost in thought!"
"Now he wags his great head in daffish fashion!"
"He reins the horse about and puts the golden spurs to her!"
"But that is the direction from which he lately came with such excess of speed!"
"No, it's slightly different! It's at an angle of about fifteen degrees to the first!"
"This breakbone pace will soon unhorse him!'

The combination of accuracy ("an angle of fifteen degrees") and opacity (who are the speakers? where are the speakers?) honors and parodies Malory while at the same time fitting neatly into the patterns of Barthelme's postmodern aesthetic. The passage creates a kind of complementary parody in which the medieval mocks the modern, while the modern returns the favor. It is a clever miniature *tour de force*. The comic potential of this interpenetration of the medieval and the modern turns grim, however, when the second chapter reveals Guinevere buttering an apple and listening to the radio.

> "Good evening, fellow Englishmen," the radio said. "This is Germany calling."
> "A fundamentally disagreeable voice," said Guinevere, "stale cabbage."
> "The invincible forces of the Reich," said Haw-Haw, "are advancing on all fronts. Dunkirk has been completely secured. The slaughter is very great. Gawain has been reported captured—" [Barthelme 3]

Lord Haw-Haw and Guinevere, the Reich and Gawain: the anachronisms pour in and are compounded. Ezra Pound and Lech Walesa, among others, make their appearance later, and Arthur has to deal with dockyard strikes and locomotives welded to the tracks, impeding movement between Ipswich and Stowmarket. Arthur with his chivalric training is pretty much incapable of dealing with this farrago of medieval and modern disasters.

As a master of language, Barthelme is naturally concerned with the imprecision and distortions of the language of Haw-Haw and Pound. He is aware too of a violent, incoherent world, a world as Lyonesse perceives that is violent *because* it is incoherent: "They must fight ever more fiercely, in order to deny what they know to be true. That they are not sane" (25). It is this violent, absurdist madness that signals the distance Arthurian novelists have traveled in their treatment of World War II. Erskine's concern about an uncharitable vision of perfection is suggested by the vision of Barthelme's Blue Knight of a disappointing Paradise composed of Wyndham Lewis' *Blast*, music by Milhaud and frescoes by the Italian futurists (78). It is the aesthetic fascism of Guinevere's vision, and merely the less dark side of the vision, the nightmare extension of aesthetic fascism, that Erskine's Galahad implicitly foreshadows, and that Barthelme's Ezra Pound expresses in demented tirades, such as "You would do better to inoculate your children with typhus and syphilis [...] than to let in the Sassoons, Rothschilds, and Warburgs" (7). Thus, Barthelme explores the grimly comic nastiness of the Nazi racism that Erskine foreshadows and that White ignores.

White also presents a neat ideological conflict that Barthelme reduces to a general madness. He also tries to deal with the other horror of the war, which he imagines as a terrible Grail. The idea is introduced by the melancholy knight, a Knight with the Blues, or, The Blue Knight. "The Grail," he says, "is that which will end the war along with a victory for the right" (76). In Barthelme's grimmest conflation of the medieval and the modern, the Grail becomes that most contemporary vision of conflict resolution, the Bomb. Both sides, the Blue Knight reminds us, are in the race to find the Grail, and adds, "Myself, I'm partial to cobalt. It's blue" (79).

Barthelme, sane in his depiction of madness, clear in his creation of confusion, moral in his vision of corruption, comic in his delineation of horror, and analytically cold in his nostalgia for the Middle Ages, comes closer than any of his predecessors in dealing with the genocidal horrors of both the camps and the Bomb. Even Barthelme, however, crumbles before the actual horrors of the war and retreats to the Middle Ages. Somewhat like Mark Twain, his more obvious precursor in the vein of nostalgic Arthurian satire, he finds (somewhat reluctantly) in the Middle Ages a purer time. In this case, the medieval has been exposed to the modern and rejects it. In the voice of Barthelme's most moral speaker, the Black Knight, Sir Roger of Ibadan, originally from Dahomey, the battle is won and Arthur has defeated Mordred, a feat made possible by Arthur's tinkering with Merlin's prophecies: "But it was the last battle of its kind, I feel. There will be other Mordreds, but Arthur will never countenance another fratricidal war. And he won't manufacture the bomb, but someone else is certain to, and then we'll have the hellish thing with us for eternity. Be like having a volcano in the parlor" (142).

Roger is poised on what might be the cusp of Barthelme's escape to the Middle Ages. He prophesies the immediate past, the dangers of the bomb and the Nazi ideology, but propels modern history into the future, turning what has happened into what will happen. This is a trick he has, of course, learned from the master, from Merlin's *Prophecies* as recorded by Geoffrey of Monmouth. Geoffrey's record, however, suffered from Merlin's inability to see past the present; Geoffrey could see the future from the perspective of 542,[7] but only the past from the perspective of 1138. He and his Merlin must suffer the limit of human understanding, the poignant inability to predict the future. Sir Roger and Barthelme, however, suffer more painfully from an inability, or a refusal, to predict the past. While Barthelme raises the issues of the holocaust and Hiroshima, he finds himself unable to deal with them, certainly unable to deal with them adequately in the tone of satire and nostalgia that he has chosen for his novel; the style captures the madness of a world that allows such things to happen, but is not equipped to deal with the human dimensions of the tragedy the world suffered. Merciless in analyzing the ineffectiveness of Arthur's goodness, neither Barthelme nor Roger can push on to deal with the consequences of the triumph of evil will. Thus, as the novel approaches the culminating horrors of World War II, it retreats back to the Arthurian perspective, a return to a past fraught with ignorance and danger, but not quite poised on the brink of universal horror.

The novel ends, then, as it seems it must, in the dream of an older age. Lancelot again, as in the beginning, is the object of anonymous discourse, but whereas in the beginning he was observed riding, he is now observed sleeping, sleeping, in fact, under the apple tree where he rests himself in the opening scene of Malory's "Noble Tale of Sir Launcelot du Lake" (149). As if in a dream, other figures appear, such as Morgan's damsel with the incinerating cloak (from "Gawain, Ywain, and Marhalt"), "fifty giants engendered of fiends" (from "The Tale of the Noble King Arthur That Was Emperor Himself Through Dignity of His Hands"), and the hitherto unknown "Margot de L'Eaux Distraits."

> "But Launcelot sleeps on, undisturbed! I wonder what he's dreaming."
> "He is dreaming that there is no war, no Table Round, no Arthur, no Launcelot!"
> "That cannot be! He dreams, rather, of the softness of Guinevere, the sweetness of Guinevere, the brightness of Guinevere, and the sexuality of Guinevere!"
> "How do you know?"
> "I can see into the dream! Now she enters the dream in her own person, wearing a gown wrought of gold bezants over white samite and carrying a bottle of fine wine, Pinot Grigio by the look of it!"
> "What a matchless dream!"
> "Under an apple tree..." [158]

Ruthless and analytic as he is, even Barthelme cannot finally reconcile, even as bitter satire, the nostalgic appeal of the Arthurian legend with the brutal realities of World War II. In fiction, as in films from Chaplin's *The Great Dictator* to Mel Brooks's *To Be or Not To Be* to the most recent and possibly most controversial of all, Roberto Benigni's *La Vita è Bella*, attempts to deflate the Nazis through parody and ridicule have only limited success. Even Barthelme, however carefully he controls the topics he allows himself to consider, finally retreats into a dream of a happier time. Arthur's ideals, however old-fashioned, possess a nobility at their core which are also, although for opposite reasons, beyond the reach of simple parody. While Barthelme begins by mocking the quaint ideals of Camelot in a basic Mark Twain mode and by critiquing the follies and cruelties of the masters of obfuscation and disinformation of World War II, he finally finds the horrors of the war too deep for parody and the magic of the legend too consoling to reject. Far less enchanted by the legend itself than were T.H. White and

John Erskine, he becomes in the end a kind of reluctant Arthurian, and he escapes from the brutal realities of World War II and the twentieth century to embrace once again that matchless dream under an apple tree.

Notes

1. Norris Lacy has already investigated some of these issues and provided a fine introduction to the work of Anderson and Barthelme. (See "King Arthur Goes to War.")

2. Erskine foreshadows some of the issues that surround World War II, although he could have known nothing of the holocaust to come.

3. It may be a bit of a stretch to think of the fairly highbrow minimalist Barthelme as a "popular" author, but he is certainly not without his fans and has inspired something of a cult. Anderson, on the other hand, makes no claim to be more (or less) than a "popular" author.

4. In a response to a version of this paper at the Fifteenth-Century Symposium at Antwerp (July 2000), Peter Field described Erskine's approach as "debunking." Insofar as the term denotes a reduction of the mystique of the hero, Field is certainly correct. Erskine, however, seems to maintain a reverence for the heroes and is not so much concerned with debunking as domesticating them. As implied in his "private lives" series (which seems to acknowledge both domesticity and Noel Coward, an uneasy coupling at best), he wants to see heroes as humans, ordinary men called into extraordinary deeds. He envisions, in effect, a world of ideals without heroes, the sort of world that collapsed with the onset of World War II, although World War I had certainly done its part to tarnish the notion of the hero. Wilfred Owen, for example, sounds the death knell of the old heroic ethos in his bitter denunciation of the claim *dulce et decorum est pro patria mori.*

5. In this respect, Merlyn may have, in fact, been prophetic. The consequences may not, however, have been as hopeful as he had intended.

6. Lacy also provides a good introduction to Barthelme's Arthurian novel. See also Hoffman's "POMOREX."

7. The date for the quest given in *The Quest of the Holy Grail.*

Works Cited

Anderson, Dennis Lee. *Arthur, King.* New York: Harper, 1995.

Barthelme, Donald. *The King.* New York: Penguin, 1990.

Erskine, John. *Galahad: Enough of His Life to Explain His Reputation.* Indianapolis: Bobbs-Merrill, 1926.

_____. *Tristan and Isolde: Restoring Palamede.* Indianapolis: Bobbs-Merrill, 1932.

Hoffman, Donald L. "POMOREX: Arthurian Tradition in Barthelme's *The King,* Acker's *Don Quixote,* and Reed's *Flight to Canada.*" *Arthuriana* 4 (1994): 376–86.

Lacy, Norris. "King Arthur Goes to War." In Debra Mancoff, ed. *King Arthur's Modern Return.* New York, NY: Garland, 1998. 159–69.

Malory, Sir Thomas. *Complete Works*. 2nd ed. Eugène Vinaver, Ed. New York: Oxford UP, 1971.

The Quest of the Holy Grail. Tr. Pauline Matarosso. New York: Penguin, 1969.

White, T.H. *The Once and Future King*. New York: Berkeley Medallion, 1966.

_____. *The Book of Merlyn: The Unpublished Conclusion to the Once and Future King*. Austin: University of Texas Press, 1977.

King Arthur and Vietnam

Barbara Tepa Lupack

Arthurian literature, especially American Arthurian literature, has long offered writers a way to comment on war. As far back as 1807, Welsh-born American Joseph Leigh, in his political pamphlet *Illustrations of the Fulfilment of the Prediction of Merlin*, drew on the prophetic Merlin tradition as found in Geoffrey of Monmouth and other authors to create his own prophecy, which speaks of a lion that wounds a "Virgin true" and which addresses the relationship between Britain (represented by the lion) and the United States (the Virgin, symbolic of "injured innocence" [Leigh 10–11]) in light of the political events leading to the War of 1812 and of a specific later incident, the attack by the British ship *Leopard* on the American frigate *Chesapeake*. Appropriating Merlin not to glorify the British monarchy, as earlier prophecies had done, but to lend the supernatural weight of prophecy to the claims of a young nation, Leigh patriotically predicted that "The Lion's might shall be undone" (18) if Britain failed to make reparations for the attack.

Arthurian legend and war were conflated again in Sallie Bridges' *Marble Isle, Legends of the Round Table, and Other Poems* (1864), which contains a sequence of fourteen poems that recast material from Malory. The most original of those poems, "Avilion," is remarkable not just for its depiction of Avalon and its call for Arthur to return but also for its implications about the contemporary events surrounding the Civil War and Bridges' concern over the possibility of "dissolution of the Union."[1] Like Bridges, Frank O. Ticknor, a Georgia physician and poet, linked the Arthurian legends with the Civil War; his poem "Arthur, the Great King," addressed to Jefferson Davis, made an analogy between Davis and King Arthur. By contrast, a Northern work, a pamphlet called *Excalibur: A Tale for American Boys*, constructed a bizarre history of Excalibur and its uses in the fighting of oppression from the time Bedivere cast it into the mere until it reached America: having been given to George Washington by Frederick the Great, it comes to be used by John Brown in his fight against slavery and then is passed on to Abraham Lincoln. Finally, upon Lincoln's death, it passes to Andrew Johnson, who the anonymous author hopes "may never blunt its fine edge" (*Excalibur* 24).

More recent authors, like T.S. Eliot in *The Waste Land* (1922) and Ernest Hemingway in *The Sun Also Rises* (1926), responded directly and immediately to the plight of the postwar world by describing the wasteland of contemporary society and the rampant spiritual decline of its inhabitants. Similarly, in *Merlin* (1917) and *Lancelot* (1920), two of his three book-length poems, Edwin Arlington Robinson modernized Arthurian legend by using it to comment on the ravages of World War I. A few years later, T.H. White in *The Once and Future King* (completed in 1958 but begun just as World War II was breaking out and written largely during the hostilities of that conflict) saw a bitter ironic contrast between the golden age of Arthurian chivalry and the villainy of Britain's enemies, most notably Hitler and his SS forces, as well as the perceived cowardice of some of Britain's own leaders. And, as Norris J. Lacy demonstrated in his excellent essay "King Arthur Goes to War," contemporary writers like Donald Barthelme in *The King* (1990) and Dennis Lee Anderson in *Arthur, King* (1995) not only suggested the pertinence of Arthurian themes to World War II but also returned Arthur himself to a Britain embroiled in war against Germany.[2]

It is not surprising, therefore, that contemporary authors have turned to the Arthurian legends as a way of commenting on the Vietnam War. Perhaps the most important such treatment occurs in Bobbie Ann Mason's award-winning first novel, *In Country* (1985), a story about the national conflict effected by Vietnam. Unlike the majority of writers who deal with the war in their fiction, however, Mason does not focus on the soldier, for whom the horrors of combat are made tolerable by easy camaraderie and genuine closeness (Durham 45); she focuses instead on the Southern working class, the class that was most profoundly affected by the war, and on the dislocations felt by the multigenerational members of that class as they struggled to cope with the psychological and social changes in American culture that were the repercussions of Vietnam. What gives *In Country* its special resonance are the multiple mythic structures upon which Mason builds, from the Homeric search for the father to the heroic naming ritual Samantha ("Sam") Hughes must engage in to discover her own identity. Among the most significant of those myths is that of the Fisher King.

In Mason's novel, it is Sam's uncle, Emmett Smith, who is a type of the Fisher King. As a veteran of an undeclared war—a war whose purpose he never quite understood, in a country whose very topography was horrifyingly alien to him—Emmett returns to Hopewell, Kentucky, a wounded and broken man who simply does not fit into the society he had so recently left. At first, Emmett appears to be one of the lucky ones; less fortunate boys like Emmett's brother-in-law Dwayne Hughes never made it home alive. But Emmett's wounds, though less obvious, are no less real than Dwayne's.

Sam suspects that Emmett has been sexually maimed, that his manhood was destroyed by some kind of physical injury suffered in Vietnam; and she raises the question of Emmett's wounding with all of her friends and family. Emmett's exposure overseas to Agent Orange, she tells her best friend Dawn, could cause him to have children with birth defects. "Maybe," concludes Dawn, "that's why your uncle never married" (Mason 41). To her boyfriend Lonnie, Sam wonders "if something could have happened to Emmett in the war, like a wound or something, that means he can't have girlfriends," to which Lonnie responds, "You mean could he have had his balls shot off?" (186). Curious, Sam asks her mother Irene directly, "Did he get wounded in the war? ... I thought maybe some reason like that was why he never had any girlfriends" (169). Irene confirms only that "not long after that [returning from Vietnam], Emmett flipped out for a while, and then you probably remember that time he lost the feeling in his legs. The doctors said he was identifying with the paraplegics, but he didn't even know anybody like that then" (234). And after Sam tries to have sex with Emmett's friend Tom Hudson, who proves to be impotent ("There ain't nothing wrong with me," he claims. "It's just my head" [128]), Sam applies the same diagnosis to Emmett. "Then it occurred to her that Emmett might have the same problem as Tom. It seemed so obvious now.... Maybe Emmett even had an actual wound, nerve damage of some kind" (130).

Emmett does have an "actual wound," but that wound—like Nick Adams' in Hemingway's *In Our Time*—is more psychic than physical. It is a survivor's guilt, a gnawing pain over the fact that he lived while his buddies died, that he survived by pretending that he too was dead, by hiding all night and all day under their corpses, until the smell of their blood in the jungle heat felt "like soup coming to a boil" (223) and until he, the lone survivor, felt more dead inside than they. That pain festers and grows: many years later, he still sleeps poorly, hears his buddies' voices calling out to him on stormy nights, and feels other strange sensations inside his head. Despite his father's prodding, he holds no job, because "ain't nothing worth doing" (45); and—apart from Sam—he has nothing or no one to distract him from his painful past.

Like the Fisher King in his blighted land, Emmett lives in a dilapidated house with a cracked foundation. "The house was damp and musty, and the humidity exaggerated ancient smells in the house. The wallpaper was coming unglued ... like some repressed life that wanted to emerge" (106). Even "the floor was rotting" (65), as were the joists; and "all kinds of things could be breeding" (73) in the basement, in which were stored several years' of unbundled newspapers intended for the Scouts, "swollen and mushy" stacks of *Reader's Digest* magazines, a trash can filled with liquor bottles, and numerous plants that finally "had given up seeking the light. She [Sam] couldn't remember what year they died. The dead stalks in the tub ... were oppressive, something useless and ridiculous" (152). As if to maintain a modicum of order in his crumbling kingdom, Emmett obsessively digs a ditch around the frame of the house hoping to contain the collapsing walls.

Emmett's memories of Vietnam are also of a blighted land—of napalm disintegrating the palm trees and of other toxic chemicals contaminating the water. "Once," Emmett tells Sam, "we came across this place that had been defoliated. And I remember thinking, this looks like winter, but winter doesn't come to the jungle. It's always green in the jungle, but here was this place all brown and dead" (95). The sole object of beauty he recalls there was an egret so white it was almost ghost-like. "That beautiful bird just going about its business with all that crazy stuff going on over there." Once, a grenade hit some trees and caused an entire flock to take wing. It was such a remarkable sight, Emmett recalls, that "we thought it was snowing up instead of down" (36). Back in Hopewell, Emmett searches everywhere for egrets, in the hope that finding such a sign of life, beauty, and vitality might restore some joy to him and some life to the wasteland around him.

Just as the Fisher King's wound is reflected in the wounded land around him, Emmett's behavior is microcosmically a mirror of the social upheaval that took place during the Vietnam era. Even Grandma Smith recognizes that fact. "Everything started to change," she says, soon after Emmett came home; and she sees the reverberations of those changes in the world around her: "Hopewell used to be the best place to bring up kids, but now it's not" (147). Yet she too has changed as a result: when Pap, complaining about Emmett's laziness, asserts that he can still "pull himself up and be proud," Grandma blames Pap's (and, by implication, society's) conventional thinking for causing Emmett's problems in the first place: "You were all for him going [to Vietnam]!" she accuses him. "You said the Army would make a man out of him. But look what it done" (149). Sam's other grandmother is also cognizant of the postwar social changes: when Sam asks Mamaw if, given the chance to go back in time, she would have let Dwayne go to Vietnam or sent him to Canada, Mamaw can only say sadly that people "don't have choices" like that (197); she implies, however, that the choices—even *her* choices—would be different today than they were two decades ago. In ways such as these, suggests David Booth in "Sam's Quest, Emmett's Wound: Grail Motifs in Bobbie Ann Mason's Portrait of America After Vietnam," *In Country* "reenacts Eliot's lament for the spiritual weariness of England in a lament for America in the aftermath of Vietnam" (Booth 100).

If Emmett is the Fisher King, then—in an interesting gender twist—Sam is the Grail knight who eventually restores him, and those around him, to health. To be sure, it is not an easy process, for Sam bears wounds of her own from Vietnam. As the daughter of a father who conceived her in the month of marriage before going overseas and who died a month before she was born, she must first come to terms with her past, a past with which she, like the rest of her generation, is mostly unaware; engage in a ritualistic process that involves remembering and then celebrating—in part by reenacting—her history; and ultimately find a mechanism for interweaving memory and imagination, the real and the idealized, in a way that will open the past to the present. Like the traditional questing knight, she must ask the questions that will effectuate the healing of the wounded land. After all, as David Booth observes, the wasteland can only be restored by "a reintroduction of the woman who in turn forces the wounded generation of men to come to terms with itself" (109).

Sam's quest begins when she graduates from high school, a symbolic and cultural rite of passage from childhood to adulthood. The commencement speaker preaches to her graduating class about keeping the country strong, words that make Sam "nervous" and cause her to "start thinking about war, ... [thoughts that] stayed on her mind all summer" (Mason 23). Afterwards, when she unrolls her diploma, she discovers only a blank page inside; "the real diplomas were mailed later" (200). The blank piece of paper that she has received is like the legacy of the Vietnam War; and, as Katherine Kinney notes, "until she can fill in the imaginative space occupied by her father and the war, her education will remain incomplete" (Kinney 40).

So Sam embarks on a journey, first metaphorical, later literal, to complete that education. But, virtually from the outset, she is discouraged in her pursuit and repeatedly admonished by others that the war does not concern her. Her mother Irene, now living in Lexington with her second husband and baby, has a new life; it has taken Irene years to break away from the unhappy memories of her former home in Hopewell and the burdens of war, including her early widowhood and her responsibility for her brother Emmett; Irene sees no purpose in dredging up the past. "Don't fret about this Vietnam thing," she tells Sam. "It had nothing to do with you" (Mason 57). Sam's boyfriend Lonnie is a sexually charged adolescent whose interest in Vietnam is as limited as his knowledge of it. When Sam tells him that, contrary to her mother's advice, the war "had *everything* to do with me" (71), Lonnie tries to silence her by saying, "Hush ... people are looking." Even Emmett, a surrogate father closer to Sam than her real father ever was, refuses to discuss Vietnam with her. "Women weren't over there," he snaps. "So they can't really understand" (107). When Sam presses him to "tell me something that happened [in Vietnam]," he deflects her request. "You don't want to know all of that" (54).

But that is exactly what Sam does want to know. Insistent upon learning about "what it was like" (94) and frustrated by Emmett's non-responsiveness, she grows "curious about the veterans he hung around with," men whom "she had known for years" but never "thought much about ... as vets" (46). Yet they too talk about Vietnam primarily among themselves, because—according to one—"nobody else could ever know what you went through except guys who have been there" (78).

Reminded by Irene of Dwayne's letters from Vietnam, Sam finds them in her mother's old room, arranges them chronologically, and reads them with great care. The letters, however, reveal little about her father beyond his delight over Irene's pregnancy and his desire to be home again; still, they help to create the first tangible bond between father and daughter. She discovers for the first time something about her own name: Dwayne had picked it out. His favorite name was Samuel; "If it is a girl," he wrote Irene, "name it Samantha" (182).

This is an especially vital bit of information for Sam, who had mused since childhood that "If she couldn't know a simple fact like the source of her name, what could she know for sure?" (53). Names and naming, moreover, assume increased significance throughout the novel and underlie part of the ritual that Sam must perform in the quest for her father, for her own identity, and for the answers that will ultimately heal Emmett, her surrogate father. The newfound knowledge that Dwayne, though dead by the time she was born, had been responsible for giving her a name, in fact his *favorite* name, prompts Sam to visit his parents, the Hughes, for more clues to the past. At Sam's urging, Mamaw locates Dwayne's diary, which she dismisses as nothing more than scribblings about "troop movements and weapons and things like that" (200). But, as Mamaw hands the notebook to her, Sam is instinctively aware that she is getting closer to the object of her search. "Sam remembers reaching just this way at graduation when the principal handed her the rolled diploma" (200). At graduation, however, the paper was blank and her name was missing; now Sam is beginning to fill in some of those blanks, to complete her education—and to pass another test that brings her closer to the achievement of her quest.

The diary does not prove as ennobling as Sam anticipates: contrary to Mamaw's idealized version of the war, Sam reads about Dwayne's making "gook puddin" (204) and his taking teeth from dead men as good luck; she learns that her father not only had killed Vietcong but also had enjoyed the experience, facts that upset her enormously. Afterwards, she is overwhelmed by a sense of rot and decay; the wasteland images described by her father—his own shriveled feet, his dead buddy, the dead V.C. corpse, the sickly-sweet smell of banana leaves—reverberate in the equally sickly reality of the Hughes' home that she has just left, with its smell of manure-sodden farm clothing, decaying bathroom mat, mangy dog, clip-eared cat, and Mamaw's rusty pea bucket. Sam "had a morbid imagination, but it had always been like a horror movie, not something real. Now everything seemed suddenly so real it enveloped her, like something rotten she had fallen into, like a skunk smell" (206).

The connection with her father that Sam makes through the diary is also a connection with the animal fact of the deaths he caused and of his own death; it is a connection so intimate yet so profound that it scares and repulses her. Unable to confront Dwayne and to direct at him the anger she feels about his conduct, she races home to confront Emmett instead. Emmett, however, is not there; having just released a series of flea bombs, he has left the house until the chemicals subside. Sam, her imagination inflamed by her father's description of Vietnam, associates Emmett's killing of the fleas with Dwayne's murder of the Vietnamese, and she leaves the diary on their kitchen table with the accusatory note, "Is that what it was like over there? If it was, then you can just forget about me. Don't try to find me" (207). She then runs away to Cawood's Pond, where she intends to "hump the boonies" and thus to discover the purpose men believe they have in going to war.

Alone in the swamp, like the Grail knight keeping his solitary vigil, she spends the night "walking point" (211), observing "first watch," and imagining the face of the V.C. in every raccoon she sees and their presence in every sound of nature she hears. Like Nick Adams in "The Big, Two-Hearted River," Sam ritualizes each of her actions. But it is not until morning, when Emmett—haggard and frightened over her absence—finds her that she gives voice to her anger, an anger simultaneously toward her father for his inability to live up to the image she has formed, toward herself for being capable of the same kind of brutality, and toward Emmett for his unwillingness to share with her the ugly truth of Vietnam. Sam's profession of hatred toward Dwayne is so intense that Emmett tries to defuse it by admitting that Dwayne "could have been me. All of us..." (222); and, overcome by emotion, he reveals his long-held secret of how he survived by hiding for hours under the bodies. Sam's disappearance, says Emmett, duplicated for him the horror of that event; it was "like being left by myself and all my buddies dead" (225).

The confrontation that Sam has forced allows Emmett to begin his healing. Having uttered the unutterable, having spilled his long-held secret, he can begin to expiate his guilt and, as a result, to heal from his wound. The moment, which binds them more closely than ever before as family, therefore proves cathartic for both, and it marks the beginning of a kind of transcendence (symbolized by the recurring references to the egret and to other birds) that they ultimately achieve in Washington, D.C., where they travel with Mamaw Hughes.

At the Vietnam Veterans' Memorial, the three generations—Sam, the fatherless daughter; Mamaw, the childless mother; and Emmett, the surrogate father to Sam and surrogate son to Mamaw—find Dwayne Hughes' name at the top of the black granite wall. Though distanced from Dwayne by accident and time, they realize that they are nonetheless inextricably linked: a father, dead before he ever became a father; a daughter, now almost the same age as her father was when he died, very much alive and coming of age, who has at last found her father and—in finding him—has found herself; a brother, which Dwayne was to Emmett by marriage as well as by circumstance, finally grieving for himself and his dead comrades, all of whom were brothers-in-arms; a mother, at last able to offer a proper farewell to her lost child. As Mamaw clutches Sam's arm and speaks of the despair she felt when she first saw the wall but the "hope" she now finds in its symbolism and as Emmett bursts into a smile that indicates his reconciliation with the past,[3] Sam goes to the directory to view her father's name once again. And there, running her finger along all the different Hughes' names listed there, she finds her own: SAM A HUGHES. Locating it on one of the wall's granite slabs, she discovers, "It is the first on a line. It is down low enough to touch. She touches her own name. How odd it feels, as though all the names in America have been used to decorate this wall" (244–45). While Sam Hughes, the Vietnam soldier whose name is etched on the wall, is dead, another Sam Hughes, the young woman who imagined herself to be a soldier in order to understand Vietnam, is alive and, by this experience, possessed "of a deeper knowledge of the dark complexities that shadow all human experience [and an understanding of] the nature of growth and regeneration" (Brinkmeyer 30).

Sam and Emmett's shared experience, which allows them to make their separate peace with the war and to move beyond the painful memories and the often violent legacy of the past, is portrayed by Mason in very gender-specific imagery that suggests the cycle of rebirth and regeneration inherent in the vegetation myths of the Fisher King and the Grail quest. At Cawood's Pond, where Sam forces Emmett to face the ghosts of his dead comrades that haunt him, Emmett breaks down sobbing and crying; he admits his desire to be a father, especially to Sam, and, having given birth to his sorrow and guilt, he leaves the swamp looking "like an old peasant woman hugging a baby" (Mason 226). By facing his terror, he can forge a new life (suggested by the image of the baby), something he has been unable to do until now; and that new life begins with his taking a job, paying off his debts, preparing Sam to go away to college, and undertaking the journey of reconciliation to Washington. A comparable image is evoked later in the novel, at the Vietnam Veterans' Memorial. Against the phallic imagery of the Washington Monument, "a big white prick" (238), and the Memorial, a deep "black gash in the hillside ... a giant grave ... a hole" (239)—imagery reminiscent of the Grail legend's spear and cup—"Sam doesn't understand what she is feeling, but it is something so strong, it is like a tornado moving in her, something massive and overpowering. It feels like giving birth to this wall" (240). Katherine Kinney writes that "In this revisionary image the daughter gives birth to the father, the future to the past, the living to the dead—but the relationship between destruction and regeneration is no longer horrific" (Kinney 48). Indeed, by locating Dwayne's name on the wall, Sam brings the missing father to life, just as her cathartic confrontation with Emmett at Cawood's Pond brings him to life; and, in the course of her search for Dwayne, Sam metaphorically gives birth to herself, as evidenced by her discovery of the name "Sam A. Hughes" on the wall. The name absent from her diploma at the beginning of her journey and hidden away from her on the documents in the Hopewell courthouse is now etched forever not only in Sam's personal and family history but also in the national consciousness. The powerful closing image of Sam, Emmett, and Mamaw thus fuses the simultaneous shame and hope of a family and of a nation and offers a sense of shared identity, at once personal, familial, and national, and of reconciliation that transcends generational boundaries.[4]

The Vietnam War, which created deep political and philosophical divisions in this country, left scars not only on the young men who fought there but also on the society that they left behind. Sam's quest to understand the meaning of Vietnam is as noble as any quest in medieval literature, and its achievement helps to heal the war-wounded Emmett and others around her as well. Moreover, in its patterns of rebirth, and especially of the rejuvenation of Emmett, the injured contemporary Fisher King, In Country suggests the national need for healing, for returning vitality and honor to the country and to the notion of America itself. Through the use of the Grail legend to undergird her very contemporary tale, Mason thus makes a noteworthy contribution to the American Arthurian tradition.

The Grail theme also underlies another novel about Vietnam, Katherine Paterson's Park's Quest (1988), a juvenile work that uses the Arthurian legends in a truly innovative way and that echoes Sam's odyssey in In Country. Paterson's Parkington Waddell Broughton the Fifth—"Park," for short—embarks on a quest to learn about his father, who died in Vietnam when Park was just a baby. Park's quest takes him first to the Vietnam Memorial in Washington, D.C., and then to the farm where his father was raised, where he discovers the family secrets that his mother has withheld from him—that she divorced his father just before his second tour of duty in Vietnam, during which he was killed; that his grandfather, a career military officer called simply "the Colonel," had suffered his first stroke when he heard the sad news. And Park learns the deepest secret of all: that Thanh, the strange and scrappy Vietnamese girl who lives on the farm, is actually his half-sister. The very contemporary Park is therefore much like the traditional Percival, whose mother kept him ignorant of chivalry, which she blamed for his father's death; who, learning of the existence of knights, ignored his mother's grief and left for court; who, in a strange castle, is witness to a strange procession but, as advised, never questions what he sees; and who eventually asks the question that cures the infirm Fisher King. Park's mother's refusal to discuss his father and her attempts to shelter him from the Colonel and the rest of the family, whose military associations date back centuries and whom she somehow holds responsible for the Vietnam War and the loss of her husband, impel Park to find things out for himself. But, upon the advice of his mother and out of his own fear of seeming forward or impolite, he rarely asks the necessary questions; when his Uncle Frank picks him up at the bus stop, for instance, Park realizes "he had used up his one question" (Paterson 43). After several visits to the farm's springhouse, where Thanh—a kind of modern-day Grail maiden—not only gives him water but also guides him to various self-discoveries, he is able at last to speak to his grandfather. His questions—"What's the matter?" "Does something hurt?" "Do you miss him?" (147)—cause the old man to break down in tears that bring healing to both of them. When Thanh reappears, she holds in her hands a coconut shell full of clear water for the two men to drink. "Then they took the Holy Grail in their hands and drew away the cloth and drank.... And it seemed to all who saw them that their faces shone with a light that was not of this world. And they were as one in the company of the Grail" (148). In entwining the Grail theme with a young boy's odyssey to understand Vietnam and discover his heritage, *Park's Quest* tells a powerful story that is at once traditionally Arthurian and uniquely American.

Set in southeast Asia a few years after the end of the Vietnam War, the British novel *The Queen's Messenger* (1982), by W.R. Duncan, the collective name used by Wanda Duncan and her husband Robert L. Duncan (who also writes under the name James Hall Roberts), has an interesting, recurring Arthurian allusion. Among the central characters is "Charlie Excalibur," a United States Marine deserter who has been hiding out in the jungles and sending vital information about military actions to the attention of Gordon Clive at Britain's MI6. About to explode his biggest story yet, Charlie Excalibur sends one last message to Clive by way of his courier, Mr. Po. Although the message reaches the diplomatic pouch en route to the Embassy in London, the unthinkable occurs: William Marston, the Queen's Messenger, vanishes. Fearful that he has been abducted or that he has defected, the Foreign Office sends Clive to Asia to investigate Marston's disappearance. It is a difficult assignment for Clive, who only a year before had been abducted himself, interrogated, and tortured almost to the point of death. Nonetheless, Clive determines—at any cost—to effect Marston's return; and although ultimately he is unable to save Marston or his daughter, Clive (with Charlie Excalibur's help) unravels the numerous mysteries and exposes the traitor, Colonel Harry Patterson, chief of British Foreign Intelligence in Bangkok. The novel, which suggests that the Queen's messengers are a kind of chivalric brotherhood, is only marginally Arthurian. "I used the name Charlie," explains the pseudonymous American informant, "because that's what the American troops called the Vietcong. And Excalibur was King Arthur's sword, and that pleased me somehow" (Duncan 347). The search for Marston, it could be argued, constitutes a quest of sorts for honor, but even that argument is a bit tenuous.

The Arthurian element is employed more explicitly and more effectively in Megan Lindholm's fantasy novel, *Wizard of the Pigeons* (1986), the story of a traumatized Vietnam veteran who is separated from his wife and son and who is living as a street person in Seattle. Named "Wizard" by his homeless friends, Mitchell Ignatius Reilly seems to be both a bard and a prophet who predicts others' futures. (He tells a lonely old man on a public bus, for instance, that his wife should cook a big turkey for Thanksgiving because their son, who has been stationed in Germany for the past year, is planning to surprise them with a visit for the holidays.) Like Merlin after the battle of Arfderydd, however, Wizard is crazed by the horrors of Southeast Asia, horrors revived by the bureaucracy of a Veterans' Administration that lists him as "missing in action" and denies him benefits and assistance. In the course of the novel, Wizard tries to take control of his circumstances by observing the "rules" demanded by his "magic": "Hold the pigeons sacred and never harm them. Listen to the ones who come to talk to you, and when you have comfort for them, speak out. Tell the Truth when it comes on you, and when you Know, admit you Know." Yet, as his beloved friend Cassie points out, he also imposes upon himself "extra rules" that become his "own petty fences, put up to keep others at a distance" (Lindholm 184): not carrying more than a dollar's worth of change in his pocket, not becoming sexually involved with a woman, and not turning his fierce "strength loose on others" (183). Ultimately, Wizard musters the strength to defeat his greatest adversary, the dark force ("this gray thing, this Mir" [185]) that threatens him, a confrontation by which he reaffirms his own mystical powers.

Lindholm not only incorporates Grail quest imagery and other Arthurian allusions throughout the novel;i in one section, she makes explicit the connection between Wizard and Merlin. As Wizard initially tries to fight the magic with which he is possessed and which seems always to "hover ... just out of his reach" (150), Cassie explains that "it happened the same way to all of us. Perhaps that's the only universal thing about it. You wake up the day after, and know that nothing will ever be the same. Some hear voices, and some are filled with the total silence of the world. Some of us are filled with awesome purpose, and some of us are emptied of ambition and opened to time" (62). To illustrate her point, Cassie tells Wizard a story about an orphaned girl who lived in a hut on the edge of the woods. To survive, the girl tended chickens and raised herbs, some of which "were quite rare, with virtues unknown to many more learned folk" (62). One day, a great company of knights and ladies rode past her dwelling; "talking and jesting among themselves," all failed to notice the girl in her garden—

all, that is, except an old man dressed in a blue robe and mantle, who "came down from his tall horse and entered the maid's garden and life." For five years and a day, the old man stayed with the girl and "taught her much of herbs and all that grows, things beyond the teachings of any other mortal. Rules he gave her that she recognized as her own. 'You can offer,' he told her, 'but not with words, and until what you offer is accepted, you cannot give it.... You can take all, except for the things that you desire most, and those you must not touch until they are given freely'" (63). But portentous events were brewing, "and so he left her, and never again was she the same person." Wizard shifts impatiently throughout the story, trying not to be touched by Cassie's words; before she can continue, he adds, "And the old man was Merlin, and the little girl was Cassie. The End." (63) The story is significant because it serves as a kind of analogy for the relationship between Wizard and Cassie, who learn from each other and who live together on the streets for a period comparable to the time that Merlin spends with the maiden. Yet, even though they share a special knowledge of magic, Wizard is not ready to accept what Cassie most wants to give him; and when portentous events occur—in this case, the appearance of the gray "Mir" that challenges Wizard—Cassie is forced to "unbalance" her own magic in order to lend him her strength. "I took it upon myself," she tells him, "to give you what you would not ask for." The unbalancing, however, compromises "the rules [that] are given us" and leaves her wounded, "never again ... the same" (211); and she disappears. His magic renewed, Wizard is left to carry on alone, with only Cassie's memory to sustain him.

Two modern short fantasy stories make equally interesting associations between the Arthurian legends and Vietnam. In the first of those stories, Owl Goingback's "Grass Dancer," Roger Thunder Horse, a full-blooded Kiowa, is serving as an American Marine in Vietnam. Before shipping out, Roger entrusts his elaborate dance regalia, which includes "forty-three golden eagle feathers ... passed down for generations, from one Thunder Horse to the next" (Goingback 115), to his wheelchair-bound eleven-year-old brother Jimmy. After Roger is killed in Vietnam (a death that Jimmy foresees in a dream), Jimmy dons Roger's regalia in order to participate in a powwow in his brother's memory. As Jimmy moves, slowly and painfully, toward the ritualistic dance circle, a miraculous transformation occurs: he drops his crutches and begins to shuffle, then to walk, and then to dance, as if animated by the spirit of his brother. "The tiny blades of grass sprouted from the ground [where he stepped, and] ... quickly spread to form a thick carpet of green" (128). Jimmy is fully healed, and so—suggests Goingback—is the land.

Were it not for the fact that "Grass Dancer" appeared in the volume of collected stories *Excalibur*, it is unlikely that readers would have made any associations between the story and Excalibur. But, given the context, Roger's dance regalia becomes like the legendary sword passed on to the chosen one. "The spirits of your ancestors are in those feathers," Roger tells Jimmy. "They'll protect you while I'm gone, keep you safe till I get back" (116). Yet, in fact, the regalia functions more like a Grail that restores health and fertility to the injured king and his land than a sword that offers protection against harm, and it ensures that a new generation will inherit the family's Native American traditions.

In the second story, S.P. Somtow's "The Steel American," a contemporary American clad in armor and named Sir Perceval comes seeking the Grail from Mali, a beautiful sorceress living in the small Thai-speaking village of Doi Xang. ("We're not actually *in* a country," explains the sorceress, "though everyone around us thinks we're in *his*" [Somtow 233].) Perceval, whom Mali calls "the steel American," has vowed to live inside his metal shell until his quest is fulfilled. Upon the advice of Father O'Malley, an American chaplain who deserted from Vietnam, she eventually turns over the Grail (currently an "old plastic bowl"—although "the Holy Grail [previously] took many forms," including a broken Coke bottle and other lowly household objects [242, 244]) to the American. Apparently, it is the custom of the village to give seekers whatever they request; the "giving people," in fact, have already given away—among other things—the golden fleece, the golden apples of the sun, and the urn of the demon's heart. Once in possession of the Grail, however, Perceval watches as "all at once the armor seemed to melt from him" (248); immediately afterwards, the pure knight makes love to Mali, then grows old and withered and "disintegrate[s] into the pool of water" with which she had earlier filled the Grail; and Mali is left to try to "exorcise" from her mind the quester she had "loved" and "killed" by relinquishing her desire in order to fulfill his. Somtow's blending of the traditional Grail story with a variety of nontraditional elements such as "the CIA and the Russians and the Vietnamese" (234) and references to American popular culture (e.g., *Twilight Zone, Leave It to Beaver*, reruns of *I Love Lucy*, Landrovers) is intriguing, although at times puzzling, even incomprehensible. But it reveals that for writers of science fiction and fantasy, as for novelists like Bobbie Ann Mason, Katherine Patterson, and W.R. Duncan, the Arthurian legends continue to be seen as a vital story that has relevance for commenting on historical events like the Vietnam War and its effects.

Notes

I am grateful to Dan Nastali for bringing *Skull, The Slayer* and *Wizard of the Pigeons* to my attention. *The Arthurian Annals* (as yet unpublished), compiled by Dan Nastali and Phil Boardman, contains a wealth of information on the Arthurian legends and is an invaluable resource for both Arthurian scholars and enthusiasts.

1. For a fuller discussion of Sallie Bridges' Arthurian sequence, see Lupack and Lupack, *King Arthur in America*, pp. 14–20.

2. And, in so doing, as Norris J. Lacy suggests, both Anderson and Barthelme "return Arthur to his roots as a *dux bellorum*," the military role accorded to him as early as the ninth century. But, as Lacy goes on to demonstrate, "beyond these similarities—the historical period and Arthur's status—the two differ radically in their approaches, intentions, and effects" (160).

3. Ellen A. Blais writes that the final image of Emmett sitting on the ground in front of the names of his buddies on the wall "becomes the iconic equivalent of Sam's recognition of herself in the Vietnam veteran who bears her name" (117). Robert H. Brinkmeyer, Jr., sees in Emmett's posture "a profound, almost phoenix-like rebirth.... In finally confronting the terrors of his past, Emmett is ready to forge a new life, something he has been resisting since his return from Vietnam" (31). Thus, as Sam does, Emmett gives birth to himself at the wall. Thomas Morrissey, in "Mason's *In Country*," also comments on the concluding image of Emmett as phoenix; Morrissey contends that it is the culmination of numerous bird images throughout the novel. Even the memorial itself, which Mason describes as a "black wing embedded in the soil," is—according to Morrissey—"a fallen bird ... [that] has nevertheless unburdened the survivors so that they can rise from the ashes of war and sorrow to meet their own destinies" (63–64).

4. Robert H. Brinkmeyer, Jr., finds links also to Southern literary tradition. He writes that "this final scene is significant not only as a strong and fitting conclusion to a fine novel but also as a revealing statement on the state of contemporary Southern fiction." He suggests that the conclusion of *In Country* "transposes a crucial paradigm of the Southern literary renascence—that to understand the present, including oneself, one explores the past—into a contemporary setting. In doing so, Mason maintains the integrity of the paradigm but alters its thrust and direction" (31)—much as she does with the Arthurian legend itself.

5. The novel is full of images of "high-born ladies" and "knights-errant" (193) and references to magical knives, quests (albeit often "ridiculous" ones (154]), and Grail maidens. ("Cassie came behind him, bearing a candelabra.... He trailed along behind her through a maze of rooms and corridors. Most of the chambers they passed through were dusty and abandoned, but some were strangely and sumptuously furnished, ... and lit by a pale yellow light that blinded Wizard until he passed into the darkened chambers beyond" [71].) Wizard himself dresses in a Merlin-like outfit that includes a pointed wizard's hat and a long flowing robe with stars upon it; and he surrounds himself with animals, from his beloved pigeons to his maimed cat, Black Thomas, which suggest his Merlin-like affinity for nature and the natural world.

6. An even more interesting confluence of Arthurian imagery, popular culture, and Vietnam occurs in a three-issue story line of Steve Englehart's *Skull, The*

Slayer (Nos. 4–6 [March–July 1976]), a Marvel Comics series. Jim Scully, a Vietnam veteran who finds himself in a time tower controlled by an alien villain in which he is able to move among different periods of time, visits Camelot. There he joins Merlin and the Black Knight in a battle against Morgan le Fay. Eventually, however, he discovers that the Arthurian figures are really robots, engaged in an endless battle. Scully employs tactics like those used at "Tet and My Lai" and the skills and instincts learned in Vietnam to escape the time tower and to save himself and his colleagues.

Bibliography

Blais, Ellen A. "Gender Issues in Bobbie Ann Mason's *In Country*." *South Atlantic Review* 56.2 (1991): 107–18.

Bridges, Sallie. *Marble Isle, Legends of the Round Table, and Other Poems*. Philadelphia: J. B. Lippincott, 1864.

Brinkmeyer, Robert H., Jr. "Finding One's History: Bobbie Ann Mason and Contemporary Southern Literature." *Southern Literary Journal* 19.2 (1987): 22–33.

Booth, David. "Sam's Quest, Emmett's Wound: Grail Motifs in Bobbie Ann Mason's Portrait of America After Vietnam." *Southern Literary Journal* 23.2 (Spring 1991): 98–109.

Duncan, W.R. *The Queen's Messenger*. London: Michael Joseph, 1982.

Durham, Sandra Bonilla. "Women and War: Bobbie Ann Mason's *In Country*." *Southern Literary Journal* 22.2 (Spring 1990): 45–52.

Englehart, Steve. *Skull, The Slayer*. Marvel Comics. Nos. 4–6 (March–July 1976).

Excalibur: A Tale for American Boys. Philadelphia: King & Baird, 1865.

Goingback, Owl. "Grass Dancer." In *Excalibur*. Ed. Richard Gilliam, Martin H. Greenberg, and Edward E. Kramer. New York: Aspect/Warner Books, 1995. 111–130.

Hemingway, Ernest. *In Our Time*. New York: Scribner, 1925.

Kinney, Katherine. "'Humping the Boonies': Sex, Combat, and the Female in Bobbie Ann Mason's *In Country*." In *Fourteen Landing Zones: Approaches to Vietnam War Literature*. Ed. Philip K. Jason. Iowa City: University of Iowa Press, 1991. 38–48.

Lacy, Norris J. "King Arthur Goes To War." *King Arthur's Modern Return*. Ed. Debra N. Mancoff. New York: Garland, 1998. 159–69.

Leigh, Joseph. *Illustrations of the Fulfillment of the Prediction of Merlin Occasioned by the Late Outrageous Attack of the British Ship of War the Leopard, on the American Frigate Chesapeake, and the Measures Taken by the President, Supported by the Citizens Thereon*. Portsmouth, NH: Printed for the Author, 1807.

Lindholm, Megan. *Wizard of the Pigeons*. New York: Ace Fantasy Books, 1986.

Lupack, Alan and Barbara Tepa Lupack. *King Arthur in America*. Cambridge: D. S. Brewer, 1999.

Mason, Bobbie Ann. *In Country*. New York: Harper, 1985.

Morrissey, Thomas J. "Mason's *In Country*." *Explicator* 50.1 (Fall 1991): 62–64.

Paterson, Katherine. *Park's Quest*. New York: Lodestar/E. P. Dutton, 1988.

Somtow, S.P. "The Steel American." In *Grails: Quests, Visitations and Other Occur-*

rences. Ed. Richard Gilliam, Martin H. Greenberg, and Edward E. Kramer. Atlanta: Unnameable Press, 1992. 230–50.

Ticknor, Frank O. *The Poems of Frank O. Ticknor, M.D.* Ed. K.M.R. With an Introductory Notice of the Author by Paul H. Hayne. Philadelphia: J.P. Lippincott, 1879.

The Documentary Arthur: Reflections of a Talking Head

Norris J. Lacy

Arthurian documentaries remain a flourishing business. Indeed, there can surely be no medieval subjects that are of more enduring interest to documentary film makers and, obviously, to their audiences than the genesis and development of the Arthurian legend. During the past decade, a new Arthurian documentary has appeared on American television about once a year, and older ones have been recycled. Most are U.S. products, though some British documentaries or joint British/American films also find their way onto the American television screen.

My intent in this essay is to provide general observations about the interests, emphases, and quality of some of these films. These remarks are based on recent re-viewings of about a half-dozen films and reasonable recollections of a few others.[1] Following general remarks, I offer some reactions drawn from my personal, albeit limited, experience as a consultant for several, and an on-screen participant in two, such documentaries.[2] And I should acknowledge from the outset that my estimation of most Arthurian documentaries, including those in which I appear, is not high, for reasons that will become apparent.

The first principle of Arthurian documentaries in English appears to be that the central role played by literature—by fiction—in the flowering and evolution of the legend is at best of negligible interest to producers.[3] One exception to that remark (though not a radical one) is "Morte d'Arthur: Legend of the King," which, as part of a "great books" series, gave at least

77

reasonable attention to Malory and, in a few instances, made passing mention of several other writers as well.

In general, we can take it for granted that these films will deal with the historical Arthur, and a number of the films either try to make a case for the King's historicity or, at least, leave the interpretation sufficiently open to allow the audience to assume his existence, even when the narration hedges by using a formula such as "Some people believe..." or "Some scholars think that...." And part of the presentation almost inevitably includes discussions of archaeology—South Cadbury, Glastonbury, and perhaps Tintagel—designed to investigate (and sometimes to imply) the existence of Arthur.

In Arthurian documentaries, there are, in addition to the discussion about who Arthur was and the nearly obligatory views of "Arthur country" (usually taken to be Somerset and Cornwall), certain other images seem to be almost universal in the genre. The most common one shows a group of men dressed as knights (usually in late plate armor) either doing battle or riding, often in slow-motion, across a hill. The obvious intent is to represent Arthur and the Knights of the Round Table. Of course, it is also essential to use medieval miniatures (and not infrequently modern book illustrations, such as those of Howard Pyle) in such films. In some instances, the images are selected with appropriate care and accuracy. That is not always the case, however, and the result may be, as it was in one film, an image of the Annunciation on the screen when the subject being discussed was Mary Magdalene.

One can sympathize, to an extent, with the producers' dilemma, though not with their carelessness: in documentaries dealing with the Middle Ages, one is left largely with three choices: reenactment, static images (e.g., manuscript miniatures), and scholarly "talking heads." Some of the choices made are better, and more responsible, than others; in the worst cases, an attempt is made merely to offer a film that will look somewhat "medieval" to an audience that, it is surely assumed, will not recognize the inappropriateness of the images.

Typically a documentary has some kind of hook intended to focus on a particular point of view, however diffuse. In "Le Morte d'Arthur: Legend of the King," there are in fact several quite diverse emphases. The result, in my view, is an impression of some disorder (see my detailed comments below); but in particular this film dwells on the uses and perversions of the legend, including the transformation of the town of Tintagel into a collection of New-Age crystal and kitsch shops.[4]

One of the most direct and persistent hooks is offered by "The Quest for the Holy Grail," which asks the question at the beginning, "Has [the Holy Grail] already been discovered?" Several times during the film, and especially before and after breaks, it is suggested that perhaps the Grail has indeed been discovered—and that it may not be an object at all, but a bloodline, and that its "descendants" may be walking among us even now. The film acknowledges that this is speculative but returns repeatedly to the notion. It is in fact Laurence Gardner's theory, presented in his book *Bloodline of the Holy Grail*, which reflects but extends the Holy Blood/Holy Grail hypothesis elaborated by Baigent, Leigh, and Lincoln. One full segment of the documentary is devoted to this theory: that Jesus married Mary Magdalene and that the "Grail" is their bloodline, perhaps continuing still today. The point is driven home by a scene, repeated several times, of ordinary people walking along a busy modern sidewalk. The image, accompanied by some version of the question concerning the survival of this particular "grail," implies that some of these very people could be descendants of Jesus. Elsewhere the film deals with more conventional subjects concerning the origin and development of the Grail legend, but the memory of it that lingers with viewers, even the most skeptical ones, is likely to be the "bloodline" notion.

At least that film clearly identifies Gardner's ideas as speculation, acknowledging even that it is "a disturbing and highly controversial theory." The same cannot always be said of other films. For example, Arthurian scholars and enthusiasts will recall the excitement that followed reports of the 1998 discovery at Tintagel of an engraved stone, offering a name (Artognov or Artognou) somewhat similar to the form that "Arthur" might have taken during the so-called Arthurian period.[5] The excitement of that discovery persists, among enthusiasts and among producers of at least one documentary, despite plausible and explicit denials that the stone has anything at all to do with King Arthur.[6] In the recent "King Arthur" on the Discovery Channel (2000), Charles Thomas, the expert selected to comment authoritatively on the stone, emphatically denies that it is even remotely related to King Arthur,[7] yet the Discovery Channel's own publicity for that very documentary had proclaimed of the stone that "this could be final proof of the existance [sic] of King Arthur."[8] It is patently obvious, and not only from this example, just what aspect of the Arthurian legend will sell to the public—and the extent to which, knowing what will sell, publicity departments may sometimes choose to ignore any elements of the film that may disappoint its viewers.

I now turn to my own experiences with Arthurian documentaries. Those experiences, at least on screen, are admittedly not extensive: I have served as a talking head in only two. Otherwise, I have been consulted at some length, by phone or in person, for perhaps seven or eight others, some of which were made, others not.[9] However, I suspect, and in some instances know, that my reactions parallel those of some other scholars who have been interviewed for Arthurian documentaries.

The first step, once it is decided that an Arthurian documentary is to be made, is obviously to talk to the "usual suspects," scholars (and others) who have some visibility in the field, owing to their publications or professional functions. At each step it is customary to ask who else should be contacted, and as a result the same half-dozen or dozen names inevitably surface. (The process is thus circular, indeed sometimes highly redundant: often, the names I name have already come to the producers' attention, and I am sometimes informed that those persons had in fact given them my name.) The producers select potential interviewees, sometimes after several extended conversations; they or their representatives may in rare cases—this has happened to me only once—ask for *curricula vitae* and samples of publications. At other times they may ask simply for *titles* of selected publications, but sometimes they show little interest in such matters, and it is not always clear whether they have already done their homework or are simply careless. Then final decisions are made and invitations extended.

I was first interviewed for the Cronkite/Ward program "Le Morte d'Arthur: Legend of the King," made for the Learning Channel and intended to be shown later on the Discovery Channel as well. I was flown to New York, put up at a fine hotel overlooking Central Park, invited to avail myself of room service (which I did liberally, since I was interviewed on my birthday), paid a fee (about which more later), and interviewed at the Pierpont Morgan Museum, a magnificent setting. So far, so good.

The interview lasted four and one-half hours, with two short breaks of five to ten minutes each. Because documentary producers reasonably enough wish to avoid "canned" or memorized responses, they ordinarily offer advance information only about the general areas and subjects they wish to explore in the interview. However, in the case of the Cronkite/Ward film, the producer neglected to send me the information he had promised. As a result, I did a very lengthy interview with no advance idea of what to expect, beyond his casual statement, by phone, that he himself was particularly interested in the *uses* of the Arthurian legend. That interview, to a good extent, involved my being asked to say something about the contributions, in turn, of Malory, of Chrétien, of Wolfram, of Spenser, of Scott, of Twain, of T.H. White, of Steinbeck, and of others, to the Arthurian legend. I was also asked more general questions about Arthurian origins, Glastonbury Abbey, the persistent appeal of the legend, and the like.

After more than four hours, lights were turned off, microphones were removed, and then, as I was preparing to leave, the interviewer suddenly said, "Oh, I forgot one question." Lights were turned on, microphones were set up, and I was then asked, "Would you tell us something about John F. Kennedy and the Arthurian legend?" Caught off guard, I said something that, although not incorrect, was less than gracefully expressed. One part of my reply seemed to me more awkward than the rest, and, predictably enough, that part made it into the film. Overall, out of four and one-half hours of interviews, the film includes about ninety seconds (in three segments of thirty seconds or so) of my voice and face. And besides talking about Kennedy, I am there on screen discussing Sir Thomas Malory—hardly my specialty, although Spenser, Scott, and others are even farther outside my domain—whereas Derek Brewer, who specializes in the British Arthurian tradition, talks about Chrétien de Troyes.

There are several other curious and disturbing facts about this film. First, the producers obviously spent a great deal of money on travel, on helicopter rental for fine aerial photography, and on other items, but appeared to care little about the small—or sometimes the large—details of the production. In fact, I was sent the final script for review—something that has not happened, at least to me, with other films. Impressed by the apparent concern for accuracy, but struck by many problems with the script, I returned a number of pages of suggestions, corrections, and explanations, and that was followed by a rather lengthy telephone conversation. To the best of my recollection, not one of my suggestions was taken.

The film contains a number of small errors and at least one large one, which is the repeated pronunciation of "Tintagel" as "Tintagua" (rhyming with "Padua") by the narrator, Donald Sutherland. All in all, it struck me as odd and very unfortunate that a production company would lavish so much attention (and money) on images and then neglect the details. That inattention to detail led, for example, to the misspelling of my name as "Lacey" and of Derek Brewer's as "Derrick." Comparatively few viewers will recognize these misspellings or care about them, but a good many have asked me why Sutherland talks about Tintagua.

And a final note on that documentary: although the subject was Malory and related areas, some of the topics were *not* in fact very closely related. The filmmakers, having located an armorer in California, spend a good deal of time interviewing him about his construction of plate armor—hardly an Arthurian subject unless the viewer's idea of the Arthurian age is taken from *Excalibur* or similar cinematic anachronisms. (Indeed, the viewer *is* informed that this is not the kind of armor that a King Arthur would have worn, but that denial is followed by a detailed description and illustration of the articulated plate armor made in California.) The film also devotes a good deal of attention to George Lucas talking about the Arthurian influence on *Star Wars*, a subject that is of significant general interest for questions of myth and legend, but that does not impart a sense of focus to an Arthurian film ostensibly devoted to Malory's work. There are in addition scenes from a modern Renaissance (= Medieval?) Festival, and there is a sizeable segment on Hal Foster's comic strip *Prince Valiant*. The impression, I fear, is that the film is a miscellany of subjects either related to or merely suggested by Arthurian themes.

But at least that program, because of its Great Books orientation, did have some literary content. That is not always true of some others, including "The Quest for the Holy Grail." This, the second film for which I provided a "talking head," is primarily concerned with the historical question: did the Grail exist? What happened to it? And (as noted above) could the Grail—that is, the descendants of Christ—be among us today? Although I had been given a very general idea of the subjects to be covered (e.g., the Church's reaction to the Grail), it quickly became clear that the interviewer had no desire to hear that the Grail legend was the product of medieval romance, that is, of narrative *fiction*.

Reacting rather perversely, perhaps, to the lack of interest in acknowledging the literary elaboration of the legend, I made it a point in a number of my answers (during a two and one-half hour interview, of which, again, no more than two minutes made it onto the screen) to refer to fictional elaboration of the legend, to the fact that the Grail story is primarily a literary construct, to which have been added many layers of speculation about historical "fact." None of my literary references made it into the documentary (other than a general allusion to the rise of medieval fiction), and indeed, in one instance the editing leaves me with a rising intonation, my literary reference having been simply lopped off after the word "romance." The remainder of the sentence had said, as I recall, something like "which was of course the original source of the Grail legend."

In my experience, it is clear that the producers of such documentaries—and my impressions drawn from the two in which I appeared are borne out from consulting I have done for other films—most often have only the most general idea, if that, of the kind of film they want to make.[10] Instead, in interviews they often make an effort to gather as many quotable responses as possible about as many subjects as possible (during an interview that may last several hours), in order to pick and choose later and mold a film out of the material at their disposal. One result, at least in my experience, is to make the persons interviewed await the eventual screening with some trepidation—and others have confirmed my experience in this regard—since they can only guess (usually incorrectly) which small excerpts will be selected from a long interview. The selections and the editing can make almost anyone look either brilliant or moronic. You are entirely at their mercy, and whereas some of the interviewers are quite knowledgeable about the Arthurian legend, others (as well as editors and writers) may have only a vague idea about that legend. And, as noted, not all of them seem to be particularly concerned about getting all the details right.

Many viewers of Arthurian documentaries will have the impression that they have already seen what they are seeing again on the screen. In some cases they are correct. There are two explanations. First, the cable networks share programs. The Malory program was made for the Learning Channel and was first shown in September 1993, but, as noted, from the beginning it was intended to be shown later on the Discovery Channel. Correspondents have informed me that they have since seen it on A&E. (And I am told that in 1996 it was dubbed into Japanese and released in Japan.)

"The Quest for the Holy Grail" was made for A&E, but it too has turned up elsewhere. Moreover, in December 1997, fitted with a new title ("The Holy Grail"), with new narration, and with a different narrator (replacing Leonard Nimoy), it became part of The History Channel's series "In Search of History."

Finally, a word ought to be said about money. Some producers of documentaries are clearly operating on a shoestring; others are not. Most will, in any event, try to economize as much as possible. And their assumption, in a good many instances, is that academics, whether for professional advancement or for love of the subject, will work for peanuts—or for nothing (and sometimes they are right). For the first documentary in which I appeared, I was offered, besides expenses, an honorarium that I thought reasonable, though certainly not princely. For the second film I was offered nothing at all until I broached the subject, and then the producer proposed a minimal honorarium—and to add insult to financial injury, it was proposed that, to save on airfare, I fly from St. Louis to Los Angeles with two intermediate stops and one change of plane. (I declined, whereupon a different airline, with a nonstop flight, was—grudgingly, I thought—proposed.) In addition to the small or nonexistent honoraria that are typically proposed, most makers of documentaries will offer no additional remuneration when the film is rerun, provided to another network, or re-edited for other use. Only in the unusual cases when, presumably for legal reasons, producers or networks decide that they need to secure permission from participants to reuse their words and likenesses is there even an opportunity for those participants to demand payment.[11]

In addition, it is simply assumed that preliminary telephone interviews will be a charitable donation on the scholar's part. In one instance, I was phoned four times in ten days by the producer of a proposed documentary for one of the major commercial networks; one of the conversations lasted nearly an hour, the others at least twenty minutes. Eventually, I informed her that I would be happy to continue to offer consultation and that I was confident that they would find my fee reasonable. I heard no more from her.

Making a documentary is surely not easy. But it is not a simple matter, either, to be a participant in one, even for ninety seconds on the screen (out of more than four hours of talk). Honoraria vary from modest to none, and, as I noted, the interviewee has no control at all over the part of his or her interview that will be used. So the question might reasonably be asked, "Why does anyone agree to be interviewed for an Arthurian documentary?" The answer I suggested above—that we do it for academic advancement—is both cynical and certainly wrong in most cases, if only because such an activity is unlikely to *bring* any advancement. Another possible explanation, that a flattered academic does it out of vanity and the desire to be seen on television, is even more cynical and is certainly incorrect in regard to the Arthurians I know who have participated in such films.

In fact, I do not know what the motivation of others may be. In my case, I have continued to offer unremunerated advice and, in two instances,[12] to consent to be interviewed because I continue to hope that one of these films, one of these days, will turn out to be a superlative presentation—engaging yet authoritative, thoughtful, and correct—of the Arthurian legend. In other words, I hope a film will eventually get it right. If such a film has been made to date, I have missed it. But hope springs eternal.

Notes

1. I concentrate here on English-language documentaries, especially American or British/American. My remarks are based primarily on participation in, or viewing of, the following documentaries: *Camelot* (FilmRoos production for A&E Network; Michael E. Katz, Executive Producer; 1995); *King Arthur* (BBC/Discovery

Channel; Toni Bednar Landy, Producer; 2000); *King Arthur: His Life and Legends* (A Satel Production for A&E Television Networks; Rod Caird, Executive Producer; Sue Hayes, Producer and Director; 1995); *Le Morte d'Arthur: Legend of the King* (Discovery Communications / Cronkite, Ward & Co. for the Learning Channel; Tim Cowling, Executive Producer; Dale Minor and Linda Duvoisin, Producers; 1993. *The Quest for the Holy Grail* (A FilmRoos production for A&E; Bram Roos, Executive Producer; Truusie Kushner, Producer; 1997). I also draw from a cursory viewing of *Merlin, Arthur and the Holy Grail* (Emdee Productions for the Learning Channel; Maria Anderton, Executive Producer; Stephen Rooke, Director, 1998; a compilation of three originally distinct episodes from the 1997 "Legends of the Isles" series). It should be noted, as I do elsewhere in these comments, that documentary films often circulate from channel to channel, occasionally with new titles and even with new narration. For example, the 1995 "Camelot" was recycled, with changes, as "The Knights of Camelot" in 1997. For additional titles and information on Arthurian documentary and commercial films, see Bert Olton's extensive listing in *Arthurian Legends on Film and Television*.

2. I do not want to misrepresent my experience here. I am, I believe, credited as a consultant in only one. Beyond that, "consultation" should be understood to refer to telephone discussions (some of them extensive, some brief) when a documentary is being planned or, occasionally, as it is in progress. In some instances I am asked "factual" questions about the Arthurian legend; in others I have been asked for advice about the way a subject might be presented or about my view of a theory (e.g., of Arthurian or Grail origins). My advice is sometimes followed but just as often ignored.

3. I confess that I use the terms "producer," "filmmaker," etc. rather loosely in these remarks. A network contracts with a production company to produce the film, but from that point on, the connections between producers, interviewers, and others are not always clear. Generally the actual interviews are conducted by associate producers or production assistants (but occasionally by the producer or by someone else). Preliminary work, including phone interviews, is usually done by persons associated with the production company, but in two instances I had several conversations with ostensible representatives, not of the producers, but of two different networks. (I say "ostensible" because I am aware of instances in which persons misrepresented their affiliation, introducing themselves as employees of networks for which they expected or merely hoped to produce programs.)

4. See James Noble's "Tintagel: The Best of English Twinkie," elsewhere in this volume.

5. See, for example, the research page of the Department of Archaeology of the University of Glasgow, at http://www.gla.ac.uk/archaeology/research/. (Click on "Christopher Morris, *Tintagel Excavations*.")

6. On a subpage to the site noted above (n. 5), we read, "Although Tintagel is often associated with the mysterious and mythical past, we must dismiss any idea that the name on this stone is in any way to be associated with the legendary and literary figure Arthur."

7. Thomas comments that "It's most unfortunate that people chose to hype up King Arthur on the strength of this." He insists that "this isn't the name Arthur any more than the names George and Geronimo are connected because they happen to start with 'Ge.'"

8. From publicity on the Discovery Channel's website, at http://dsc.discovery.

com/tv/tvschedule/episode.jsp?episode=20005017. In addition, in the film itself, scholarly denial of any connection with Arthur is preceded by the narrator's question, "Could this have been the earliest evidence of Arthur the King?" And even after that denial and other statements to the contrary, including the acknowledging that "the true identity of Arthur is likely to remain a mystery," the conclusion of the film still appears to imply the historicity of Arthur.

9. Among those not made (to my knowledge) is a documentary proposed on the subject of Laurel Phelan, the woman who claims to be Guinevere reincarnated. Asked my advice, I suggested that the project be abandoned. To the best of my knowledge, it was, though I have no reason to think that my recommendation was instrumental in that decision. See Phelan's book *Guinever*, and Jacqueline Jenkin's "The Once and Future Queen: Guinevere in a New Age," in this volume.

10. As noted, the producer of the Malory film did inform me in advance that he was interested in the "uses" of the Arthurian legend. Although that is all the information I received (thus leaving me in an awkward position), that focus no doubt justifies the question about the JFK-Arthur connection.

11. A reasonable solution would of course be for the scholar to make it clear from the beginning that he or she will sign the customary release (i.e., permission to use his or her words in the film) *only* if it authorizes a single showing and stipulates payment for additional use. Almost certainly, though, the producer would not accept such a stipulation and would locate a different expert.

12. And curiously, for three others that never happened. More precisely, two were never made, and the producers of the third invited me to participate, suggesting that they fly me to Europe for an interview. Those plans were eventually abandoned, perhaps owing to expense, and the film was made without my participation.

Works Cited

Baigent, Michael, Richard Leigh, and Henry Lincoln. *Holy Blood, Holy Grail.* New York: Delacorte Press, 1982.
Gardner, Laurence. *Bloodline of the Holy Grail: The Hidden Lineage of Jesus Revealed.* Shaftesbury, Dorset; Boston: Element, 1996.
Olton, Bert. *Arthurian Legends on Film and Television.* Jefferson, NC: McFarland, 2000.
Phelan, Laurel. *Guinevere: The True Story of One Woman's Quest for Her Past Life Identity and the Healing of Her Eternal Soul.* New York: Pocket Books, 1996.

Was That in the Vulgate?
Arthurian Legend in
TV Film and Series Episodes

Bert Olton

From vague to explicit, from inferential to direct, uses of Arthurian legend in television programming are far more extensive and varied than one might first imagine. They also display the full spectrum, from high end to low, of faithfulness to source and quality of production. The following essay attempts to provide an overview or a representative sample of these TV shows, and to point out some of their strengths and limitations.

While there are numerous TV shows with episodes having Arthurian titles or brief Arthurian references within the show, I am not attempting exhaustive coverage here. The famous (or infamous) series *Dallas*, for instance, boasts three episodes with Arthurian titles. All airing in the show's tenth season in 1986, they were "*Return to Camelot*" parts 1 and 2 and "*Once and Future King.*" *Today's Special*, a Canadian sit-com of the 1980s, aired an episode titled "*A Runaway Spell*" (1987), in which an accident turns the people in a department store into Captain Hook, Alice in Wonderland, Little Red Riding Hood, King Arthur and others. *The Good Life* (not the British series which came to the U.S. as *The Good Neighbors*), featured an episode titled "*Maureen's Play*" in 1994 in which the protagonist directs a play about King Arthur.

Since a complete discussion of Arthurian references on television, while perhaps not impossible to do, would be nothing short of an Herculean task, the primary targets of this essay are the shows to which some sort of reasonable access is possible (either from video stores, online auctions or private collectors) and which contain comparatively strong Arthurian material.

American television programs are not generally known for their subtlety, and Arthurian content is usually blatant. Some however, manage to incorporate marvelously evocative detail in deceptively simple ways. An episode of ABC's *Naked City* is a good example.

With a one-season break after its first year on TV, *Naked City* ran from 1958 to 1963. A very popular crime show about the detectives of New York City's Sixty-Fifth Precinct, the program was based on a 1948 movie of the same title, which in turn drew on the book of the same name, a collection of photographs by the author and crime photographer Weegee (Arthur Fellig), who became famous for his brutally candid and explicit pictures of crime scenes and victims. The TV show was noted for having retained something of the *film noir* feel of Weegee's work and the subsequent movie.

The episode entitled "*King Stanislaus and the Knights of the Round Stable*" from *Naked City* opens with the following narration: "His mother drowned one summer at Far Rockaway and his father who couldn't swim vanished trying to save her. The nine-year-old boy entered the world of his Grandpa. Grandpa's world was full of wonderful things. For instance, King Stanislaus and the Knights of the Round Stable, which Grandpa proved was Polish, not English history. The polite English made the Knights sit around a table, yet everybody knows that Knights rode horses. Obviously they gathered not around a table but in a stable. And only Polish kings had round stables because corners bred demons."

So, in a Polish neighborhood of New York city, a version of the Arthurian romance is played out. A fellow named Steve Werminski (John Larch) is troubled by the thought that the child about to be born to his wife and himself is not actually his. As his poor wife Gloria (Joanna Merlin) struggles through the early stages of labor in the hospital, Steve unloads his suspicions that the real father of the child is Gloria's former boyfriend Pete Kammik (Jack Klugman). In a drunken confrontation and battle involving a butcher's cleaver instead of Excalibur, the two men ultimately clear up the situation.

Through a series of flashbacks we learn that years ago Pete had been called the king of the neighborhood. His Guinevere, Gloria, had always had eyes for Steve. When Pete got involved with loan sharks and even asked Gloria to pawn her engagement ring to help pay his debts, she ended the relationship and wound up marrying Steve, her Lancelot.

Superficially we have the correlations of Pete/Arthur, Steve/Lancelot and Gloria/Guinevere. However, this story mixes things up a bit. Steve turns out to be the good one, the Arthur of the story. His mother drowned—not the same as being raised as a foster child, but close enough. That his father drowned as well fits roughly with the disappearance of Uther from Arthur's life. Steve entering the world of his Grandpa—which was "...full of wonderful things," including the quirky story of a Slavic origin to King Arthur—is not unlike Arthur's rearing at the hands of Merlin and Ector.

Pete, though king of his neighborhood in his youth, is the interfering Lancelot and perhaps even more strongly the would-be Meleagaunce of the show. This was no pure-intentioned Arthur, but a man who wound up in trouble and nearly dragged his fiancé into it along with him.

But this is a show right out of the late 1950s and early 1960s, a period when America was on the verge of major political and social changes. This episode aired in December of 1962, and some of the influences of the times can be seen in the program. On the one hand, the show struggles to remain decent and to present homey, traditional family values. By contrast, the book it is based on addresses some of the grittiest material available from police files and records. Infidelity, alcoholism, attempted murder, loan-sharking, to name a few, are not the stuff of *Father Knows Best* or *Lassie*. This was a real departure for television, particularly from the myriad westerns that dominated the programming of the period. The amalgam of cop show with the Matter of Arthur is an even further departure.

More typical of television are the uses of Arthuriana in episodes of shows like *Lost in Space, Fantasy Island, Highway to Heaven, Red Dwarf,* and to an extent *Babylon 5* and *Hercules: The Legendary Journeys,* among others. In these programs Arthurian characters or Arthur himself are either made slightly ridiculous or marginalized in some manner.

Though a number of texts portray Arthur as an elder statesman dependent upon his knights for tales of interest and excitement, it is not too often that he is made out to be a complete idiot. This theme of weak or dotty men in Arthurian television does include one example that is not centered on Arthur but instead on a character named Sagramonte in *Lost in Space:* "The Questing Beast."

Lost in Space, of course, is the cult classic science fiction series which ran from 1965 to 1968 on CBS. It projected a version of the Wyss's Robinsons (from their nineteenth-century novel *The Swiss Family Robinson*) into the galaxy-hopping future of 1997. Thrown off course on their way to Alpha Centauri this Space Family Robinson experienced many odd adventures, one of them an encounter with a space knight.

This knight named Sagramonte (Hans Conried), clothed in full chain mail and partial armor (gauntlets and helmet), had been for years chasing a dragon around the universe, for reasons unclear. He grew old and rickety on the long quest and his fighting skills became comically ineffectual. He tips over under the weight of a lance as often as he is able to stand upright. Finally cornering the dragon on the planet the Robinsons currently inhabit, Sagramonte learns for the first time that the beast is an intelligent and sympathetic female. With the counseling of the Robinsons, he winds up thinking better of killing her.

The name Sagramonte is reminiscent of Malory's Sagremore le Desirous. A knight of the Round Table, Sagremore appears in several romances. A questing beast also appears in many texts, but Sagremore is not usually associated with it. In Malory for instance (book 1, chapter 19) it is Pellinore who pursues the strange animal, and after Pellinore's death Palomides takes up the odd quest. In film and television it is most often Sagremore who captures the Yankee in adaptations of Twain's *A Connecticut Yankee in King Arthur's Court*. It is hard to imagine what this mistaken fixation on Sagremore might stem from.

In spite of all the inconsistencies, however, this television Sagramonte/ Pellinore is amusing to watch, being as doddery and comical as T.H. White's Pellinore from his novel *The Once and Future King*. The campy dragon he chases is typical *Lost in Space* fare.

Similarly, the mature Arthur of *Fantasy Island*'s "King Arthur in Mr. Roarke's Court" is embarrassingly dunderheaded. The original *Fantasy Island* (ABC, 1978 to 1984) had the omniscient and omnipotent Mr. Roarke (Ricardo Montalban) presiding over a resort island where guests could live out their dreams and desires.

In 1982's "King Arthur in Mr. Roarke's Court," a guest named Ralph Rogers (Tom Smothers) shows up on the island with a copy of Twain's *A Connecticut Yankee in King Arthur's Court* in hand. His wish is to visit Camelot and meet King Arthur. Roarke obliges by causing Excalibur in the stone to appear. As soon as Rogers pulls the sword, his fantasy begins.

Rogers materializes in Camelot for a moment, but both he and the fully armored King Arthur (Robert Mandan) vanish, reappearing on Fantasy Island. Arthur is enraged at being taken from his castle, primarily because he is worried that Lancelot is romancing Guinevere (Carol Lynley). Guinevere has been missing for some time and Arthur is convinced that Merlin and Lancelot have conspired to get him out of the way permanently.

On the island Roarke places Arthur's safety in Rogers' hands—no mean assignment. The King immediately gets into trouble with traffic and soon thereafter into a nearly fatal bar fight. Eventually it is learned that Guinevere has not been hiding out with Lancelot, but is herself on Fantasy Island by way of escape from the troublesome politics of Camelot and her husband's jealous railings.

When Rogers takes Guinevere to an innocent dinner, Arthur walks in and nearly kills him. Guinevere stops the attack, walking out in frustration. Rogers and Roarke give Arthur a stern lecture. Finally, at a masquerade ball thrown in their royal honor, Arthur declares his love for Guinevere and apologizes to all for his bad behavior. Guinevere is reconciled, Arthur dubs Rogers a Knight of the Realm and the King and Queen ride happily off to Camelot. At the close of the show Roarke reveals that it was his "old friend" Merlin who had requested this marital counseling session.

Many of the usual erroneous concepts about Arthurian legend are included in this episode. Among them are Arthur calling himself the King of England and upon seeing the effects of a hand gun being fired, commenting that he could use such weapons to conquer the Vikings. More disappointing than these minor details, though, is the portrayal of Arthur himself. The show posits that Arthur is only imagining an affair between Lancelot and Guinevere, and that therefore his jealousy is unfounded. This Arthur does not handle the problem in a very kingly fashion, but rants and raves, gets into fights and makes a general nuisance of himself. Like Sagramonte in *Lost in Space*, Arthur needs the guidance of others to figure things out. It takes his being lectured to like a child to get him to stop the nonsense.

In turning from *Fantasy Island* to the show *Highway to Heaven* (NBC, 1984 to 1988), we switch from an Arthur insane with jealousy to one who is just plain insane. *Highway to Heaven* was a series about an angel named Jonathan Smith (Michael Landon) who had come to Earth in human form to help people in need. In "A *Divine Madness*," episode seven of the show's first season, Smith meets Arthur Krock (Ron Moody), a widowed and retired construction company owner.

Krock however is not the typical hard hat. Instead, he now wears a crown along with full chain mail and other knightly accoutrements. Having spent his life building his business, he let family life go by the boards. He had fulfilled at least one promise to his wife before she died—he had built a castle for her. Now rattling around in the place by himself, Krock had gone slightly mad, imagining himself to be King Arthur.

Smith comes along as Arthur Krock, Jr. (Jonathan Frakes), is about to take over the land of a neighbor to complete a $20 million building project. The neighbor, Gwen Halstead (Jean Allison), is the mother of the local veterinarian, but also takes in and cares for stray animals. Krock Jr. not only controls his father's business, but he ruthlessly ignores any pleas to work something out with Halstead and is simultaneously making plans to have his father committed to an institution.

Krock Sr.'s depression and fear of the outside world immobilize him until Smith tells him one night that if he doesn't enter the battle, he is no king. Krock Sr. prays "...Give me courage to dream dreams and strength to make them real, and if this be madness, let it only serve your purpose and I'll envy no man the world calls sane." A distant lightening bolt seems to answer him.

The next day Krock Sr. shows up at the job site in full armor, mounted on horseback and carrying a lance. He charges and damages a bucket loader, temporarily stopping work. His son forces a competency hearing and Krock Sr. names Smith to represent him in court. With a couple of small miracles Smith turns the judge's sympathies towards the old man, but the clincher comes when Krock declares his love for his son and admits his error in having wasted so many years on only business. Krock Jr. is won over, the case is dismissed and things return to normal—including Krock Sr.

Hercules: The Legendary Journeys (Syndicated, 1995 to 1999) verges on this same theme in "*Once Upon a Future King,*" with an Arthur who is turned to the dark side (to use a phrase popularized by the Star Wars films) by a sorceress. Just as in the shows mentioned above, it takes the intervention of a wise, friendly guide to get Arthur back onto the right path.

The manner in which the main characters all come together in this program is also through a sort of "Connecticut Yankee" scenario. In fact, a working title for the show before it aired was "*A Greek Hero in King Arthur's Court.*" The only real similarity to Twain's novel however is the element of time travel.

The episode opens in a different AD 500 than one would expect. Britannia is a wasteland, the population decimated not by invading Angles, Saxons or Picts, but by a marauding King Arthur (Neill Rea). Arthur's advisor in this horrific turn of events is the evil sorceress Mab (Sara Wiseman). The elderly Merlin of AD 500 (Norman Forsey) realizes that he won't be effective in combating the Arthur/Mab team so he manages to send them back in time 1,000 years. The young Merlin of this earlier age (Tim Faville) finds Hercules (Kevin Sorbo) and convinces him to travel to Britannia. Once there, the mage and the legendary son of Zeus meet up with an Irish demigod named Morrigan (Tamara Gorski), who tags along to insure that this evil Arthur doesn't initiate any expansionist ideas against her home-land.

In the Britannia of 500 BC the evil duo immediately raise another army, then Mab takes Arthur to what has to be the most voluptuous Lady of the Lake (Asa Lindh) on record. Even though it is 1,000 years too soon, she is convinced by a birthmark on his neck that this is indeed the true Arthur, so she gives him Excalibur. Amidst the requisite action-packed encounters which follow, Mab kidnaps Merlin, but Hercules and Morri-gan manage to capture Arthur. Much of the humor typical of this frequently tongue-in-cheek series ensues at the expense of Excalibur. In combating their foes, Hercules uses it variously as a bat, a golf club and as a post on which to spin to aid his gymnastic Kung Fu fighting techniques. As if it were an automobile, he quips, "Hmm, solid construction, handles well, turns on a dinar."

In quieter moments, Hercules uses logical reasoning and a discussion of moral principles to plant doubts in Arthur's mind about the course he has chosen. Arthur is finally won over when it is made obvious that Mab is only after power and couldn't care less what happens to Arthur. Mab is destroyed, and Arthur, now properly tutored on the finer points of good leadership, is returned to his own time.

A number of series episodes which I have not discussed here incor-porate the idea of lunacy in bringing Arthur into the picture. In both "A Late Delivery from Avalon" from *Babylon 5* (for a more in-depth discussion of this see Kristina Hildebrand's article elsewhere in this book) and "A Knight to Remember" from the TV western series *Bonanza*, a modern indi-vidual becomes mentally unstable, imagining himself to be King Arthur. Add to these *Highway to Heaven*: "A Divine Madness," and the collective the-sis might be that only a disturbed person can be an Arthur-like hero, and that only through the help of the people around him can he either aban-don this misapprehension or incorporate the positive aspects of Arthurian chivalry into an acceptable life style.

Similarly, in "Once Upon a Future King" from *Hercules: The Legendary Journeys* and *Fantasy Island*'s "King Arthur in Mr. Roarke's Court," the real King Arthur has gone astray and is causing problems either for his king-dom or for his marriage. Again, it is only through the intervention of oth-ers that these Arthurs manage to return to the right path. Though in all of these shows good is ultimately achieved, in none of them does Arthur start out as the just and moral leader to whom we have become accus-tomed. This modern Arthur of TV is not a Father who Knows Best.

An interesting character from the *Hercules* episode seems to have originated in the made-for-TV movie (or more accurately, miniseries) *Merlin*, starring Sam Neill. Mab, or Queen Mab (Miranda Richardson) is new to Arthurian motion pictures. She seems to bring to modern film renderings a character who can successfully deflect the onus of evil away from Morgan le Fay. Mab may be based on the mortal but decidedly rambunctious Queen Maeve of Connacht from Celtic legend, or she may be derived from Dryden's poem *Nymphidia* and Shakespeare's *The Tragedy of Romeo and Juliet*. Historically, she has been understood to be the Queen of the Fairies and the one who causes dreams.

Hallmark Entertainment's 1998 production of *Merlin* is admirable for its ambitious scope. Not since the theatrical release *Excalibur* (1981) has such a complete sweep of the Arthurian saga been attempted. *Merlin* in fact outstrips Boorman's film in that it starts further back in time and legend than *Excalibur*. Merlin is also a special-effects tour de force.

On the other hand, *Merlin* tracks with the TV versions of Arthurian stories already mentioned. The Britain of *Merlin* is like the mythical Lake Woebegone from Garrison Keillor's weekly NPR radio program, *A Prairie Home Companion*, a place "...where all the women are strong, the men are good looking and the children are above average." The main male characters in the film seem to be a bunch of bumblers who continuously thwart and become problematic to the women. The elderly King Constant (John Gielgud), Uther's father, is described as the first Christian king of England (few films call the place Britain), but he is killed at the opening of the story by none other than Vortigern (Rutger Hauer). Vortigern isn't much more than a buffoon, albeit one with a pretty good sense of humor. Uther (Mark Jax), though majestic in Roman garb sallying forth from Normandy to attack Vortigern, is nonetheless so weak of character that instantly upon crowning himself he begins lusting after someone else's wife. He winds up going insane and committing suicide. Merlin himself (Neill) constantly resists taking an upper hand and is battered about by the women in his life. Frik (Martin Short), the pointy-eared, shape-shifting assistant to Mab is thoroughly dominated by his female boss. The recumbent Mountain King/Rock of Ages (voiced by James Earl Jones) is happy to sleep through the nonsense swirling around him, and even Arthur (Paul Curran) is a callow youth dependent on the magic of Excalibur for his strength. Mordred (Jason Done), though a powerful force, is henpecked into his role and often verbally spanked for misbehaving.

By contrast, the female figures, particularly Mab, dominate this story. Mab is the sole surviving proponent of the Old Religion, fighting the spread of the new Christianity. Speaking in a strange, whispering rasp, this off-the-wall woman starts out sounding good, but soon proves that she'll stop at nothing to preserve her place in the universe.

The feisty Ambrosia (Billie Whitelaw) raises Merlin. Though only human, she doesn't hesitate to let Mab know what she thinks of her activities. Ambrosia's death at the hands of Mab causes Merlin to finally decide on a path for himself—namely battling Mab. So here we do not have a Merlin with an altruistic world view or even one with great political ambitions. Instead he's just a guy like a character in a B Western, out to avenge the death of his Ma.

The Lady of the Lake (Miranda Richardson) is of considerable help to Merlin, warning him of Ambrosia's impending death, then later giving him Excalibur. Incredibly though, Merlin fouls up a crucial bit of her advice when he misinterprets one of her statements. He picks Lancelot instead of the knight's less fickle son Galahad to protect Camelot in Arthur's absence.

Probably the weakest of the female characters, Morgan seems to be in the movie only to bear Mordred and to display an incredible speech impediment. Odd that two women in this movie appropriate such peculiar vocal characteristics. In any case, Frik loves Morgan , in spite of the fact that only Mab's magic has kept Morgan beautiful. It is good to see this film rid Morgan of the dishonor of being the primary evil force in the story. It's a shame though, that in making Mab the villain, the *Merlin* production made Morgan so peculiar.

In terms of using the sentiment of Arthurian legend, as opposed to specific versions or details, certainly the best film produced for TV to date has been Disney's 1995 *The Four Diamonds*, which tells the story of Christopher Millard, a youngster who died at the age of 14 in 1972 of a now-curable nasal cavity muscle sarcoma, after fighting the cancer for three years. During his freshman year of high school, his class was assigned a writing project to describe their summer activities. Not caring to address his hospitalizations specifically, Millard created an allegorical Arthurian story about his battle with the disease.

The movie does a fine job of weaving the stages of Millard's real life struggles with Arthurian parallels in his story. Millard (Thomas Guiry) translated himself, his family and his oncologist into the characters of his tale. He became Sir Millard, squire and seeker of the Four Diamonds of Courage, Wisdom, Honesty and Strength. His oncologist, Dr. Burke (Christine Lahti), became the evil Queen Raptemahad, holder of the Four Diamonds and namer of the quests Millard had to complete to achieve each of the gems.

In real life Millard conquers his fear of the grim diagnosis and the horrors of chemotherapy by making friends with other young patients in the hospital and even eliciting conversation with his unsociable doctor. Squire Millard in the meantime is captured by Raptemahad. He challenges her to a fair fight, but she declines, stating that if instead he completes her four tests and achieves each of her gems, he can go free. Squire Millard succeeds on the first quest by overcoming his fear of unseen cave demons on a mountain, finding the tree of life there and bringing a fruit from the tree to the sorceress.

Millard's next quest is initiated when his illness upstages his sister Stacey's winning the leading role in a production of *Swan Lake*. Frustrated by her rejection of his attempts to apologize, he learns wisdom when his mother advises him that Stacey (Sarah Rose Karr) is just afraid and that he must let her come to him. Raptemahad sends Squire Millard out to capture the Stacia Swan which is guarded by a Wise Hermit (Jayne Brook, also Millard's mother). The Squire tries to catch the Swan first by chasing it, then by building a decoy, but only succeeds when he heeds the Hermit's words, "You get to keep what you set free" and simply stands still allowing the Swan to approach him. The Squire wins the second diamond, Wisdom.

As Millard's medical condition deteriorates, his father (Kevin Dunn) becomes more and more surly, remote and unable to face the situation. A friend visits Millard at his home and his father overhears Millard telling his friend that should he die, he wants him to have his baseball card collection. Mr. Millard breaks down at this and, weeping, is finally able to talk with his son and accept his condition. Raptemahad challenges the Squire to get the Athene Medallion from the strange but just wizard Charles the Mysterious. In trying to find him, the Squire comes across a man (also Millard's Dad) whose cart wheel has fallen off. Squire Millard helps the man fix the cart, but refuses any payment, stating that he is on a quest for his future. The man asks that the Squire help him with one more small task, cleaning his gold coins. When Squire Millard discovers that one of them is the Athene Medallion, the man gives it to him, also revealing that he indeed is Charles the Mysterious.

Squire Millard is awarded the third diamond, Honesty, but Raptemahad next gives him the quest she thinks most impossible of all. The Squire must bring her the head of the Black Cavalier. Millard's tumor has grown, taking his sight as it hits the optic nerves. He rejects further chemotherapy, and enraged at Dr. Burke's callousness, finally brings even her to sympathetic tears. Squire Millard finds the Black Cavalier at the seashore. The two joust, but the Squire is unhorsed at the second pass. The Cavalier, still mounted, attacks with a fearsome battle axe. Millard and his father return home from the hospital and his dad carries Millard up to his room. Squire Millard manages to unhorse and disarm the Black Cavalier, then calls for the knight to yield. The Cavalier will not and the Squire raises his sword for the death stroke. At dinner Millard can't eat, but he talks of happy memories of a Thanksgiving vacation the family had enjoyed at a quiet seaside cove. Not feeling well he asks his father to carry him upstairs. With a weak grin he gives his mother and sister the "Victory" sign. The film closes with Millard now a Knight, riding victoriously towards the gloriously transformed castle of Raptemahad, carrying the shield and pennant of The Four Diamonds.

Though of uneven quality, the variety and frequency of the uses of Arthurian themes in television shows confirms how deeply these legends are embedded in the Western psyche and culture. The shows which include Arthur, Merlin or any of the other characters from the Round Table are often of questionable merit. Even more often, they make clear departures from the accepted traditions handed down in the literature which culminates with Malory. Occasionally however, innovations crop up, like the character Mab or the exceptional *The Four Diamonds*, proving that King Arthur is among us and well and sometimes living on TV.

Appendix

The following is a partial list of the primary series episodes and made-for-TV movies which include Arthurian material. By no means complete as yet, it at least gives a basis for further research and a starting point for further cataloging.

Series Episodes

Naked City: "King Stanislaus and the Knights of the Round Stable" (1961), Screen Gems, Columbia Pictures Television, Producer—Charles Russell, Director—James Sheldon, Writer—Abram S. Ginnes.

Bonanza: "Knight Errant" (1962), RCA/NBC Television, Producer—David Dortort, Director—William Claxton, Writer—Joseph Hoffman.

Bonanza: "A Knight to Remember" (1964), RCA/NBC Television, Producer—David Dortort, Director—Vincent McEveety, Writer—Robert V. Barron.

Lost in Space: "The Questing Beast" (1967), Space Productions, 20th Century Fox Television, Producer—Irwin Allen, Director—Don Richardson, Writer—Carey Wilbur.

The Time Tunnel: "Merlin the Magician" (1967), Kent Productions, Inc., 20th Century Fox Television, Irwin Allen Productions, Director—Harry Harris, Story Editor—Arthur Weiss.

Fantasy Island: "King Arthur in Mr. Roarke's Court" (1982), Spelling/Goldberg Productions, Columbia Pictures Television, Producer—Don Ingalls, Director—Philip Leacock, Writer—A. Bass.

Highway to Heaven: "A Divine Madness" (1984), Michael Landon Productions, Inc., Executive Producer—Michael Landon, Director—Michael Landon, Writer—Dan Gordon.

The New Twilight Zone: "The Last Defender of Camelot" (1986), CBS, Inc., Producer—Harvey Frand, Director—Jeannot Szwarc, Writer—Roger Zelazny (Teleplay—George R.R. Martin).

Dr. Who: "Battlefield" (1989), BBC, Producer—John Nathan-Turner, Director—Michael Kerrigan, Writer—Ben Aaronovitch.

MacGyver: "Legend of the Holy Rose" (1989), Henry Winkler/John Rich Productions, Paramount Pictures, Inc., Executive Producers—Stephen Downing, Henry Winkler and John Rich, Director (Part 1)—Michael Coffey, Director (Part 2)—Charles Correll, Writer—Stephen Downing.

MacGyver: "Good Knight MacGyver" (1991), Henry Winkler/John Rich Productions, Paramount Pictures, Inc., Executive Producers—Stephen Downing, Henry Winkler and John Rich, Director—Michael Vejar, Writer—John Considine.

Land of the Lost: "Day for Knight" (1991), Krofft Entertainment, Inc., Republic Pictures, Spelling Entertainment Group, Inc., Producers—Sid & Marty Krofft, Director—John Carl Buechler, Writers—Jules Dennis and Richard Mueller.

Northern Exposure: "Wake Up Call" (1992), Falahey/Austin Street Productions, Universal Television, Executive Producers—Joshua Brand and John Falsey, Director—Nick Marck, Writers—Diane Frolov and Andrew Sneider.

Babylon 5: "Grail" (1993), PTN Consortium, Producer—John Copeland, Director—Richard Compton, Writer—Christy Marx.

Babylon 5: "A Late Delivery from Avalon" (1995), PTN Consortium, Producer—John Copeland, Director—Michael Vejar, Writer—J. Michael Straczynski.

Sabrina the Teenage Witch: "Oh What a Tangled Spell She Weaves" (1996), Viacom Productions, Inc./Paramount, Heartbreak Films, Inc., Producer—Kenneth R. Koch, Director—David Trainer, Writers—David Weiss and Joan Binder Weiss.

The New Adventures of Robin Hood: "Miracle at Avalon" (1997), Weintraub/Kuhn Productions, Executive Producers—Tom Kuhn and Fred Weintraub, Director—Rober Tucker, Writers—Claudia Lonow and Larry Felix, Jr.

Red Dwarf: "Stoke Me a Clipper" (1997), Grant Naylor Productions/BBC North, Producer—Ed Bye, Director—Ed Bye, Writers—Paul Alexander and Doug Naylor.

Field Trip: "Sticks in Stones" (1998), ProCreations/Western International Syndication, Producers—Scott Madden and Andrew Jones, Director—Scott Madden, Writers—Andrew Jones and Scott Madden.

The New Adventures of Robin Hood: "Return to Camelot" (1999), Weintraub/Kuhn Productions, Executive Producers—Tom Kuhn and Fred Weintraub, Director—Colin Bucksey, Writers—Jaq Greenspon and Sandra Weintraub.

Hercules: The Legendary Journeys: "Once Upon a Future King" (1999), Studios USA, Renaissance Pictures, Flat Earth Productions, Producer—Bernadette Joyce, Director—Mark Beesley, Writers—Gene O'Neill and Noreen Tobin.

GvsE (Good vs Evil): "Gee Your Hair Smells Evil" (1999), Chum Television/USA Network, Producer—Paul Biddle, Director—Jonas Pate, Writers—Josh Pate and Jonas Pate.

Sir Arthur Conan Doyle's The Lost World: "Camelot" (1999), Canada, Inc., Coote/Hayes Pty Ltd., Producer—Darryl Sheen, Director—Colin Budds, Writer—James Thorpe.

The Made-for-TV Movies

A Connecticut Yankee in King Arthur's Court (1978), Metropolitan Pittsburgh Public Broadcasting, Inc., Once Upon A Classic, Producer—Chiz Schultz, Director—David Tapper, Dramatization—Stephen Dick.

The Moon Stallion (1978), BBC Corp. and BBC Enterprises, Ltd., Sudfunk Stuttgart, TABU, Executive Producer—Anna Home, Director—Dorothea Brooking, Writer—Brian Hayles.

A Connecticut Yankee in King Arthur's Court (1989), Consolidated Productions, Schaeffer Karpf Productions, Producer—Graham Ford, Director—Mel Damski, Writer—Mark Twain (Teleplay—Paul Zindel).

Merlin of the Crystal Cave (1991), BBC Corp./BBC Enterprises, Ltd., Producer—Shaun Sutton, Director—Michael Darlow, Writer—Mary Stewart (Television Adaptation—Steve Bescoby).

Guinevere (1994), Alexander/Enright and Associates, Weintraub/Kuhn Productions, Producer—Joi Broido, Director—Jud Taylor, Writer—Persia Woolley (Television Story and Teleplay—Ronni Kern).

Teklab: Tekwar (1994), Grosyenda Park LI Ltd. Partnership, Universal/MCA/Atlantis Films Ltd., Executive Producers—William Shatner and Peter Sussman, Director—Timothy Bond, Writer—William Shatner (Screenplay—Chris Haddock, Screen Story—Westbrook Claridge).

Ymadawiad Arthur (1994), S4C/Cynhyrchiadau'r Bae Ar Gyfer S4C, Director—Marc Evans [My apologies, but the cast and crew credit titles for this film are entirely in Welsh.

A Young Connecticut Yankee in King Arthur's Court (1996), Cabin Fever Entertainment, Inc./Timeless Adventures, Filmline International/Images Television International, Producer—Nicolas Clermont, Director—R.L. Thomas, Screenplay—Frank Encarnacao and R.L. Thomas.

The Four Diamonds (1995), The Walt Disney Company/O'Byrne Productions, Producer—Jean Higgins, Director—Peter Werner, Writer—Chris Millard (Teleplay—Todd Robinson).

Merlin: The Magic Begins (1997), Seagull Productions/KMG, Kaleidoscope Media Group, Wynn Entertainment, Cromwell Productions, Director—David Winning, Writer—Tom Richards.

Babylon 5: A Call to Arms (1998), Warner Bros., Producer—John Copeland, Director—Michael Vejar, Writer—J. Michael Straczynski.

A Knight in Camelot (1998), Disney Enterprises, Inc., ABC Television, Rosemont Productions International, Inc., Producer—Nick Gillott, Director—Roger Young, Writer—Mark Twain (Teleplay—Joe Wiesenfeld).

Merlin (1998), NBC/RHI Entertainment, Hallmark Entertainment Productions, Producer—Dyson Lovell, Director—Steve Barron, Story—Edward Khmara.

Knights in Space:
The Arthur of *Babylon 5*
and *Dr. Who*

KRISTINA HILDEBRAND

Moving with the times, Arthur and his story have always been able to flourish in new genres and media, from poetry and romance to drama, comic books, and film. As Bert Olton has shown us, TV has been as unable as any other genre to resist Arthur. This essay will explore the Arthurian matter in two science fiction series, *Babylon 5* and *Dr. Who*, especially in the episodes "Grail" and "A Late Delivery from Avalon" from the former and "Battlefield" from the latter.[1] These two series differ greatly from each other, and therefore I will briefly introduce them before analyzing the function of the Arthurian motifs.

Babylon 5 comprises a little over a hundred episodes, stretching over five seasons. The story arc is consistent and the entire series was mapped out before writing commenced. Despite later changes, this arc remains coherent, involving first the fight against an ancient race known as the Shadows, and later the struggle to free Earth from a dictator and unite the space-faring races into a federation. The format allows for extensive character development, and considerable effort seems to have gone towards keeping both characters and plot believable. Furthermore, the series frequently addresses existential and religious issues: for example, the struggle of one character, G'kar, to forgive his enemy, Londo Mollari, is a persistent theme through the last two seasons.

The series is set at the diplomatic space station *Babylon 5*, which is crewed by human military personnel but inhabited by representatives of

101

numerous races. The main characters are the command staff and the alien ambassadors; while some of these change, most remain the same. The human characters relevant for the episodes discussed here are Captain Sinclair, played by Michael O'Hare, who is later replaced by Captain John Sheridan (Bruce Boxleitner), Commander Susan Ivanova (Claudia Christian), Head of Security Michael Garibaldi (Jerry Doyle), medical officer Dr. Stephen Franklin (Richard Biggs) and the Ranger Marcus (Jason Carter). The alien ambassadors who feature most prominently are the Minbari Delenn (Mira Furlan) with her aide Lennier (Bill Mumy), the Centauri Londo Mollari (Peter Jurasik), with his aide Vir Kotto (Stephen Furst), the Narn ambassador G'kar (Andreas Katsulas) and the Vorlon ambassador Kosh (Ardwight Chamberlain).

Unlike *Babylon 5*, *Dr. Who* is primarily a comedy series, which has run, with some interruptions, through twenty-seven seasons since 1963. It does not have a coherent story arc, and the main character, the Doctor, has been played by several different actors. The stories center on the Doctor's space ship, known as the TARDIS, which can move through time. In appearance, it resembles a phone box of a type common in Britain in the 1960s, which enables the Doctor to put it down in different places without attracting attention. However, since the ship persists in malfunctioning, those places are not necessarily of the Doctor's choosing.

Although the Brigadier Lethbridge-Stewart, played by Nicholas Courtney, recurs frequently, the only consistently appearing character is the Doctor, in his many different shapes. Instead, different characters are introduced and may reappear in other episodes. In "Battlefield," the Doctor is played by Sylvester McCoy, who is the seventh actor to portray him.

Whereas "Battlefield" is the only episode of *Dr. Who* to feature the matter of Arthur, in *Babylon 5* Arthurian references abound even outside the explicitly Arthurian episodes. Captain Sheridan functions as an Arthur figure: he establishes a Camelot in space, "a shining beacon" full of loyal knights, with the Vorlon ambassador Kosh and later the strange being Lorien, played by Wayne Alexander, for his Merlins. The idea of Babylon 5 as Camelot is explicitly formulated at the end of "A Late Delivery," when Marcus comments that Kosh is Merlin: as Merlin lives backwards in time, "maybe he had Arthur establish the Round Table by remembering us—we're forming one of our own, after all."[2] Sheridan also shares with Arthur the mystery of his disappearance: at the end of his life, he takes a ship out into space, and there Lorien appears and takes him beyond the rim of known space. While nothing is said of his eventual return, the parallel with Arthur's journey to Avalon is clear.

There are other features reminiscent of the Arthurian tradition in *Babylon 5*. Sheridan's wife, Delenn, has an aide, Lennier, whose love and service makes him a Lancelot to her Guinevere. Eventually, he is driven to betray Sheridan by his impossible love, turning into a Mordred figure—a position previously held by an agent of evil with the suggestive name Morden.

In addition to this permeation of Arthurian allusions, two episodes make specific reference to Arthur and the stories surrounding him. One of these, "Grail," concerns itself with the quest for the Grail, which here comes to signify the search for meaning, empowerment, and the willingness to embrace spiritual values. In this episode, a quester, Aldous Gajic, played by David Warner, comes to the station to question the alien ambassadors on the whereabouts of the Grail. He refers to the search as having restored meaning to his life after the death of his family, and conveys this meaning to an inept thief, known only by the nickname Jinxo (Tom Booker), whom he befriends. Jinxo, whose name refers to his bringing bad luck to people, is in a sense a Fair Unknown, a knight in hiding. He stays on Babylon 5 out of a conviction that it will be destroyed should he leave it, that having happened to Babylon 1 through 4. His goodness and ability is hidden from everyone, including himself, behind the persona of the pickpocket. The meaning of his life has so far been negative: only by not acting can he assure the safety of those around him. The quest for the Grail offers a more active meaning to his life.

The quest is also empowering: for example, Gajic possesses power over a half-sentient alien that preys on the homeless. Faced with this creature, the quester alone is able to subdue it with, as it seems, sheer force of character. The Grail quest here provides both meaning and power: due to the clearness of the quester's vision, he has power over the forces of dark and evil. His successor, the thief, also experiences empowerment: at his assumption of the role as quester, he rejects his nickname Jinxo, and reassumes his real name, Thomas Jordan.

Furthermore, the Grail symbolizes spiritual values as opposed to materialistic ones. The reactions of the various characters clearly delineate their spiritual status: the Minbari, Delenn, and Lennier treat Gajic with courtesy and respect, whereas the Centauri ambassador Mollari casually dismisses him. The later development of the Centauri ambassador's aide, Vir Kotto, into a character torn by his conscience is here anticipated by his greater respect for the Grail seeker. The station's human staff is portrayed as growing in spiritual understanding through their encounter with the quester: from a curt welcome they move to respectful farewells at his coffin.

Despite the many Arthurian features of *Babylon 5*, the only episode that features Arthur himself is "A Late Delivery from Avalon." In this episode, a man claiming to be Arthur, played by Michael York, shows up on Babylon 5, carrying a sword which he uses to fight for the protection of the helpless. It is eventually discovered that he is a former spaceship gunner, whose guilt over firing the shot that started the Earth-Minbari war has caused him to have a nervous breakdown.

When Arthur is introduced into the already richly Arthurian setting of *Babylon 5*, he becomes a symbol of honor, compassion, and responsibility. This position is repeatedly emphasized: his first act after escaping surveillance is to help an old penniless woman. Arthur is here contrasted with the harsh underworld of Babylon 5 not only through his willingness to fight for the helpless, but also through his courtesy to the old woman: he tells her that "eyes as lovely as yours were never made for tears." The fight also brings Arthur together with the Narn ambassador G'kar, who is at this point in the series on his way towards becoming a representative of good. G'kar's decision to join Arthur's side both emphasizes his own movement towards enlightenment and establishes Arthur as a warrior for good. G'kar's subsequent knighting by Arthur is consistent with his increasing understanding of honor and responsibility.

This issue of responsibility is further stressed in the conversation between G'kar and Arthur. Arthur states that he formed the Round Table to prevent the strong from preying on the weak, and then moves to the story of his own responsibility. Expressing deep guilt and sorrow over the death of his knights, he recounts the story of how, on Camlann field, a knight drew his sword to kill an adder, thereby inadvertently signalling the battle to start. When the true identity of Arthur is discovered to be Gunnery Sergeant David McIntyre, he is even more closely linked to the story of Camlann: having fired the shot which started the Earth-Minbari war, he is unable to handle the burden of guilt and responsibility he feels for all the death. On the space ship *Prometheus* he was not Arthur: he was the knight drawing his sword without thinking. The narrative implies that McIntyre, who only followed orders to fire, cannot accept that he is free of guilt: the court martial that freed him of responsibility has, paradoxically, made him unable to deal with the result of his actions. McIntyre believes himself to be Arthur, as that will allow him to act with the responsibility he has been denied.

Whereas in "A Late Delivery from Avalon" Arthur represents honor and responsibility, in "Battlefield" he symbolizes no such thing. In this episode, the Doctor is called to Lake Vortigern, under which Arthur rests, together with Excalibur, awaiting the time to return. The situation is made more dangerous by the accidental breakdown, next to the lake, of a transport containing a nuclear missile. Drawn to the lake in the same way as the Doctor, Morgaine le Fay (Jean Marsh) and Mordred (Christopher Bowen) hope to succeed in killing Arthur this time, despite the defense of the one remaining Arthurian knight, Ancelyn (Marcus Gilbert). The Doctor, the Brigadier, and the Doctor's companion Ace, played by Sophie Aldred, join forces with Ancelyn. So does the leader of the military group escorting the nuclear missile, Brigadier Bambera (Angela Bruce). In the end Morgaine and Mordred are defeated, but King Arthur turns out to have died at Camlann.

The episode includes several Arthurian characters, though Arthur himself is present only as an inert body, around which Morgaine le Fay and Mordred wage battle against Arthur's defenders for possession of the sword. Ancelyn is the only Round Table knight present. So far as I have been able to ascertain, this name does not appear in the Arthurian story; however, in sound it resembles Lancelot, a similarity further strengthened by the knight's devotion to the Brigadier Bambera, whose first name is Winifred, reminiscent of Guinevere. As a Lancelot figure, who refers to himself as the best knight of the world, Ancelyn represents Arthur on the battlefield. Furthermore, the Doctor is, to his own surprise, immediately recognized by Morgaine as Merlin—something which, he says, must refer to his personal future.

Arthur himself, in his underwater resting-place, becomes a powerful central figure due to his very absence. Were he to return, Morgaine's desire to kill him and Ancelyn's to see him restored would involve Arthur directly. As long as Arthur remains unawakened, the potential for great change is still present; his presence would, in a sense, be anticlimactic. The importance of this absence is evident at the discovery that Arthur is dead: the Doctor's note, found in Arthur's dust-filled helmet, states that he died at Camlann and "all the rest [is] propaganda." The power of Arthur is dependent on his absence or his death and on the stories surrounding it: a dead king is not a bad subject for political exploitation. Rather than symbolizing compassion and responsibility, Arthur represents the power of propaganda and a political tool.

"A Late Delivery from Avalon" and "Battlefield" differ markedly not only in their representations of Arthur, but also in their presentation of information to the viewers, and the final position in which they leave the audience. "A Late Delivery from Avalon," while privileging the audience's perspective, keeps information from the viewer; "Battlefield" more openly privileges the audience, offering the viewer information withheld from the characters.

In "A Late Delivery from Avalon," the audience is allowed to share Arthur's perception of the world, yet this is initially more confusing than clarifying. The first view of Arthur shows him dreaming: he is running through a ship corridor with doors leading from it. This dream environment will return repeatedly in Arthur's mind, waking or sleeping, and seems to symbolize the locking away of truth: when the doors blow open, he sees a battle. The battle is at first not visible to the audience, who see only the reflections of fire on Arthur's face. As this vision of opening doors returns, the viewer is allowed to see brief glimpses of the battle, and may, if thoroughly familiar with earlier episodes, identify it as the last battle in the Earth-Minbari war. The truth is, one may say, out there.

Despite this inside view of Arthur, he is not the only "focalizer" available to the audience.[3] Others include the sceptical Dr. Franklin and the Ranger Marcus, who discover the identity of Arthur. The use of other focalizers enables the narrative to question the identity and sanity of Arthur; through the introduction of scepticism, the viewer is not left with only Arthur's perception of himself.

The viewer is offered an ambiguous perspective, due to the multiple focalizers and the depiction of Arthur's mind. This perspective includes a double vision of outside/inside reaction: to Dr. Franklin, Arthur suddenly becomes catatonic, to Arthur, he is struck down from behind by a dark knight. The solution of Arthur's dilemma also takes this double form: whereas from the outside perspective it is the Minbari ambassador Delenn who appears at his sickbed, in Arthur's vision she is the Lady of the Lake accepting Excalibur back.[4] The rational quality of the outside view is qualified by a measure of reality granted to the inside view. Arthur's visions are always presented from a third person point of view: the audience sees him experience them, rather than seeing them through his eyes. This lends an objective quality to the visions which prevents the viewer from dismissing them as hallucinations.

This double vision allows the viewer to accept Dr. Franklin's view of Arthur/McIntyre as a man driven by unendurable guilt rather than a king returning from the dead, but avoids resolving the issue entirely. The visions of Arthur's, which include the finding of a sword, can be read as metaphors for his running from the truth, but, just as the objective quality of these visions has been implied, the sword is undeniably real. When Arthur arrives on Babylon 5 he is carrying a sword, yet there is no explanation of how he got it. In the dream he has aboard ship coming to Babylon 5, he finds the sword at the end of the corridor and takes it. The unreal quality of the dream is contradicted by the undoubted existence of the sword.

"A Late Delivery from Avalon" avoids closure, leaving the viewer with several unanswered questions. The final scene is Arthur/McIntyre's departure from Babylon 5, and here it is implied that though he may not be Arthur, he is more than McIntyre. The Vorlon ambassador Kosh appears to see him leave: throughout the series, the presence of the Vorlon ambassador signifies something of importance. As stated above, Kosh functions as a Merlin figure to Sheridan, and this is twice emphasized in this episode. First, Marcus at one point suggests that since the Vorlon have earlier visited Earth, abducted and changed humans, they may have done that with Arthur, too. Second, as Arthur is leaving, Marcus comments on Dr. Franklin's scepticism by indicating Kosh and saying, "next thing you'll be saying is he's not Merlin." The presence of Kosh/Merlin at this point implies that there is more to Arthur/McIntyre than a delusional spaceship gunner.

"Battlefield" does not include the ambiguities of view found in "A Late Delivery from Avalon." The narrative unfolds from an omniscient perspective, relying more on cliff-hanging at the end of episodes than on withheld information to keep the viewer in suspense. The audience's perspective is privileged above the characters' and includes information unavailable to them. For example, the ruthlessness of Morgaine, as well as her sense of honor, is conveyed in a scene where the main characters—the Doctor, his helper Ace, the brigadier, Ancelyn and Bamberra—are absent. Morgaine's killing of the brigadier's pilot and her curing of the blind wife of the hotel owner are known only to the viewer. Similarly, the survival of brigadier Bamberra and Ancelyn is known to the viewer while the other characters assume them to be dead. The exception is the death of Arthur, which is kept from audience and characters alike for most of the episode

Morgaine's character in particular is more available to the audience than to the other characters. Her decision to cure the hotel owner's wife and her anger at discovering that her knights have gathered in a cemetery, showing the dead dishonor, are not witnessed by any of the "good" characters. This shifts the viewers' sympathies in her favor. Since she has already been established as evil, malicious actions, such as her killing of the brigadier's pilot, do little to modify the audience's understanding of her character. Her unexpected acts of charity and honor, on the other hand, provide the viewers with insight not available to the other characters in the production. Thus her cheerful greeting of the brigadier as a fellow warrior and her request for a cease-fire to allow her to honor the dead make sense to the audience, though not to the brigadier.

"Battlefield" achieves closure. The ending leaves the audience with no questions unresolved, except possibly how any ordinary prison will be able to hold Morgaine and Mordred. Arthur is dead, his enemies defeated, and the threats to humankind have been defused.

Despite these differences between the episodes, there are also intriguing similarities in the depiction of Arthur and the return of the once and future king. Both episodes contrast Arthur against his surroundings, introducing an element of strangeness into the familiar tale. They also focus on the potential return of Arthur, yet that return is rejected or, possibly, postponed. The underlying theme in both episodes is similar: that dwelling on the past must be rejected in favour of looking forward.

The contrast of Arthur against the setting is emphasized in both episodes. Arthur of *Babylon 5* is dressed in medieval style clothing, wears chain mail and carries a sword, which clashes with the space station environment. In *Dr. Who*, the contrast is at first less obvious. The setting is the English countryside, complete with a country pub. Some scenes take place in the home of the retired brigadier and show him involved in gardening with his wife. This idyllic environment seems highly appropriate for the introduction of a returning Arthur, yet the resting-place of the king, and of Excalibur, is a space ship, and the knights carry space-style firearms.

These contrasts introduce a feeling of incongruity, which serves to remind the viewers that the return of Arthur is unlikely. The return of Arthur from the dead would contradict the laws of nature, which *Babylon 5* normally avoids violating: that Arthur looks like a medieval king further emphasizes that he is out of place. In *Dr. Who*, Arthur is explained as coming from another dimension and so, even were he to return from a state of suspended animation, he is not the Arthur of Malory or Tennyson. He is as out of place in the familiar surroundings as the familiar king of *Babylon 5* is in his. The viewers are first introduced to the Arthurian element with this incongruity strongly realized. The knights of "Battlefield" arrive in space capsules and carry firearms; Arthur in *Babylon 5* simply steps into the station carrying a sword.

The potential return of this out-of-place Arthur is also treated in similar fashion by both episodes. The portrayal of the return of Arthur in modern times, rather than the medieval Arthur, is, in the case of *Babylon 5*, unavoidable, considering the structure of the series: with one exception, it does not involve time travel. *Dr. Who*, however, could easily have included an episode set in the Dark Ages, as time travel is the central feature of the series. The choice not to involve Arthur directly must therefore be considered a deliberate one. Both episodes reject the possibility of the return of Arthur, yet "A Late Delivery from Avalon" does so ambiguously and with regret, whereas "Battlefield" is emphatic and clear.

The title "A Late Delivery from Avalon" is deliberately many-layered. Throughout the episode runs a subplot on problems in the post office, where deliveries are delayed and expensive, but there is also a hint of 'deliverance' and salvation. Arthur's arrival promises deliverance from the current conflict, yet this promise is false: Arthur is no Arthur—or, as he goes, at the end, to help another race fight their battle for freedom, he is not mankind's Arthur.

The episode leaves the viewer with a double message: McIntyre is not Arthur, but the dream is a worthy one. The future must be faced without salvation from the past, yet the real Arthur's return remains a possibility. Though the episode rejects the returning king as a route to salvation, his importance as a symbol of compassion and responsibility is consistently emphasized: the episode remains ambiguous.

The message of "Battlefield," on the other hand, is clear. The death of Arthur occurred at Camlann, preventing all return: when the main characters find the body, it has gone to dust inside its armour. The note stating that all the rest is propaganda makes it obvious that expecting help from the past is vain, and that the future must be faced without such hope. Furthermore, dwelling on the past may be dangerous: Morgaine has devoted centuries to avenging herself on Arthur, in the process alienating her son, only to find that her revenge is impossible and its object beyond reach. Whereas in "A Late Delivery" the past is a source of strength and moral values, in "Battlefield" it may lead to lost hopes and wasted lives.

Babylon 5 and *Dr. Who* are very different series, originating in the U.S. and Great Britain respectively; the differences point to the plasticity of the legend and to the potential Arthur still holds as a symbol. Whether he is rejected as a false symbol based on propaganda, or embraced as a source of hope and strength, he has gained a foothold in space, and among all the Avalons where Arthur may sleep, we must now include those beyond the stars.

Notes

1. "Battlefield," *Dr. Who*, dir. Michael Kerrigan, BBC 1998. "A Late Delivery from Avalon," *Babylon 5*, written by Michael Straczynski, dir. Michael Vejar, Warner 1997. For practical reasons, "Battlefield" will be treated as one episode, though it is in fact four consecutive episodes.

2. All quotations are transcribed from the video tape of the episode.

3. A focalizer is a character "whose perception orients the presentation. See Shlomith Rimmon-Kenan, *Narrative Fiction: Contemporary Poetics* (London: Methuen, 1983), 74.

4. It should perhaps be noted here that Delenn also is the one who decides who is to be the first captain of Babylon 5; in a sense, she provides him with his weapon, as did the Lady of the Lake with Arthur.

Arthurian Animation at Century's End

MICHAEL N. SALDA

It is not uncommon in today's competitive animation market, with its high costs and low profit margins, for minor, direct-to-video filmmakers to attempt to capitalize on new theatrical releases from major studios. If Disney is about to premiere a film, several videos with approximately the same title will inevitably hit the shelves at Blockbuster and Wal-Mart even before Disney's film opens. The logic that guides these smaller studios is that Disney's advertising dollars will create a market for *anything* about, say, *Beauty and the Beast*, and that consumers won't be all that picky when the moment to choose a video actually arrives. One cartoon is as good as another to most people, so this logic continues, and even if the big studio's film is likely to be better produced, how discriminating will an impatient nine-year-old and his disinterested parent be, anyway? Rental outlets and retailers play along, making it easy for consumers to substitute a minor release for a major one by arranging films in convenient "If you like this, why not try that?" shelving, which further fosters an impression that there's no real difference between one animated feature and the next.

Any minor studio wanting to capitalize on Warner Bros.'s 1998 *Quest for Camelot* had plenty of time to prepare an Arthurian knockoff. Even as *Space Jam* (1996), the first film to make use of Warner Bros.'s newly formed Feature Animation unit, was in production, rumors swirled in internet newsgroups about the difficulties the studio was already experiencing with *Quest for Camelot*, the unit's first fully animated film. Production staff, writers, and voice talent seemed to change weekly. Would Christopher Reeve, paralyzed in a 1995 riding accident, accept the rumored offer of Arthur's voice? How closely could the writers adhere to Vera Chapman's adult novel of rape and revenge in a film that had to stay within PG guidelines? And all the while delays with *Space Jam* were moving *Quest for Camelot*'s production timeline into an ever more distant future. The tumult became the subject of parody even inside the studio perimeter as writers at Warner Bros.'s other animation unit, the one responsible for television hits such as *Tiny Toon Adventures*, *Pinky and the Brain*, and *Animaniacs*, couldn't resist a dig at their colleagues across the lot with a reference to a disastrous hodgepodge of a film that "crashed on take-off" called *Jamelot*, an obvious lampoon of both the already-released *Space Jam* and the still-in-production *Quest for Camelot*.[1]

Smaller studios should have observed the harbingers warning that *Quest for Camelot* would not be another *Lion King* with ample skirts to ride. The lure of Arthuriana, however, apparently proved too great for some. Three production companies rushed to release films in 1997 and 1998, all with the word "Camelot" figuring prominently in the title and all available before *Quest for Camelot*'s May 1998 release. Although the three films do not constitute great moments in cinematic history, along with *Quest for Camelot* they provide an index to what was thought marketable Arthurian animation fare for children at the close of the twentieth century.

***

Sword in the Stone meets the 1967 *Camelot* meets *First Knight* is a quick summary of the major themes of *Camelot: The Legend* (Tundra Productions, 1998). This 70-minute film examines a particular moment during Arthur's reign. Twenty-year-old Mordred is about to make a play for the throne. Morgan, whom Merlin has imprisoned in a mountain cave because she tricked Arthur into fathering Mordred,[2] tries to further Mordred's plans, though she's more of a Disneyesque bumbling Madame Mim than a real threat to anybody. Lancelot, having left France in search of adventure, comes to the land just in time to save Arthur and wife Guinevere from the first of many attacks by Mordred's thugs. Arthur is busy trying to unite the realm, though the film spends much more time following Mordred's and Morgan's plots than the king's actions in pursuit of his goal.

The story unrolls to include Lancelot and Guinevere's growing friendship (but no more), Arthur's decision to build his ranks by knighting any townsman Lancelot deems worthy of knighthood, Guinevere's desire for a child and unhappiness with her inattentive husband, Arthur's suspicion that his wife has stopped loving him, Merlin's generally ineffectual role as the king's adviser and magician, the uncovering of Mordred's scheme, a battle of shape-shifting magicians, Arthur's recognition that he can't treat his wife like a child, and a *First Knight*–type conclusion that closes not with Arthur's death but instead with the king, queen, and Lancelot happily singing together on the platform that only a moment before had served for a mock trial of Guinevere. And through it all is the slapstick of everybody falling down, sneezing uncontrollably, dressing in drag (with the consequence of a same-sex attraction designed to play as homophobic "humor"), and enough overamplified sound effects of slide whistles, sproings, and cuckoo clocks to make this film almost unwatchable.

Confused? It's hard not to be. *Camelot: The Legend* lacks a consistent tone. Maybe it's the "additional writing" credited to Elizabeth Logun that conflicts with the original script by Lisa Moricoli Latham, maybe it's the thematically unrelated song lyrics from Jim Latham, or maybe it's Michael Aschner's "story development." Regardless of cause, rather than a steady plot with a clear intent we find a film that at base can't decide whether it is drama or comedy and whether its audience is old or young. On one hand, we have Morgan and Mordred conspiring to kill people and relishing detailed thoughts of their enemies' deaths, suspected adultery, Arthur's plan to banish Guinevere to the forest despite her plaint that she'll die if thrust into the wild alone, Lancelot's role of teacher to both king and queen, and such high-sounding ideas as Arthur's "Even if you kill us both, Camelot will live on forever" and Morgan's declaration that "Mordred is a spell I formed in flesh." It's difficult to reconcile those serious elements with, on the other hand, the film's many awkward gambits at humor. Item: Morgan's repeated use of a Clapper to turn off and on her makeshift sword-in-the-stone projection television that she employs to keep an eye on the events of Camelot. Item: Lancelot's song about what it means to be a "parfit, gentil knight," which manages to bring together in a single stanza one's chivalric duties to "ride all night and fight all day" and (the astonishingly insensitive) "teach the pagans how to pray" with the more mundane tasks to "free kittens from the trees" and "save children from deep wells," as everyone gets together and dances like Rockettes in a chorus line. Item: a damsel-toss going on at the local watering hole. Item: a much overused gag that derives from the accidental substitution of sneezing powder for a love potion. And so on.

After as little as half an hour of oscillating randomly between drama and low comedy, the film becomes largely incoherent. When Merlin's voice reminds us at film's end of the goal the production team apparently once had in mind—Camelot as a symbol for "all those true believers who want equality, justice, and opportunity for all people"—one has to wonder why these themes were scarcely explored. Although Arthur does elevate some of locals to knighthood, and although he eventually does recognize that his queen can handle a sword, the conclusion seems unrelated to the film we've just seen.

A few other notes are in order for *Camelot: The Legend*. Arthurians can't help but giggle as Lancelot is assigned the Siege Perilous, despite the alleged work of the "historical consultant" hired for the film. Literary critics will ponder the Freudian significance of gifts that Morgan sends: a phallic sword to Guinevere and vaginal gloves to Lancelot in a scheme that she hopes will make them lovers. On the technical side, the animation from Color-land Animation Productions (Shenzhen, China) is occasionally crudely drawn and lacking in continuity; the audio, especially in the musical sections, is muddy; and Lancelot's French accent is ridiculous.

***

Imagine the 1967 *Camelot* framed by Marion Zimmer Bradley's *Mists of Avalon*, with a few touches from *The Sword in the Stone*, and you have the intriguing mix brought together in *Camelot* (Sony Wonder, 1997). The dense, 48-minute film covers Arthur's entire career, from the moment that Merlin saves an abandoned baby—parentless, as far as we ever learn—from a modest hut in war-torn Britain to Arthur's journey to Avalon at the end. In between Arthur grows up in Avalon, returns to Britain, and founds, rules, and finally watches the collapse of Camelot.

In Avalon, Arthur is raised by Viviane, her sister Morgause, and the other wiccans who inhabit the isle. The women teach him to fight, ride, and dance, while Merlin transforms the boy into various animals à la T.H. White and Disney to show him the connectedness of all things in nature. Morgause also teaches Arthur about love, and then marries him in accord with the gynecocracy's hope that Arthur will carry the rational, peaceful spirit of Avalon back to his testosterone-ravaged homeland. Shortly after the marriage, a white stag appears and Morgause vanishes—events, like many others in this film, completely without explanation—as Merlin emerges from a tree to take Arthur to a cave. The magician orders Arthur to pull a golden Excalibur from a stone and so become king of Britain. Then he is told he must leave Avalon and Morgause, too, for she cannot accompany the mortal Arthur to "the real world."

Arthur has aged enough to sprout a beard by the next time we see him, now rescuing Guenevere from a dragon. Guenevere is a runaway—escaping from parents who would have married her to a wealthy landlord twice her age—and so she becomes his riding partner. He explains his Avalonian plans to stop the strong from oppressing the weak, which she believes will be a difficult task on British soil.[3] Arthur rides about the land gathering knights, one by one, and eventually settles in Cornwall—because sometimes through the mists Avalon can be seen from there—where the locals band together to help him build a castle and then democratically "choose" him to be their king. Merlin's spirit appears behind Arthur at the Round Table to turn all the knights' swords gold, thus underscoring their equality, as dark-skinned Palomides, Arthur's tactical adviser (think: Azeem from *Robin Hood: Prince of Thieves*), leads them in shouting "Might for right!" At Merlin's urging, Arthur marries Guenevere, bigamy apparently not being a problem if your other wife lives in the mists. Then Arthur sets off to solidify his control over the kingdom by fighting battles and arranging treaties. Guenevere feels slighted by her inattentive husband and quickly falls for a mildly resistant Lancelot, as autumn leaves blow across the screen to signal the beginning of the end.

A now graying Arthur realizes that Guenevere is attracted to Lancelot, but his only response is sadness. Meanwhile the lovers become more reckless and are discovered together at Meliagrance's castle, where only Viviane's magical intervention prevents Lancelot from killing his host. Viviane tells the lovers that she has come not to help them, but solely Arthur, and exits with the cutting remark, "If you can't be faithful, try to be kind." The words set the stage for the surprise arrival of Mordred of Avalon, hitherto unrevealed son of Arthur and Morgause, who will also be unable to balance the demands of faithfulness and kindness as he righteously and without hidden agenda reveals to Arthur the affair that the king has intentionally ignored for over twenty years. Echoing the 1967 *Camelot*, Arthur is powerless to stop the growing gossip, the plan to take Lancelot and Guenevere in her chambers, and the deaths of several knights as the lovers escape to Joyeuse Garde. Arthur and Lancelot meet privately to arrange a treaty, yet both know that Mordred won't let the two men find peace. At a public ceremony the next morning, Mordred goads Lancelot until the latter pulls his sword and the catastrophe ensues. Arthur is wounded by an unidentified knight. Before he loses consciousness, he appears to reconcile with Lancelot, Guenevere, and Mordred, and tells his son that it is now his responsibility to "carry the peace of Camelot forward." Mists rise, Viviane and Merlin come for Arthur, and they sail to Avalon where the king is reunited with Morgause. Merlin's voiceover recalls Arthur's accomplishment—"hope of a world at peace, beyond all fear"—and reminds us that Arthur waits on Avalon until his time comes again.

Arthur has no overt foes in this film. Instead, conflicts arise as Arthur tries to make Camelot mirror Avalon. Near the film's close, as Arthur realizes that the end of his dream must come soon, he tells Merlin, "I blame only myself. I don't blame Guenevere and Lancelot for anything. I don't even blame Mordred. I am the one who lost Camelot." It takes Merlin's reply to reveal a higher plane of reality: "Nonsense. You are the one who built it. No one else could have done that. The Lancelots can't build. They can only defend. And the Mordreds have good intentions but can't see the bigger picture.... Because of you there is now a Camelot to remember, and rebuild, and fall, over and over. You are one with Avalon. Avalon is always."

Sony Wonder's *Camelot* is much better constructed than *Camelot: The Legend*. The storyline is more coherent, despite a number of telegraphic references to Bradley that only Arthurians are likely to understand; the dialogue makes sense; Merrill Farnsworth's three songs are appropriate to the tone of the film, even if one calls to mind the theme song of the 1967 *Camelot* and another echoes "Colors of the Wind" from Disney's *Pocahontas*; and the work from Hong Ying Animation (Suzhou, China) pleases the eye. The narrative fusion of Bradley's world with more traditional treatments will surely pique the interest of Arthurians, though whether this complex, allusive film could hold a child's attention is a much different matter.

***

At the same time that Sony Wonder's *Camelot* was appearing on shelves, another animated film with the same title and the almost identical runtime of 50 minutes appeared right next to it: *Camelot* (Burbank Animation Studios, 1997). The bulk of the animation was rendered at Colorland Animation Productions, the same company that did the work for *Camelot: The Legend*, though the general artistic competence is much higher than in the Tundra Productions film.

Unlike the films already discussed, Burbank's *Camelot* appears to have few borrowings from previous Arthurian films, with the exception of some surface similarities to *The Sword in the Stone*, which may be inevitable because both films focus primarily on the actions of young Arthur leading up to the moment he becomes king. The *The Sword in the Stone's* opening movement of the dangers and rapaciousness of the forest—symbolic of the political conditions of the land—is clearly exploited in *Camelot's* opening scene of a storm ripping through the forest outside a darkened castle in which King Gerdlach, Arthur's father, breathes his last commands. Gerdlach, knowing that chaos will follow his death, orders Merlin to watch over his son until the boy is twelve, old enough to claim Excalibur and the land for his own. Merlin takes Arthur to Stonehenge, sets the sword in the stone, then removes to a cave where quick vignettes show Camelot falling into ruins and Arthur growing to adolescence. Along the way Arthur acquires four animals (that later will speak to one another) and gal-pal Cynthia, an adolescent foundling who turns up one day inside Stonehenge and is taken in by Merlin.[4]

Arthur longs to be a magician, but when it becomes clear that Cynthia is the one with the gift, he leaves home in search of a destiny that Merlin knows yet has pledged Gerdlach not to reveal. Merlin transforms Cynthia into a falcon and sends her to protect Arthur. Then the magician issues a message heard across the country that tells all clans to stop fighting and assemble at Stonehenge in order to determine who can pull Gerdlach's Excalibur from the stone and thus replace the dead king. Enter the complication: thick-headed bully Sir Baldrick, who has learned from squire Runcibel that Arthur can move the sword (a fact unknown even to Arthur himself, who accidentally falls against it while Runcibel is watching) and wants the throne for himself. Although Baldrick captures Arthur, he is rescued by falcon Cynthia and the other animals, arriving at Stonehenge in time to pull the sword from the stone and thereby demonstrate to all that he is king. Arthur rebuilds Camelot, banishes Baldrick, establishes the Round Table "to insure no knight would ever abuse his powers again" as Baldrick had, and accepts Cynthia as his new court magician when Merlin retires to write his story, "The Secret of Camelot," a title introduced so clumsily that one can only assume that at one time it must have served as this production's working title.

Burbank's *Camelot* has a good sense of its youth audience. The storyline proceeds cleanly from start to finish with a single, simple complication. Potentially frightening threats to Arthur, even while in prison, are innocuous, and are further undercut with wise-cracking Runcibel and goofy talking animals at the future king's side. There are no songs, which is probably for the best unless you have the budget to acquire top musical talent. I do not mean to suggest, however, that Burbank's *Camelot* is a good Arthurian film; rather, it sets a modest goal and attains it, and that alone sets it apart from the two films examined above.

***

Quest for Camelot (Warner Bros. Feature Animation, 1998) was a disappointment for most Arthurians. It purports to be based on Vera Chapman's

The King's Damosel. Yet anyone familiar with Chapman's adult romance of rape, torture, revenge, forgiveness, personal redemption through love, and spiritual regeneration through a Grail quest, had to wonder why Warner Bros. ever bought the rights in the first place if it wanted to make a children's film. Indeed, only a few similarities to the novel remain in the 85-minute film. There's a strong heroine, Kayley—essentially Malory's Damsel Maldisant, whose tale Chapman rewrites and enlarges in her novel. There's a blind man, Garrett—an important character for the development of Chapman's heroine, but far less important in the novel than the film. There's a villain—several from Malory and Tennyson via Chapman, all compressed into the film's Ruber. There's a falcon in this film, too—Chapman's belongs to the heroine, the film's to first Merlin and then Garrett. And finally there's a quest—for the spiritual Grail that will heal the heroine's psychic scars and potentially restore the blind man's sight, here reduced to an adventurous secular search for the stolen Excalibur. For the record, there's no Devon and Cornwall, two-headed, talking, toy-spinoff dragon, anywhere in the book.[5]

The film's primary action takes place almost entirely at the periphery of what most would consider the matter of Britain. Although it opens with a brief introduction rehearsing how (once again) a parentless Arthur (once again) pulled the sword from the stone at (once again) Stonehenge, we soon find ourselves in a story that seems to have little to do with familiar Arthurian themes. One of Arthur's knights, Lionel, is killed by rogue knight Ruber in a battle at Arthur's court. Ten years pass and his daughter, Kayley, matures into a young woman as Arthur builds the kingdom. One day Ruber steals and loses Excalibur and then kidnaps Kayley's mother, causing Kayley to begin seeking the sword so that her mother can be rescued. So begins the main narrative line of the film.

The adult Arthur himself turns out to be a minor, impotent character in *Quest for Camelot.* He is introduced to the audience in a long shot that immediately deemphasizes his importance and then remains spatially and narratively distant throughout the film, never receiving the close-up treatments reserved for the principal, non–Arthurian characters, Kayley and Garrett. An almost powerless Merlin at the king's side is superfluous. In fact he tells Arthur at one point that magic cannot help them, but that instead they will have to rely on the citizenry to solve the national crisis that arises with the theft of Excalibur. Evidently Arthur and Merlin cannot rely on the Round Table knights either, a virtually indistinguishable bunch of noble-looking men who spend most of their time within Camelot's walls instead of out seeking the sword. Although the castle's occupants swear to uphold the monarchy by pursuing a random mix of democratic ideals—liberty, justice, trust, freedom, peace, honor, goodness, strength, and valor—we rarely see them actually acting on these pledges. The king himself, an apparent proto–Marxist, seems to have yet another political agenda as he explains to Ruber that "land will be divided according to each person's needs." The fastidious viewer will also note that despite the film's title, the quest is for *Excalibur*, not *Camelot*.[6] In fact everyone *knows* where Camelot lies—there are literally roadsigns in Arthur's well-organized kingdom.[7] In sum, the film's Arthurian dimension is superficial and even incoherent if given more than five minutes' thought.

In the film's defense, it may be argued that *Quest for Camelot* isn't supposed to be Arthurian. Rather, it's supposed to be Warner Bros.'s attempt to create a strong heroine movie to rival Disney's *The Little Mermaid, Beauty and the Beast, Pocahontas,* and *Mulan* (released five weeks after *Quest for Camelot*). Yet it still fails to satisfy, and for all the same reasons Disney's films are often criticized. Kayley is without doubt the same plucky mainstream heroine we've seen many times before: a young, goo-goo-eyed brunette; strong and confident, but always less so than the males in her life; beautiful and tomboyish at once, though ready to trade her pants for a (wedding?) dress by movie's end; a girl who wants to be a boy, at least until she meets one. Her signature song, Carole Bayer Sager and David Foster's admittedly pretty "On My Father's Wings," overtly reveals Kayley's reliance on the patriarchy at the beginning, just as the "Just Knighted" sign on the horse's tail as she and the male lead ride off together at the end suggests the connubial "just hitched" even if we've witnessed no marriage ceremony.

Garrett, Kayley's companion on the quest, serves a predictable function as her antagonist, then teacher, and finally love-interest. Throughout their adventures it is obvious that to succeed she must learn to follow his ways, and in particular must master Garrett's Sun Tzu–inspired (or, more probably, *Karate Kid*–inspired) battle tactic—take position, face fear, and hold ground until the last possible moment—to defeat Ruber and return Excalibur to Arthur. In large measure, Garrett serves merely as a replacement for Kayley's dead father, new wings for her to fly on. In the process, rather than offer us a truly independent heroine, the film ultimately shows us only hackneyed ideas of female strength as it reaffirms Hollywood's usual paradigm of correct behavior for girls.

The animation, voice work, and music are much better than we find in the other three *Camelots*. Even so, one might have expected more given the resources available at Warner Bros. Feature Animation. There are lip-

sync problems, some jarringly choppy animation sequences, musical interludes that charm the ear but have little to do with the action on screen,
and a CGI ogre that is visually disjunct from everything else in the film.
It came as little surprise to insiders that Max Howard, president of Warner
Bros. Feature Animation, resigned his post just a few weeks after the premiere of *Quest for Camelot*.

Film history will record that the years of 1997 and 1998 provided a
bumper crop of long-format Arthurian animation. Closer inspection will
reveal, however, that the harvest failed to fulfill our desire for well-told, well-
animated stories about the Arthurian court. Despite a huge marketing push
with toy tie-ins, deals with a fast-food chain, and a (now defunct) website
to promote the film, *Quest for Camelot* lost big at the box office, then virtually vanished when Disney released its own strong heroine film, *Mulan*,
the following month. When *Quest for Camelot* was released on video later
in 1998, alongside it could be found the three also-rans that hitched their
hopes to the wrong star. Three years later, all four films routinely appear
on video clearance tumble tables and eBay for as little as $1.99, often still
sealed in their original shrinkwrap packaging. Meanwhile, children and
their parents are still waiting for a good animated version of the story of
King Arthur.

Notes

1. "Hooray for North Hollywood."
2. That's all we know of the circumstances of his engendering. Arthur's parent-
age is even more obscure and agentless: according to the synopsis that appears on
the screen as the film begins, "A young lad named Arthur came along" one day
and was able to remove the "sword that magic had firmly wedged in a stone," thus
becoming king.
3. Merlin expresses similar pessimism in *Camelot: The Legend* in response to
Arthur's plans for uniting the people. Merlin: "It's very noble of you, but not very
realistic. People fight. It's human nature."
4. No further attempt is made to explain her origins.
5. An earlier version of my remarks on *Quest for Camelot* appeared as a review
in *Arthuriana* 8:4 (1998): 176–78.
6. Hence the alternate title used in English-speaking lands beyond America:
The Magic Sword: Quest for Camelot.
7. So, too, in *Camelot: The Legend*, which even adds mile markers so that we
know at one point that the king is precisely 180 miles from Camelot and 99 miles
from Cornwall.

Works Cited

Camelot. Dir. Greg Garcia. Videocassette. Sony Wonder/Golden Films, 1997.

Camelot. Dir. Richard Slapczynski. DVD. Burbank Animation Studios, Sydney, Australia/Anchor Bay Entertainment/Madacy Entertainment, 1997.

Camelot: The Legend. Dir. William R. Kowalchuk. Videocassette. Tundra Productions/Goodtimes Home Video, 1998.

"Hooray for North Hollywood." Part 1. *Animaniacs*. WB. 3 January 1998.

Quest for Camelot. Dir. Frederik du Chau. Videocassette. Warner Bros. Feature Animation, 1998.

Salda, Michael N. Rev. of *Quest for Camelot*, dir. Frederik du Chau. *Arthuriana* 8:4 (1998): 176–78.

Sing a Song of Arthur

JEROME V. REEL, JR.

The year was 1901, the first of the new century, and two of the great lights of the nineteenth century were extinguished. One, the Italian opera composer Giuseppi Verdi, had put his artistic stamp on theatre music. His last two works, *Otello* and *Falstaff*, were drawn from British drama. The second great light was the British queen Victoria, the first to carry the title "R et I," *Regina et Imperatrix*. The coming age would be very different. Photography would replace sketchbooks as the visual medium for the middle and upper classes. And the phonograph and then the CD component system would replace the parlour piano and harmonium for music makers.

Would the coming age register equally great changes in the amount of music inspired by the Arthurian legend, another great canon of Britain? From the vantage point at the end of the twentieth century and the end of the second millennium it is tempting to answer affirmatively. Indeed, there have been major changes in the forms of delivery and also, although perhaps to a lesser extent, many changes in the thematics. In terms of audience, earlier twentieth-century Arthurian music was differentiated on the basis of social class; as the century progressed, age group rather than social status defined the target audiences.

The first two decades of the twentieth century marked the cataclysmic political and social changes begun about the same time as the death of the old queen. Her son, Edward VII, would be the last forceful sovereign of Britain, and imperial stress and war marked his reign. The awesome majesty associated with the British Empire began unraveling quickly in the reign of his son George V. To some degree, the high culture associated with composers like Richard Wagner would continue, as would middle-class entertainments such as *Lancelot the Lovely*, a London musical review and burlesque. Other turn of the century examples such as *King Arthur, or Lancelot the Loose, Guin-ever the Square and the Knights of the Round Table and Other Furniture*, and Hugh Clendon's *Little Lohengrin, or the Lover and the Bird* were regularly produced.

For the upper middle and upper classes, one of the most popular pieces of *fin de siècle* writing was *King Arthur*, a musical drama with words by Joseph K. Comyn-Carr. The music was composed by and on opening night (12 January 1895 at the Lyceum Theatre in London) conducted by Sir Arthur Sullivan. King Arthur was portrayed by Sir Henry Irving and Guinevere by Ellen Terry, with Johnston Forbes-Robertson as Lancelot. The scenery, costumes, and property were by Edward Burne-Jones, who remembered "jingo bits about the sea and England which Carr should be ashamed of " (Fitzgerald 257). Comyn-Carr had written the text at Irving's request when an earlier effort would not do. He claimed that the text was based on Malory rather than Tennyson. Nonetheless the Tennysonian tension between the moral and the romantic are intermixed in the text (Goodman 240–242). The six choruses are the only sung pieces. In the final funeral march the chorus opens

> Sleep! oh sleep! till night outworn wakens to the echoing horn
> That shall greet the King newborn ... King that was and is to be
> [Sullivan and Carr, 36–37]

The reviews were enthusiastic and the annual retrospective in the *Times of London* noted

> Much more successful was Mr. Comyn-Carr's equally literary handling of the subject of King Arthur and the Knights of the Round Table [3 January 1896, 12].

In the entire initial run in London, there were over one hundred performances. Irving took the production on tour to North America. After the company returned to Great Britain, Comyn-Carr turned his attention to a libretto for a desired but never achieved full opera by Sullivan (*Athenaeum* 27 March 1897, 12). It was a triumph but the work did not endure; in 1898, the costumes, scenery, and properties were destroyed in a warehouse fire.

A second high- to mid-culture venture was with Joseph Bédier's retelling of the Tristan story. Almost as an antidote to Richard Wagner's "Schopenhaurerian" setting, a number of Claude Debussy's friends urged him to compose an opera based on the Bédier text. Debussy dashed off a twelve bar motif. Unfortunately for the music world Bédier had promised the theatre rights elsewhere (Lacy and Ashe 268). Eventually the Bédier text would be rendered into a dramatic work by L. Artus, and the work would be supported by the incidental and vocal music of Paul Ladmirault, a noted Breton musician and composer. This *Tristan* was premiered in Nice 30 January 1929 (Newberry Library A54.513 no. 231).

Debussyan Arthur lovers would have to be satisfied with the setting of Maurice Maeterlinck's *Pelléas et Mélisande* in 1907. Of course it may be argued that the Pelleas of that tale is a different Pelleas from the one who sat at the Round Table. The same issue could be raised with Maeterlinck's marionette play *Mort de Tintagiles*, set first as an instrumental piece by Charles Loeffler in 1897, revised in 1901 and recorded (New World Records 332). Jean Nougues, a French composer from Bordeaux, composed an opera score for the brooding symbolist drama. Ralph Vaughan Williams was able to attend a private production of another *Death of Tintagiles* for which he composed the incidental music. Unfortunately, the production went badly. The music, to hear it now as a suite, could hardly have been at fault. The most recent setting of *Mort* was by Laurence Collingwood 16 April 1950 in a concert production in Sadler's Wells.

From the last decade of the nineteenth century through World War II "popular Arthurian entertainments" attracted all ages but mainly the lower middle classes to the music halls and mainly children and their guardians to the holiday pantomimes. Opera, theatre incidental music, and instrumental music was the strength of the upper middle and upper classes. The lower classes would make do with industry and union sponsored bands and choirs. While much of this would carry across the war years and continue in one form or another, World War I brought about a new division based on the age of the audience, rather than its demographic niche. At the same time, the emphasis in the themes changed as well.

In the nineteen-twenties society of cocktail lounges and piano bars inhabited by the "bright young" people, one of the best of the British pianists was Bill Mayerl. The son of musical and immigrant parents, Mayerl studied at the Trinity College of Music. In 1929, he composed for the piano the *Legends of King Arthur*, which include the "Prelude," "Merlin the Wizard," "The Sword Excalibur," "The Lady of the Lake," "Guinevere," and "The Passing of Arthur." The music exudes a sense of elegance and wit. These same features were present in Richard Rodgers' *Connecticut Yankee in King Arthur's Court* with Lorenz Hart providing the lyrics. The musical opened in New York at the Vanderbilt Theatre 3 November 1927. The producer, Lew Fields, was not sold on the show. However, the music, the lyrics and the script were in turn applauded. No better example of fun in music can be found than in "Thou Swell." And for lyrics, Hart, in "On a Desert Isle," rhymed "nonce" with "honi soit qui mal y pense." It ran for almost a year and it is an example of King Arthur changing to be a part of new popular culture. It was noted that King Arthur began to sound like Woodrow Wilson while Merlin combined so-called Old English with Broadway slang (Nolan 84).

As would be the case from 1919 on, the Christian elements faded in these works designed for general audience, but were maintained in presentments for the young. Of note are a series of pieces that celebrate the special intellectual characteristics of the "Gleam." Early in the twentieth century, Josef Holbrooke, more famous for his large pieces, composed "Follow the Gleam," using the Tennyson text, for his *Six Characteristic Songs*. In 1920, Sir Charles Villiers Stanford composed a piece for the same words.

The most curious example of the "Gleam" is a hymn for youths whose tune, composed by Helen Hill Miller, is set to a college poem written by Sallie Hume Douglas. Written as a competition entry for a Christian youth conference in New York the hymn is set as a grail narrative:

> To the knights in the days of old
> Keeping watch on the mountain height
> Came a vision of Holy Grail
> And a voice through the waiting night:
> Follow, follow, follow the Gleam;
> Banners unfurled, o'er all the world
> Follow, follow, follow the Gleam
> Of the chalice that is the Grail

Sallie Hume Douglas looked upon this as a high point in her life while Helen Hill Miller stated that she offered to pay the Young Women's Christian Association if they would detach her name from the piece.[1]

Other efforts, which took the form of short operas, were frequently designed to be performed in a hall or a church, and frequently employed children or youths in the production. Martin Shaw, the noted British hymnologist, and Barclay Baron created a forty-minute musical play in 1932 entitled *Thorn of Avalon*. The plot involves the coming of Joseph of Arimathea to the Isle of Avalon around 63 A.D. In three scenes, it is a story of three times: the coming of Joseph, the high Middle Ages, and the seventeenth century. Contemporary reviewers thought it excellent but too short (*Musical Times* 7 January 1931, 6). The Joseph of Arimathea story functions not only in the Grail narrative but also in the Anglican "high church movement." Thus it is not surprising that at least two other works deal with it. Douglas Coombes composed the music while a well regarded poet, John

Emlyn Edwards, wrote the text for *Scatterflock and the Glastonbury Thorn*. It relates the syncretistic characteristic of Christianity, which "baptizes" non–Christian custom, such as the "decking of the halls," the wassail bowl, and the Christmas tree. The second piece, by Matthew Dubroski and Kevin Fromings, is *Shadows: The Life of Joseph of Arimathea*. While the tale contains Christian history, it is also infused with cultural tension that can be understood as not only representing ethnic tension between the Celts and the Anglo-Saxons, but also as commenting on contemporary British problems.

The adult world, with a few exceptions, focused not so much on the "Christianism" but on the nature and function of love. For example, the plight of Elaine, Fair Maid of Astolat, touched many hearts and numerous popular examples survive. Paul Ambrose contributed a slow waltz "Elaine" in 1900, as did other British composers such as G.H. Ward Humphries and Albert Straus. John Arthur Behrend offered "Little Elaine" in 1901 and in 1902 Healey Willan composed "Elaine's Song." American composers such as Homer Newton Bartlett, S.R. Henry, and Reginald de Koven did also. The theme would remain strong until the late 1920s and then slow down. Nonetheless in 1986, Japanese composer Chinatsu Kuzuu wrote "Elaine the Fair," and in 1991, Loreena McKennitt composed, sang, and produced a Celtic style musical version of *The Lady of Shalott*. Her album, entitled *The Visit*, is still in pressing. Interestingly, although pertaining to elite rather than popular culture, there have been a few ballets on the character "Elaine." One, in 1932, was created by Frederick Ashton using Jean Sibelius's piano music. Then in 1958, Ashton collaborated with Sir Arthur Bliss in a work variously entitled *The Lady of Shalott* or *Two Towers*. The composition had been commissioned by the University of California for the May T. Morrison Festival. The British premiere was in Leicester in 1975 (Bliss 4). So the plight of unrequited love, mistaken intentions and pride touched every level of European and North American society and was not without its aspirants in other parts of the world.

Of course, love and sex, especially outside of marriage, whether it is the Tristan story or Elaine, also fascinated adherents of the Lancelot and Guinevere tale in the first part of the century. In the mid-twentieth century, the most important retelling of that story was Frederick Loewe's setting of Alan Jay Lerner's *Camelot*, based on T.H. White's *Once and Future King*. Its premiere in New York 4 December 1960 was lavish, and the musical play ran for 873 performances (Green 56–57). The work was not well received by the critics, although most agreed that it was "sumptuously mounted" (Ewen 110–113). The public disagreed; the conflicts of fraternal love and sexual love and of love in marriage and love beyond marriage directly touched the audiences. The cast itself was ideal, with Julie Andrews as Guinevere and Robert Goulet as Lancelot, pairing up two of the very best voices in theatre, while Roddy McDowell as Mordred brought a simpering and sneering vocal style in sharp contrast to the other principals. Richard Burton, who had very little in the way of musical talent, interpreted the king. Those critics who found the casting too similar to *My Fair Lady* missed the points—who gets the girl and the denouement. In *Camelot*, everyone loses. A long run in London led to a darkening of the score by Loewe and his orchestrators Robert Russell Bennett and Phil Lang. A movie and several recordings followed. Touring companies continue to offer staged versions in various part of the world. But unlike the Comyn-Carr and Arthur Sullivan version, *Camelot* discarded the Grail theme and the tales of the knights' exploits to focus on what was the primary concern of the world in the middle of the twentieth century—love. In this musical, the staged show played to upper and upper-middle classes, while the film was seen by a more universal audience, and recordings of individual songs as well as the complete soundtrack were of much interest to all youthful and adult classes.

Camelot was not, however, the first lengthy narrative of the story in the twentieth century. The British Broadcasting Corporation had contracted with a rising young British composer, Benjamin Britten, to write the incidental music for D.G. Bridson's *King Arthur*, which was broadcast 23 April 1937, St. George's Day. This version attempted to tell the entire story including Lancelot and Guinevere and the Grail. Clarence Reybould conducted the BBC Chorus and the London Symphony orchestra. While the work was respected, it was not widely performed. Britten would later reuse the passacaglia theme in a concerto (Palmer 413), and the music has since been reshaped into a suite.

In 1939, BBC approached Britten for a score for a second radio play, this one aimed at a youthful and perhaps not so sophisticated audience. Based on the first of four Arthurian books by T.H. White, *The Sword in the Stone*, the music is spriteful and charming, while at the same time parodic. It opens with a series of "Tinny" horn fanfares followed by a jaunty boy's march that owes some thanks to Rudolph Friml's *Vagabond King* (1925). Richard Wagner's *Ring* music was an inspiration as well. Merlin, for example, is announced by music kin to the Prelude to *Das Rheingold* while other moments of Wagner's nature music were also used. The broadcast was a six part serial 11 May to 16 July 1939. With the political situation on the European and Asian continents worsening, it is hard not to hear Fafner's music and the sword motif as warnings coming from one of the United Kingdom's pacifists.

The focus of much of Arthurian music in the twentieth century is on the young audience. Subteenaged groups were also exposed to Arthurian music from Restoration and more modern composers. The British Library holds nearly one hundred twentieth-century reissues of Purcell's "Fairest Isle" from *King Arthur* in editions for lower school use. Most of these are for youthful performers. Early in the twentieth century, Rutland Boughton composed "King Arthur had Three Sons" (1905), while in 1917 Thomas Keighly set the same traditional rhyme. In 1958 Imig and Simon did also. And in 1948, one of the United States' leading African-American composers, Ulysses Kay, composed his version of the ballad.

Just as Britten and Lerner and Loewe set parts of T.H. White's work for the public, Walt Disney also recognized a good thing and produced an animated retelling of *The Sword in the Stone*, for which the well-developed incidental music was written by Richard Sherman, whose brother, Robert, wrote the lyrics for the six set songs in the film. (The Sherman brothers followed in the footsteps of their father Al as in-house musical artists for Disney.) While the *Sword in the Stone* score is lyrical and expressive, it is not memorable. Its best moments are the "housecleaning" sequence, which owes much to Disney's *Fantasia*, and the animal transformation sequences. As is the way with most of the Disney work, the aim might have been a youthful market but the product was widely observed and enjoyed.

The emphasis on a broader audience is confirmed in the work of Timothy Porter, a British composer, musician, and historian who focused much of his effort into folk opera that appeals not to the Covent Garden audience but to the audience of adults, young adults, and children in the village and town hall. The earliest of his Arthurian works, *Sir Gawain and the Green Knight* (1970), required the vocalists to double as percussionists. Porter weaves folk tunes, some well known to the audience but others less familiar, into the score. Porter is clearly drawn to the mythic legends of the Celts both Britannic and Gaelic, and he emphasizes the wondrous elements of nature, so that in *Sir Gawain* the young nephew of King Arthur seems Adamic in his efforts to embrace the natural world. The structure is in four scenes set apart by three interludes. The prologue conveys the wonderment:

> Can we with simple tunes and rhymes
> Untie this knot of ancient times?
> The grim Green Knight from out the wood,
> Can be labeled "bad" or "good"?

A production in 1975 was described as a "lot of fun." An anonymous reviewer commented

> ...in Mr. Porter's interpretation of the Celtic myth everything was building up to the final scene. Throughout, he dwelt on the dark forces at work behind the rebirth of every year and every season and this was all put into context by the Green Knight's speech [*Salisbury Journal* December 1973, 4].

Porter's second Arthurian work was *The Entertaining of the Noble Head* (1973), which is really a philosophical work that contemplates very accessibly the relationship of myth to history. The tie with Arthur is a double exhumation: that of Bran the Blessed's head from Tower Hill by Arthur, and that of Arthur by the monks of Glastonbury. Porter notes that the musical structure is based on the ogham letter rendering of "B-R-A-N, which, when translated, formed the first four notes of the hymn tune "Lead Kindly, Light," which I [Porter] had already decided to use in the score" (Cole, 704).

Porter wrote three other Arthurian works. The first, *Tristan and Essylt* (1980), a darker work than the other four, also uses folk tunes, and its audience was both young and adult. The second, *The Marvels of Merlin* (1981), is a summer pantomime of the order beloved by children. As is typical of that style, the pantomime is formed by two tales joined together and occasionally mingled. In *Marvels*, the first tale is of Vortigern, a fascist tyrant, forced from his throne by Uther, a socialist. Uther's fascination with Igraine, wife of Gorlois, leads to the engendering of Arthur. The first half ends with the sword being extracted from the stone. The second plot is based on Culhwch and Olwen wherein the gaining of Olwen from the horrid giant allows Culhwch to join the Round Table. The pantomime played in eight towns, Gloucester, and London in its 1981 run.

Porter's most recent Arthurian work is *Lancelot, or the Tale of the Grail*. Produced in 1985 and billed as a "Malory Quincentenary Production," it begins with Arthur's wedding "by proxy" (Lancelot) to Guinevere. Then it adds King Pelles, Galahad, and the Grail and concludes with Arthur leaving in a rowboat crewed by Morgan le Fey. Music plays a significant role described as "silvery pure tones [that] appear with the grail and linger on as the evening draws to a close" (Sian Davies, 11 May 1985, 3).

There are also the two Gawain operas written by Richard Blackford, both of which use children's and youths' voices with a very few adults. The first, *Sir Gawain and the Green Knight*, from its 1978 premiere in Blewbury, Oxford, has had a number of performances and has been recorded. The second, *Gawain and Ragnall* (1984) has not been recorded.

At still another layer in the complex development of Arthurian music is the opera written specifically for elementary and middle school performance. The pedagogical purpose of school opera includes rhythm, percussion, and music in the performance and almost any field in subject matter. In the Arthurian arena, legend, history, literature, art, and music are significant. The concept of school opera grows out of modern educational theory including the works of Frederick Wilhelm August Froebel and John Dewey. The model begins in the nineteenth century and is part of a societal recognition of childhood. A few early twentieth-century Arthurian subjects are notable but it was not until post–World War II that the medium was well used. In 1952, George Kleinsinger and Paul Tripp, as composer and librettist, created *Tommy Pitcher*. In brief, it is of a boy during the era of the building of the Tennessee Valley Authority, who imagines himself to be a Knight of the Round Table desperately trying to conquer a giant (the Tennessee River) and make the world (or, at least, part of it) a better place. The key musical motive is "Ashgrove." Since its initial performance in 1952 in Stockbridge, Massachusetts, it has had a number of subsequent productions.

A second example of the school opera is Kevin Stites's musical play *Adventures with Young King Arthur*, with words by David Lewman (1995). This work owes its origins to T.H. White by opening with Arthur in tutorial with Merlin. The contrasting tension between knowledge to wage war and knowledge to wage peace is present and at the base of the Arthurian dilemma. However, the dramatic turn is not in changing Arthur into animals, which has already occurred, but rather in importing future youth, a brother and sister named Matt and Sara, into Camelot. The lyrics to the set pieces are fast-paced and designed to raise chuckles. The plot is based on the sword in the stone with the desolation of the land in the person of the Green Knight, who is in league with Morgan le Fay. After Arthur defeats these forces of evil, he is free to pull the sword from the stone and commence the age in which "right rules, not might."

Another example is *The Computer Whiz at King Arthur's Court*. The work is the result of collaboration between Karen Jean Reynhout Zylstra and her husband, Dick Williams Zylstra. Its parallels with *Connecticut Yankee* include the Wiz, "a young, brilliant, glib computer whiz dressed in a dark business suit and tie, and the lovely Lady Sandrevere, also know as Sandy." The famous eclipse scene from *Connecticut Yankee* has already happened when the musical opens. The musical follows the usual patterns of lovers, villains, and rapid jokes, so that though written with youth in mind it is more suitable for middle and high school. It is apparent that the age of "youth" is expanding upward, not only in the commercial but also in the music world as the biggest development is in the "rock opera" and its major agent the "concept album."

Another example of popular youth musical theatre is *Pendragon*. Composed by Peter Allwood to a script and lyrics by Allwood, Joanna Horton, Jeremy James Taylor, and Frank Whatley, the work is designed to be sung by youths and adults. It has had eleven separate productions in London, Edinburgh (where it received several Edinburgh Festival awards), Asia, Wales, and North America. The first half of the work is set during Uther's reign. Arthur has been fostered into Ector's household. His half sister, Morgan le Fey, is in the abbey of Glastonbury, where she meets the Lady Guinevere. The second part of the script begins with the pronouncement of Uther's death and moves quickly to the sword-in-the-stone episode. A special twist is Morgan's placing a spell on Guinevere that turns her into a "loathy lady." In this version of the story, it is Arthur who is faced with the fateful question as to whether he wishes her to be faithful but hideous, or wandering and beautiful. By acknowledging her sovereignty in the matter, Arthur gains a wife both beautiful and loyal. The opera ends with Morgan banished and the kingdom at peace, providing the hopeful ending characteristic of traditional Arthurian works for young audiences.[2]

Aimed at a slightly older but still youthful audience was Rick Wakeman's 1975 *The Myths and Legends of King Arthur and the Knights of the Round Table*. Educated in clarinet, piano, and composition, Wakeman has been a noted solo performer considered by many "as the finest solo pianist in popular music" (Gale Biography Research Center). First released as a concept album following his great success in *Journey to the Centre of the Earth*, *King Arthur* was written during Wakeman's recovery from collapse during a staged production of *Journey*. It carries the long look back that a person who has faced such a crisis can bring to creativity. *King Arthur* has nine parts: "Arthur," "The Lady of the Lake," "Guinevere," "Lancelot and the Black Knight," "Merlin the Magician," "Sir Galahad," "Reunion," "His Sword" and the "Last Battle." The sacred parts, whether Celtic or Christian, such as the Lady of the Lake, Merlin, and Galahad, remain joined in the Chivalric, although the deep entanglements of the love triangles are not well explored.

The number of Arthurian concept albums following Wakeman is astounding and made more complex by the rich tapestry of styles ranging from minimalist to New Age to Celtic to folk and on to heavy metal. The New Age and Celtic appeal to young and old while the heavy metal appeals to a young and middle-aged audience. In this same volume, Dan Nastali details many of these, but a few groups and landmarks need to be noted here.

Examples could include the 1995 Netherlandish group Ayreon's concept album, *The Final Experiment*. Composed in four acts with a prologue by Arjin Lucassen, the work has titles such as "Sail Away to Avalon," "Merlin's Will," and "Merlin's Prophecy." Even the disc is decorated with the Winchester Round Table.

Grave Digger is a seven member German musical group that has produced a rock opera *Excalibur* (1999), which they describe as a "metal opera in twelve chapters" (Grave Digger). Like others, it tells many of the tales but carefully avoids the Grail legend. Interestingly, the German group's album cover includes a Round Table scene set within the nave of Wells Cathedral with its scissor arches forming the backdrop. Of course, the cathedral is just a few miles from Glastonbury, the center of the Grail observance and often called the Isle of Avalon. Even light rocker and composer Kenny Loggins offered an Arthurian message with a song entitled "Back to Avalon" released in 1988.

Arthur remains a popular king. Throughout the twentieth century, he has been a musical topic beginning with the "serious" music of composers like Sir Arthur Sullivan. Throughout the first seventy-five years, cost and equipment may have limited the modes of musical reproduction, but with new technology in the past twenty five years musical production has changed the business of King Arthur. There is still a high culture that follows the king. Sir Harrison Birtwistle, Iain Hamilton, and Olivier Messaien have created Arthurian monuments to high culture. Middle culture received a large number of new compositions ranging from Al Jolson's "Avalon" to the many "Elaine" songs that poured forth. Opera for youth and "school opera" are, to a great extent, two of the new artistic developments. However, most of the composers were much older than their audiences. The decisive moments of division include the significance of Rick Wakeman *Myths and Legends of King Arthur*. It is the most accessible of the Arthurian rock pieces; probably the accessibility owes much to Wakeman's musical skills and education.

Still a second change occurred. The rise of American and Celtic folk music is a natural venue for Arthur. Maire Breatnach, Colin Rudd and others have reached into the distinctive shapes and colors of Celtic music. Its fingers reached out into new age music and in an aspect to the sacred. The Grail, a solid link to Christianity in the first three quarters of the century, broadened in literary analysis to envelop additional versions of the "sacred other." A few modern popular composers, Wakeman included, have attempted to bring the Grail into all music; not a successful venture, all told.

Because of the pervasiveness of the Arthurian legend and of its message, its story is generally known. Ballads and operas, symphonies and concept albums have carried the tale. The operas have included works for the opera house (not dealt within this study) but more importantly for this study, for the school auditorium, the church, the village hall, and the rock arena. When Sir Thomas Malory told of the sword in the stone, it was the crowd of the commons who demanded that the boy Arthur should be their king. Today's musicians have set Arthur to contemporary language, to languages that speak to the old, the very young, and the new youth culture—our version, perhaps, of Malory's crowd of commoners.[3]

Notes

1. The information on Helen Hill Miller is based on undated correspondence to Bryn Mawr College Library. The reference was supplied by Professor Isabel Cazeaux and the text by the Librarian.

2. I am grateful to Kevin Harty, LaSalle University, for the reference and for providing me with the compact disk and the libretto.

3. The research for this article was facilitated by two Provosts at Clemson: Steffan Rogers and Doris Helms. Edmee Reel, my wife, did research at a number of sites, including the Library of Congress, The British Library, the Music Library of the University of California-Berkeley, and the Clemson University Library. In addition Tim Porter, the composer, has answered many of my questions.

Compositions Cited

Akhurst, William M. *Arthur the King, or the Knights of the Round Table*. London: T.H. Lacy, 1871.

Ambrose, Paul. "Elaine: Valse Lente." Library of Congress.

Ashton, Frederick (editor of music by Jean Sibelius). *The Lady of Shalott*. Library of Congress, 1931.

Bartlett, Homer Newton. "Elaine." Words by Leontine Stanfield. New York: Maxwell Music, 1902.

Behrend, John Arthur. "Little Elaine." Words by F.L. Stanton. London: Boosey and Hawkes, 1901.

Blackford, Richard. *Gawain and Ragnall*. Words by Ian Barnett. Oxford: Oxford University Press, agent, 1984.

_____. *Sir Gawain and the Green Knight*. Words by John Emlyn Edwards. Oxford: Oxford University Press, 1978.

Bliss, Arthur. *The Lady of Shalott*. London: Novello, agent, 1958.

Boughton, Rutland. "King Arthur Had Three Sons" in *Barkshire Tragedy*. London: William Reeves, 1905.

Britten, Benjamin. *King Arthur*. Words: D.G. Bridson. Oxford: Oxford University Press, 1996.

_____. *The Sword in the Stone*. Words: Marianne Helwig. London: British Broadcasting Corporation, unpublished, 1939.

Clendon, Hugh. *Little Lohengrin; or the Lover and the Bird*. Words: Frederick Bowyer. Premiere 1881. Unpublished.

Coombes, Douglas. *Scatterflock and the Glastonbury Thorn*. Words: John Emlyn Edwards. Potton, U.K.: Lindsay Music.

Crook, John. *Lancelot the Lovely; or the Idol of the King*. Words: Richard Henry. London: Charles Jefferys, 1889.

Debussy, Claude. *Pelleas et Melisande*. Words: Maurice Maeterlinck. Paris: Editions Musicales, 1901.

Fromings, Kevin and Matthew Dubroski. *Shadows, the Life of Joseph of Arimathea*. Words: Kevin Fromings. Kent, U.K.: Lynton PCP, 1992.

Grave Digger. *Excalibur*. Germany: Gun Records, 1999.

Henry, S.R. "In the golden autumn time, my sweet Elaine." Words: Richard H. Gerard, 1905.

Holbrooke, Josef. "Follow the Gleam" in *Six Characteristic Songs*. Words: Alfred, Lord Tennyson. London: Boosey and Hawkes. Mss.n. d.

Humphries, G.H. Ward. "Elaine." London: Gould and Co. c. 1910.

Imig, W. and B. Simon. "King Arthur Had Three Sons." New York: C. Fischer, 1958.

Kay, Ulysses. "King Arthur Had Three Sons." New York: Pembroke Music Company, 1978.

Keighley, Thomas. "King Arthur Had Three Sons." London: Stainer and Bell, 1917.

Kleinsinger, George. *Tommy Pitcher*. Words: Paul Tripp. New York: Chappell, 1952.

Kochiss, Joseph. *The Kids from Camelot*. Words: Joseph Kochiss. Venice, Florida: Eldridge Publishing, 1973.

Koven, Reginald de. "Elaine." New York: J.H. Einack, 1910.

Kuzuu, Chinatsu. *The Lady of Shalott*. Words: Alfred, Lord Tennyson. 1985.

Loeffler, Charles Martin. *Mort de Tintagiles*. New World Records 332. composed 1897; revised 1901.

Loggins, Kenny. "Back to Avalon." Columbia Records CK40535, 1988.

Lucassen, Arjen Anthony. *Ayreon: The Final Experiment*. Netherlands: Transmission Records. TM-110, 1995.

Mayerl, Billy. *Legends of King Arthur (Six Impressions for Piano Forte)*. London: Keith Prowse and Co., 1929.

McKennitt, Loreena. "Lady of Shalott." Warner Music. WEA 17-51514, 1991.

Miller, Helen Hill. "Follow the Gleam." Words: Sallie Hume Douglas. Philadelphia: Westminster Press, 1921.

Nougues, Jean. *Mort de Tintagiles*. Words: Jean Nougues, after Maurice Maeterlinck. Private, 1906.

Porter, Timothy. *Entertaining the Noble Head*. Words: Timothy Porter. Unpublished, 1973.

_____. *Lancelot, or the Tale of the Grail*. Words: Timothy Porter. Unpublished, 1985.

_____. *The Marvels of Merlin*. Words: Timothy Porter. Unpublished, 1981.

_____. *Sir Gawain and the Green Knight*. Words: Timothy Porter. Unpublished, 1970.

_____. *Tristan and Essylt*. Words: Timothy Porter. Unpublished, 1980.

Purcell, Henry. "Fairest Isle." Words: John Dryden. Multiple, but for example, New York: Mills, 1934.

Riddick, Mark and Michael. *May the Blood of Many a Valiant Knight Be Avenged.* Herndon, VA: 1997.

Rodgers, Richard. *A Connecticut Yankee in King Arthur's Court.* Words: Lorenz Hart. New York: Chappell, 1927.

Shaw, Martin. *The Thorn of Avalon.* Words: Barclay Baron. Oxford University Press, 1931.

Sherman, Richard. *The Sword in the Stone.* Words: Robert Sherman. Anaheim, CA: Wonderland Music, 1961.

Stanford, Charles Villiers. *Merlin and the Gleam.* Words: Alfred, Lord Tennyson. London: Stainer and Bell, 1920.

Stites, Kevin. *Adventures with Young King Arthur.* Woodstock, IL: Dramatic Publishing, 1995.

Straus, Albert I. *Elaine Waltzes.* Words: Alfred, Lord Tennyson, n.d.

Sullivan, Arthur S. *King Arthur.* Words: Joseph Comyn-Carr. London: Novello, 1903.

Wakeman, Rick. *Myths and Legends of King Arthur and the Knights of the Round Table.* London: Rondor, 1974.

Willan, Healey, "Elaine's Song." Not published, 1901.

Williams, Ralph Vaughan. *Death of Tintagiles.* Words: Maurice Maeterlinck. Unpublished, 1913.

Zylstra, Karen and Dick. *A Computer Whiz at King Arthur's Court.* Louisville, KY: Aran Press, 1990.

Works Cited

Athenaeum. London, 27 March 1897.

Bliss Arthur, *Lady of Shalott.* London: *Artifact*, 3 May 1975, 4–5.

"Carr and Sullivan's *King Arthur.*" London: *Musical Times*, 1 February 1895, 5.

Cole, Hugo. "Musical Scene: Sprung from Celtic Roots." *Country Life*, 14 September 1978, 704.

Davies, Sian. "Turning the Table on Arthur." *Bath and West Evening Chronicle.* 11 May 1985, 3.

Ewen, David. *The World of Twentieth Century Composers.* Engelwood Cliffs, NJ: Prentice Hall, Inc., 1968.

Fitzgerald, Penelope. *Edward Burne Jones.* London: Michael Joseph Ltd., 1975. Revised: Stroud, Gloucestershire: Sutton Publishing Co., 1997.

Galenet: Biography Resource Center. www.galenet.com, Rick Wakeman.

Goodman, Jennifer. "Last of Avalon: Henry Irving's *King Arthur* of 1895." Cambridge, MA: Harvard Library Bulletin, 12 (1984), 239–255.

Grave Digger. *Excalibur.* Compact disc. Senden/Münster, Germany: Edition Drakkar, BMG UFA, 1999.

Green, Stanley. *Encyclopedia of Musical Theatre.* New York: Da Capo, 1976.

Lacy, Norris J. and Geoffrey Aske. *The Arthurian Handbook.* New York: Garland, 1988.

Newbery Library, Chicago, Illinois A5A, 513 no. 231.

Nolan, Frederick. *Sound of Their Music: The Story of Rodgers and Hammerstein.* New York: Walker and Co., 1978.

Palmer, A. *The Britten Companion.*
Salisbury Journal. Wiltshire. UK: Salisbury, 12, 1975, 4.
The Thorn of Avalon. Musical Times. London, 1 July 1934, 645.
Times of London. 3 January 1896, 12.

Arthurian Pop:
The Tradition in Twentieth-Century Popular Music

Dan Nastali

When Al Jolson sang, in 1920, that his heart belonged in "Avalon," he very well may have had in mind the town on Catalina Island or the city in New Jersey rather than King Arthur's island of repose. That clearly is not the case with his counterparts of today, however, whose visions of Avalon in countless songs unmistakably identify it with the fortunate isle of Arthurian legend. Avalon, Camelot, the Holy Grail, Excalibur—all have found a place in the popular music of the twentieth century, as have Merlin, Guinevere and other familiar figures from the old stories. And while the identification of several hundred Arthurian songs raises hopes of rich and wondrous new musical treatments of the great themes—the tragic fall of the king, the golden age, the famous love affairs, the quests—the reality is somewhat more mundane.

The last thirty years, and especially the last decade, have produced the most bountiful trove of Arthurian song, but it must be recognized from the outset that it is rarely the nature of pop music to be either profound or sublime. Arthurian material, it will be seen, is generally confined to only a few of the many types of pop music, the content is very selective, and the truly memorable examples are exceedingly rare, which is not to say that some genuine pleasures cannot be found.

Histories of pop music invariably begin with attempts to distinguish the field from "serious" music, which for purposes of exclusion here may be deemed to be classical music in all of its forms and works composed for the musical stage and concert hall. Pop music is created to be sold: in the early 1900s, sold in the form of sheet music and piano rolls, from the second decade of the century to the present as recordings, and now digitally distributed via the Internet, a process that has caused consternation precisely because of the difficulties it poses in collecting money for the music. If pop music has a single defining feature, it is that it always has been aimed at the marketplace and thus has catered to the tastes of mass audiences.

Composers of popular music in the early years of the twentieth century, for example, created their works for a general public that actually read poetry, a staple feature of the magazines and newspapers of the era. When they drew on Arthurian themes, they often selected those made familiar in the literature of the day, and no one was more influential than Tennyson. Even though the poet's popularity in print faded after World War I, composers continued to find inspiration in his works, notably in the story of Elaine and her alter ego, the Lady of Shalott. As the sentimental subject of countless paintings, plays and poems, the beautiful young woman who surrenders to sin and then to death for love of a flawed but noble knight also proved irresistible to songwriters. Of some 40 songs published or recorded in the first three decades of the century that are clearly inspired by Tennyson's poetry, 31 deal with Lancelot's forsaken lady. Tennyson's Guinevere and Merlin vie for a distant second place.

The concept of an enchanted Avalon was appealing as well, although its Arthurian origins are not always reflected in such titles as Jack Wells' "When Roses Bloom in Avalon" (1914), M. Wingate's "When Abbots Ruled at Avalon" (1923), E. St. Claire's "You Were My Love in Avalon" (1927), and J. Cherney's "The Bells of Avalon" (1927). The Arthurian association may have lent the name a mythic quality, but usually it was enough to depict Avalon as an alluring land of peace and comfort, separate yet accessible. Its popularity early in the century may have been little more than nostalgia for a lost pastoral world in an increasingly industrialized period, and it eventually fell out of fashion and faded from view for decades. Avalon would reappear, however, in dozens of songs as the century came to an end.

In the 1930s, there were few Arthurian popular songs beyond works for the musical stage, orchestral performance, and pieces written for choral groups. A few more "Elaine" songs signaled the end of that particular vogue, and some published works carried such forgettable titles as "I'll Go to Camelot" (1937) by R.E. Mitchell and "That Night in Avalon" (1938) by Harry Ruby. In the 1940s, Arthurian films contributed songs that found their way into the repertoires of popular singers, notably tunes by Manning Sherwin and Val Guest from the British comedy *King Arthur Was a*

Gentleman (1942) and Jimmy Van Heusen and Johnny Burke's score from the Bing Crosby film, *A Connecticut Yankee in King Arthur's Court* (1949). A revival of the stage version of *Connecticut Yankee* (1943) produced several new songs by Richard Rodgers and Lorenz Hart that also became popular through the renditions of vocalists on radio and recordings, but there is little Arthurian content in any of these works from the movies and theater.

The 1950s were the bleakest period of Arthurian popular music, surprisingly, perhaps, since the decade saw a renewed public interest in medieval subjects in both films and literature. There were a number of "serious" musical treatments of Arthurian themes—largely such literary material put to music as John Duke's "When I Set Out for Lyonesse" (1953), based on the Thomas Hardy poem, and Robin Milford's "The Summer Stars" (1957), inspired by Charles Williams' Arthurian verse cycle—but the period most notable in pop music history for the beginnings of rock and roll and the development of contemporary folk music was not yet looking to Arthurian sources for material. That would change at the end of the decade with the Broadway show that proved to have the most potent impact of any musical Arthurian material to that time, Alan Jay Lerner and Frederick Loewe's *Camelot* in 1960.

Now famous for lending its golden age aura to the Kennedy administration, *Camelot* spun off an enormously successful original cast album featuring Robert Goulet, Julie Andrews and Richard Burton. Such songs as Lancelot's "If Ever I Would Leave You" and Guenevere's "I Loved You Once in Silence" immediately became favorites of popular singers, and the score itself was covered by treatments as varied as the lush arrangements of the 101 Strings orchestra and jazzy piano improvisations by the Andre Previn Trio. Through performances of touring companies and regional productions, the film adaptation, and major revivals in New York and London, songs from the musical settled comfortably into the repertoire of modern romantic classics.

Although there have been many other Arthurian theatrical productions incorporating music, none has found an audience as wide as that of *Camelot* nor will they enter the discussion here (see Jerome V. Reel, "Sing a Sony of Arthur," in this volume). Even a brief reference to songs born on the musical stage but popularized by lounge singers raises the issue of classifying types of modern popular music, a realm in which all categories are problematical. In pop music, as in every art form of the century, categories have shifted, expanded and multiplied with changing tastes, the development of new media, and the fragmentation of audiences. Only a few years ago, popular music could be neatly compartmentalized into jazz, rock, country western, soul music and a few other familiar types. Today, to illustrate how vast and various the world of pop music has become, the All Music Guide, an Internet reference site, subdivides "new age music" alone into 20 categories, each with its own artists and audiences, and including such groupings as "adult alternative," "ethnic fusion," "healing," and "techno-tribal."

The marketing strategies of recording companies, ever in search of novel ploys to distinguish their products, complicate the matter, of course, as do the musicians themselves. In their zeal to establish unique identities, pop performers are often ingenious, pretentious, and at times, plain silly.[1] While passionate fans, musicologists, and perhaps sociologists might find the many subcategories of modern pop meaningful, the survey of recent music that follows groups its subjects into the three broad and familiar classifications in which treatments of Arthurian material have found some common ground: modern folk music, new age music, and, by far the largest, most diverse and most interesting, rock music.

Other modern categories yield little of Arthurian interest and, not surprisingly, the types of music most resistant to the appeal of the tradition are those with the deepest American roots and well-defined, exclusive conventions: country-western, which developed its modern form in white southern culture, and music with African-American origins such as the blues, rhythm and blues, soul music and their modern derivatives. While all have themes in common with the Arthurian legend—personal tragedy, failed love affairs, sin and salvation—the cultural traditions they arise from are so alien from the Anglo-European literary tradition that gave us the Arthurian story that they are not even metaphorically compatible.

Some exceptions prove the rule. "Merlin" (1986), a rap single by the New York group Legion, is nothing more than a novelty item, a rhythmic narrative in which the speaker tells of traveling into the past where he must slay a dragon at the command of Merlin. And the only identified blues treatment of Arthurian material, "The Return of Arthur" (1971) by Graham Bond, owes only its instrumentation and style to the blues. Bond, who was one of many British musicians who fell under the spell of black urban blues in the 1960s and whose life and career slipped into a mystical phase before mysteriously ending beneath the wheels of a London train, used Arthur's return as a symbol of the artistic revival that the Age of Aquarius would introduce.

Jazz also would seem to be a bad match with the Arthurian tradition, even though in its modern forms it has evolved away from its origins in black culture to become the cosmopolitan big brother of pop music. Arthurian motifs that are discernible in jazz recordings are typically little more than starting points for compositions. The fact that much jazz is purely instrumental further confounds attempts to identify the few Arthurian influences suggested by song titles. A case in point is trumpeter Donald Byrd's "King Arthur" (1998), in which brass and percussion lend the song a martial air that could suggest Arthurian pageantry. The album's liner notes, however, simply identify the piece as a tribute to the jazz drummer Art Blakey.

The Arthurian tradition, born in stories from the distant past, has always been driven by narrative, but beyond such venerable forms as the traditional ballad, popular music is predominantly lyrical, trading on the emotional moment, evocative images, and isolated themes. In all of the categories of modern pop music, it is the folksingers, the most direct inheritors of the ballad tradition, who have remained most faithful to that tradition in both sound and content. The folk music revival of the late 1950s, in fact, consisted largely of new interpretations of rediscovered songs. By the 1960s, however, American folksingers, like their counterparts in rock, were performing more original material, with themes that embodied social and political comment, and they increasingly moved towards more rock-oriented electric instrumentation and away from the acoustic sounds of the 1950s recordings.

In Great Britain, however, the transition was somewhat slower and the ties to traditional music somewhat stronger. Among the first Arthurian works to appear on a popular album was "King Arthur's Servants" (1965) by the family folk band The Watersons. A musical rendition of the old nursery rhyme about King Arthur's three sons, it is hardly mainstream Arthuriana. Another singer, Allan Taylor, turned to older sources for his version of "The Boy and the Mantle" (1971), the chastity test ballad that may date to the fifteenth century. The guitarist John Renbourn, also exploring earlier musical forms in the 1960s, recorded his original instrumental "Morgana" in 1966, inspired, reportedly, by *Sir Gawain and the Green Knight*.[2] His next venture into Arthurian subject matter was with the folk-rock group Pentangle, which recorded the "The Hunting Song" in 1969. An original piece, though very much in the old narrative mode, the song tells of the adventures of a young knight transporting the magic drinking horn—the chastity test motif again—from Morgana the Fay to Arthur's court. And yet another new ballad was Peter Coe's adaptation of "The Wizard of Alderley Edge" (1972), the tale of the discovery of Arthur's sleeping knights behind the Iron Gate.[3]

Subsequent songs by folk and folk-rock musicians which embody strong narrative content were Bill Caddick's "Gawain and Ragnell" (1979), The McCalmans' "Avalon" (1984), a story of a princess who abandoned her lover for a life in Arthur's court, and David Buskin and Robin Batteau's "Lancelot's Song" (1988) in which the knight confesses his role in Camelot's fall. Other original pieces with more modern touches are Doug McArthur and Garnet Rogers' "Merlin" (1989), in which the wizard, speaking from the cave from which he is shortly to be disinterred by the builders of a shopping center, reveals a grim secret about Guinevere, and Dave Carter's "Lancelot" (1997), in which medieval imagery is curiously blended with that of the old west as a modern Lancelot who has lost his Guinevere rides into town to find solace with a Lady Elaine. In the recent evolution of modern folk music, the folk-rock artists have taken the most adventurous turns with Arthurian material while those most bound to tradition have been the "Celtic" musicians, most often performing on acoustic and regional instruments. Typical of the modern Celtic trend are Judith Pintar's song sequence, "In Defense of Guenevere" (1985), performed on Celtic harp, "Tristan hag Isild" and "Viviane" (1977) by the Breton band An Triskell, "Rose of Avalon" (1996) by the Cornerboys, a Canadian band, and "Tintagel" (1998) by the Scottish group Avalon.

Many folk songs bearing Arthurian titles are instrumentals and thus draw on the legend's increasingly popular mystique merely for an evocative focal image, but the narrative impulse in the Arthurian tradition continues to appeal to modern folksingers. While Tennyson's Elaine was clearly the favorite object of musical sympathy in the early years of the century, it is the Lady of Shalott who has appeared most often in recent recordings. The familiar poem itself has been set to music in full or abridged versions by several folksingers, including Loreena McKennitt (1991), Anne Lister (1993), and Krysia Kristianne (1996). She is also the inspiration for an original "Lady of Shallot" (1989) by Eleanore MacDonald and Paul Kamm, while Mancy A'lan Kane, in her "Camelot" (1998), offers a lament by a woman who sees herself as the same sorrowful Lady.

Lancelot, of course, is the figure who unwittingly or not is the agent behind the woes of the Lady, and if he remains in the distance in her songs, he is much more prominent in songs where he shares the stage with the queen, who typically is portrayed as suffering from love. Such is the case in "Lancelot and Guinevere" (1986) by the Australian singer Eric Bogle, "The Walls of Caerleon" (1989) by MacDonald and Kamm, "Guinevere" (1994) by Lucy Kaplansky, "Guinevere" (1995) by Edwin McCain, "Secret Hearts" (1998) by Judy Kamminga, and "Guinevere's Lament" (1998) by

Sandra Parker, in which the queen's torment is unabashedly attributed to her lust for her champion.

Tragic love is a preferred Arthurian theme of the traditional folk-singers, but the practitioners of folk-rock have shown a fondness for the more fantastic elements of the legend. Here, Merlin is a favorite figure, as in Sally Oldfield's "Merlin's Song" (1994), and Avalon, arising from the misty past like Brigadoon, is a favorite destination, as in Eliza Gilkyson's "Key to Avalon" (1994), the Swedish singer Idha's "Fields of Avalon" (1997), and Ritchie Blackmore's celebration of an idyllic time in his own "Avalon" (1999). Arthurian artifacts with supernatural associations also find a place in such songs as Heidi Berry's "Holy Grail" (1996) and the Dutch group Purple Shadow's "Excalibur" (1998).

Recent years also have seen a number of folk-oriented Arthurian concept albums, or collections of musical pieces linked by unifying themes. In 1995, the entire central Arthurian story was told on *Merlin's Arthur*, a double album of 44 songs with incidental narration performed by a large aggregation of Welsh folk musicians gathered for the project. Created for sale at British Heritage tourist sites, the album contained both traditional and original music that unfortunately varied widely in quality, a result of the expedient conditions under which the musicians recorded, with little opportunity to polish the material or performances.

The earliest Arthurian concept albums to draw extensively on folk music traditions were by French musicians, signaling a growing interest in Arthurian material on the continent. In 1976, the group known as Lyonesse released *Tristan de Lyonesse*, an album of eleven songs on the Tristan legend, with most of the music adapted from traditional sources. In 1991, the highly regarded harpist Alan Stivell produced his *Mist of Avalon*, a Marion Zimmer Bradley–inspired collection of both instrumentals and vocals (in English, French and Breton). The culmination of the traditional folk strain of Arthurian music was an album equally at home in the "serious" category known as "early music": *Perceval: La quête du Graal, Vol.1* (1999) by La Nef, a Canadian group of singers and musicians who perform on instruments of the Middle Ages and who here set the text of Chrétien de Troyes' story to traditional British and Celtic melodies as well as to original compositions by Sylvain Bergeron.

Folk music has divided into traditional and contemporary/folk-rock camps over the past few decades, and, through a mating with progressive rock, has produced the thriving offspring known as "new age" music. Associated with the broader cultural movement of the same name, new age music embodies philosophies and attitudes that derive from contemporary interest in ancient religions and mythologies (real and imagined), Jungian psychology, and several varieties of spiritualism, all often colored with a spectrum of post–Tolkien fantasy. Mostly instrumental, the music marketed under the new age rubric exploits the favorite themes of the subculture that supports it—personal fulfillment, healing, reverie for a better time and place—and musically it is typified by simple melodies with repetitious elaborations performed on electronic and traditional acoustic instruments, often with an ethereal, soothing quality.[4]

Arthurian themes have always been popular with new age artists, as are themes drawn from other legendary and mythological sources. Although the genre was not exploited as a separate market until the mid–1980s, an Arthurian-related work that can be considered a precursor to the genre appeared as early as 1965 in Robbie Basho's guitar instrumental "The Grail and the Lotus." The earliest Arthurian work by an acknowledged new age musician was probably "Guinevere's Tears" (1972) by David Arkenstone. Because the song is an instrumental piece, to speak of Arthurian "content" is strictly inaccurate, but concepts taken from the tradition have become a commonplace in new age recordings.

It is no surprise to discover a special fondness among new agers for the isle of Avalon, an inspiration for more than a dozen individual songs, including Jana Runnall's "Spirit of Avalon" (1985), Kay Gardner's "Avalon" (1989), recorded in Glastonbury during a "women's mystery tour," songs of the same title by Jay Scott Berry (1992) and the pianist known as Micon (1997), and Frank O'Connor's "Mystic Moon of Avalon" (2000), performed on Celtic instruments. The appeal of that therapeutic island is even more apparent in at least seven concept albums. Among them are *Legends of Avalon* (1988) by Thierry Fervant, *The Magic World of Avalon* (1991), an album released in Germany by Helene Lind and Michael Taylor, *Avalon* (1992) by Roger Calverly, described as an impressionistic approach to Celtic music, and *Dreams of Avalon* (1996) by Mike Simmons. Vaguely Arthurian themes connect the songs in each of these albums.

Some predictable characters from the legend also strike a sympathetic chord with new age composers, and the most popular figure by far is Merlin, whose name appears in the titles of over 20 songs and who serves as the focal point for several concept albums: *The Enchanter* (1986) by Tim Wheater, "inspired by the legends of Merlin, the Bard, Kingmaker, Magician," *Land of Merlin* (1992) by Jon Mark, who cites T.H. White's *Once and Future King* as his source, *Broceliande* (1994), an interpretation of the legend by Patrick Broguière on keyboards, guitar and flute, and *The Merlin Mystery* (1998), an album issued by a group identified as Alkæmy as a marketing tie-in with a book of the same title that challenged readers to solve an elaborate puzzle. Guinevere, a favorite of folksingers, also has been an inspiration to new age musicians, her plight as distressed lover resonating in such works as the Canadian Greg Joy's instrumental "Lady Guinevere" (1986), "Gwenhwyfar" (1996), an electronic piece by David Arkenstone, and "Guinevere's Lament" (1997), performed by Nancy Rumbel and Eric Tingstad on keyboards, guitars and horns. Reflecting the more mystical interests of the genre, the Lady of the Lake is also a recurring figure, the title character of songs by Lisa Thiel (1992), Bill Douglas (1998) and Brendan McCloud (1999).

Of all the new age composer/performers to treat Arthurian themes, the most prolific by far has been the self-taught musician Medwyn Goodall, who records in his home in rural Cornwall on a broad array of acoustic and electronic instruments, often stirring natural sound effects into the mix as well. Although he has released many albums based on mythological concepts, his "metaphysical" renditions of Arthurian material first appeared on two albums, *Excalibur* and *Merlin*, issued on his own label in 1990. By 1995, Goodall's recordings were being produced by Oreade Music, a Netherlands company with a large new age catalog, and in a span of three years he released the five albums that constitute his Arthurian Collection: *The Grail Quest* (1996), *The Gift of Excalibur* (1996), *The Fair Queen Guinevere* (1996), *Tintagel, Castle of Arthur* (the fourth in the series, although dated 1995), and *The Round Table* (1998). Each of the albums includes six to nine tracks, with brief impressionistic liner notes explicating each piece, for an Arthurian oeuvre that consists of some 50 songs.

Other new age concept albums are similar in their approach to the Arthurian legend, providing sequences of evocative aural images rather than coherent narratives. *The Holy Spirit and the Holy Grail* (1993) is a cycle of fourteen songs on the quest theme performed by Adrian Wagner on organ and Elliot Mackrell on violin. *Arthur* (1994) by Alex Otterlei is an album of 21 pieces of electronic music with such titles as "Modred's Madness" and "The Downfall of Merlin." Simon Cooper's *Celtic Heart: The Story of Tristan and Iseult* (1996) is a collection of nine songs performed on traditional and electronic instruments. Perhaps the most unique in sound of all new age treatments—not to say the oddest—is William Wilde Zeitler's interpretation of the *Parzival* of Wolfram von Eschenbach on *The Passionate Quest: A Romance of the Grail* (1998), an album of fourteen pieces performed by the composer on the eerie glass armonica, harp and bass recorder.

The Arthurian concept album, however popular with new age musicians and audiences, originated in another branch of pop music with a 1975 release by a rock musician that still has admirers after 25 years: *The Myths and Legends of King Arthur and the Knights of the Round Table* by Rick Wakeman. A classically trained pianist, Wakeman had already earned a reputation as an extraordinary keyboard musician with the British band Yes when *Myths and Legends* appeared. It was rock music on the grand scale, and as if the orchestra and chorus supporting his own ensemble were not enough, he introduced the work to the public by putting the Arthurian characters on skates in an extravagant London ice show—an ill-advised event which reportedly cost him a fortune.

The continuing popularity of Wakeman's Arthurian creation can be attributed to his enduring presence as a performer and also to the elaborate production of the album itself, which in the style of the time was handsomely packaged with an illustrated booklet of lyrics and striking cover graphics. Of the seven songs on the album, only "Merlin the Magician," inspired by T.H. White's *Sword in the Stone* and performed on keyboards that shift between soaring synthesizer and sprightly music hall piano, has much musical merit, and all of the songs suffer from lyrics that are banal by even the most generous standards of rock music. Yet the album remains in print, and Wakeman has continued to include selections from it in solo concerts and in his performances with Yes.

Although Wakeman apparently was the first rock musician to devote an entire album to the Arthurian legend (he had earlier played keyboards on "The Vision of the Lady of the Lake" by the Strawbs in 1970), he was not the first rock musician to draw on the tradition. In the late 1960s, fantasy and even science fiction themes were expanding into popular music as they were into films and fiction. The Arthurian story, laden with familiar characters and motifs, powerful symbols and the rich patina of the distant past, offered obvious potential to the songwriters of the rapidly developing rock music market. The first notable Arthurian production in the genre was the song "Guinevere" by the Dylanesque British singer Donovan. His gentle portrait of the queen appeared on the popular soft-rock album *Sunshine Superman* (1966) as well as on later compilations. In 1968, a less specifically Arthurian turn was taken by the British band Deep Purple, which asked the listener, in medieval imagery, to be guided by the words of the bard Taliesyn in "Listen, Learn, Read On" on the album entitled *The Book of Taliesyn*.

The year 1969 saw three Arthurian rock songs introduced, two of which still receive occasional airplay on "classic rock" radio. The all-but-forgotten song is "Stones for Avalon," by the early version of the British band Tyrannosaurus Rex (later T. Rex), but a song with greater staying power, inviting the listener to enter an Arthurian world, was the Moody Blues' "Are You Sitting Comfortably?," performed with the dreamy lyricism the band was noted for. David Crosby's "Guinnevere" (variously spelled on later recordings), in which the singer compared his own lady to the queen, also continues to be performed, not only by Crosby but also in cover versions by other singers.

Merlin was the Arthurian character most appealing to the rock musicians of the 1970s—a protean figure equally at home in such soft-rock songs as "Merlin" (1973) by Climax, in progressive rock tunes such as "Merlin, the Magic Man" (1974) by If, and in one of the earliest continental treatments, "Merlin" (1976), by the German band Amon Düül, practitioners of what aficionados have labeled "Kraut rock." In 1974, the band Phantom had Merlin sing of his glorious past from his tree-prison in their own "Merlin," and in 1980, Al Stewart portrayed him as the "Scottish warrior poet" in "Merlin's Time," another song still occasionally heard on the air. The following year, the Dutch progressive rock band Kayak outlined the wizard's career, including his role in Arthur's life, in a five-song suite on their album *Merlin*.

The 1980s saw many more treatments of Arthurian material by European and American musicians, including some rather idiosyncratic takes on characters and places that reveal little regard for the integrity of the literary tradition. The pop singer Rick Springfield, for example, asked his "Guinevere" (1984) to return to her Galahad in Camelot, and Jim Matheos and John Arch, in their "Fata Morgana" (1986), had a lover appeal to Morgan le Fay to join him in a passionate fantasy. The concept of Avalon, without reference to Arthur, continued to inspire songwriters, notably Bryan Ferry, whose "Avalon" (1982), on the album of the same title by Roxy Music, alluded to an unknown destination while background vocalists repeated the word "Avalon" again and again in refrain. In "Back to Avalon" (1988), another pop singer, Kenny Loggins, sang of a retreat for lovers among the gardens and towers of Avalon.

One of the more striking musical treatments of Arthurian material and one that found its largest audience on the continent was Valerie Dore's concept album *The Legend* (1986). This recording of European dance club music, with the singer's frail vocals gliding through a mix of electronic keyboards and drum-machine percussion, outlined a narrative thread in songs devoted to "The Wizard," "King Arthur," "Guinnevere," and "Lancelot." A danceable beat also took precedence over the Arthurian concepts in "Avalon" (1983) by the English "house rock" band Quartz, and "Sir Lancelot"

(1989) by Calloway, an American urban dance band led by the brothers Reggie and Vincent Calloway.

It should be noted that the major Arthurian character least mentioned to this point is Arthur himself. In fact, beyond a few songs that depict his passing, such as Boris Grebenshikov's "Death of King Arthur" (1989), which is actually the conclusion of the *Stanzaic Morte Arthur* set to music, and songs anticipating his return, such as Beltane Fire's "King Arthur's Cave" (1985), the king has kept a rather low profile among the composers of folk, new age and pop rock music. But if those relatively nonthreatening pop genres have not proven congenial to Arthur, that is not the case in the world of heavy metal rock, where the image of a betrayed but vengeance-seeking, sword-wielding ruler is prominent both in songs and on album covers. At the opposite end of the pop spectrum from new age music, heavy metal generally aims at an audience of young white males and delivers its messages with impact—simple chords played on amplified guitars against pounding percussive beats, the artistry residing in the pyrotechnic skills of lead guitarists. It is aggressive, some say violent, music for the most part, often glorifying the heroic pose, both in its performers and its subject matter. What it found to admire in the Arthurian tradition was a cast of larger-than-life warriors, magical weapons, themes of betrayal and revenge, and no small amount of spilt blood.

One of the earliest heavy metal groups to exploit the tradition was the French band Blaspheme, which included the song "Excalibur" (1983) on their first album. The song's title has been a popular one, appearing on subsequent pieces by the British "skinhead" band Skrewdriver (1988),[5] the German band Stormwitch (1991), the appropriately named Morgan Lefay (1994), and as the title of the Arthurian concept album *Excalibur* (1999) by the German "power metal band," Grave Digger. Because the names of the groups as well as the titles of their songs reflect their personae, a few more Arthurian works may be cited: "Knights of the Round Table" (1987) by Commander, "The Last Battle" (1990) by the British group Mordred, "Mordred" (1991) by Grinder, "King Arthur" (1994) by Cement (which here unplugged its instruments to set a song of murder and despair to acoustic guitar accompaniment), and "Haunted Shores" (1996), in which Arthur summarizes his story from his grave, by the "Black, Gothic, Romantic Metal" band from Suffolk known as Cradle of Filth.

Happily, other musicians of the 1990s found more in the Arthurian story than slashing, bashing, and heroic posturing. Robert Fripp, a guitarist known for his experimental work both with instruments and with recording studio techniques, produced an inventive "Connecticut Yankee in King Arthur's Court" (1991), and a trio known as the Hellecasters released the instrumental, "King Arthur's Dream" (1993), an ominous, plodding melody with soaring guitars behind it. The lure of Avalon continued, attracting Van Morrison, in his mystical Christian mode, for "Avalon of the Heart" (1990) in which images of the Holy Grail and Camelot lend an Arthurian atmosphere to the enchanted vale that is the spiritual destination in the song. Other pop performers who have traded on the Avalon mystique are Cindi Lauper, apparently inspired by Marion Zimmer Bradley's fiction, who sang of a sort of initiation into womanhood in imagery that suggests primitive rituals in her "Sisters of Avalon" (1997), and Christopher Cross, who in "Walking to Avalon" (1998) celebrated a love affair by envisioning the couple as heroes residing in Avalon where they propose a toast to Guinevere and irreverently drink beer from a grail.

The Holy Grail itself, that amorphous vessel that in modern literature may represent anything from Christian salvation to Jungian self-fulfillment to success in a sporting event, has often appeared in rock imagery in more romantic manifestations. The Chicago band Shimmer, for example, compared a lover's forlorn condition to an empty Grail in their "Holy Grail" (1996), and the band Superdrag compared the loved one herself to the vessel in "She is a Holy Grail" (1998). Other musicians who have symbolically seized the cup include the British alternative rock band Electrafixion in "Holy Grail" (1995), the heavy metal band Raven in a song of the same title (1997), the progressive rocker Martin Darvill in "In Search of the Holy Grail" (1999), and Gene Farris, a performer of electronic "house music" in his "Grail" (2000).

While modern rock musicians tend to use the Arthurian legend merely as a convenient source of themes, concepts and symbols, it should be pointed out that the tradition's narrative origins have not been totally ignored. Indeed, a number of musicians have followed the lead of Rick Wakeman by attempting to tell Arthurian stories in song sequences and in concept albums, although they often depend on accompanying notes to establish the narrative framework. One composer who has made frequent trips into the Arthurian world is T. Owen Knight, who with his Cincinnati "fringerock" band Blacklight Braille released *Zauzomank Castle* in 1984. In narration and song, Arthur here battles the forces of darkness at Badon Hill before arriving at the hall of Oger Bran, father of Guinhwyvar and keeper of the Round Table. The band followed this recording with *The Carbonek Album* (1991), *Carmarthen* (1993), and *Camelot Palace* (1993)—all Arthurian-themed works.

More inventive uses of Arthurian material have been made by the

Dutch group Ayreon, whose creative leader, Arjen Anthony Lucassen, produced a rock opera of sorts in *The Final Experiment* (1995), in which a blind minstrel runs afoul of Merlin in King Arthur's time. In 1998, the group released a musical narrative with a science fiction plot, *Into the Electric Castle*, which included among other characters the Knight who believes he is in Avalon seeking the Grail. The American brothers Mike and Mark Riddick, who perform as The Soil Bleeds Black and who occupy a niche somewhere between folk music and Gothic rock, have frequently incorporated Arthurian content in their albums, especially in the collection of songs based on the medieval tale of Sir Gawain and the Green Knight: *May the Blood of Many a Valiant Knight Be Avenged* (1998). And an "Arthurian rock symphony" is what the composer/performer Stephen Caudel calls his *Earth in Turquoise* (1996), a one man show in which he presents episodes from Arthur's life in sonic layers consisting of an electronically simulated orchestra, choir and rock instruments.

In contrast to this solitary effort, one of the most ambitious Arthurian musical projects of recent years has been the collaborative *Excalibur, La Légende des Celtes* (1999), developed and produced by the French composer/musician Alan Simon and performed by a large international cast, including the British band Fairport Convention, the Breton vocal group Tri Yann, and many prominent solo musicians, all backed by an orchestra and chorus. The theme of *Excalibur* is the transformation of Arthurian characters into figures of myth, and the songs range from folk-rock to anthemic orchestral productions. The album was extremely popular in Europe, and a second recording of an elaborately staged concert version of the show was released as *Excalibur: Le Concert Mythique* in 2000.

If Rick Wakeman can be credited with introducing the Arthurian story to rock audiences with a theatrical flourish in 1975, it is fitting that the century should end with another Arthurian stage extravaganza. In 1999, the English writer/director Victoria Heward collaborated with the Italian progressive rock musician Fabio Zuffanti to create *Merlin: The Rock Opera*. Another spectacular production, featuring over 30 actors, singers, dancers and musicians, the show was performed throughout Italy in 1999 and 2000, and the music was released on a handsome double album. Heward based her libretto primarily on Geoffrey of Monmouth, though with cleverly expanded roles for the Devil and Vivian, and Zuffanti's music blended folk song, Celtic and medieval influences into a symphonic rock score. *Merlin* stands—with Wakeman's *Myths and Legends* and Simon's *Excalibur*—as a pop music work that by its scale alone aspires to be something more than a commercial commodity.

The reality that confounds such aspirations is the same problem that bedevils all popular art in the twentieth century—the lack of normative standards for judging works that arise from and cater to the aesthetic senses of many cultural subgroups. The only meaningful standard may be the test of time. And what will survive of the Arthurian pop music of the past one hundred years? Will it be Jolson's "Avalon," undoubtedly the most frequently recorded work with Arthurian associations, however slight?[6] Songs from Lerner and Loewe's *Camelot*, although their content is not explicitly Arthurian? Some new age or heavy metal piece? Our perspective is too short to tell.

Yet a few judgments are possible. Unlike modern fiction, popular music has added little substance to the tradition, and it has scarcely extended the body of Arthurian narrative at all. Traditional Arthurian elements, it seems, are treated either with too much reverence or with complete disregard. For all the images of Arthurian lovers and locales conjured in all the songs, few attach themselves to melodies and linger in the mind. In terms of staying power, one looks in vain for a musical equivalent of a T.H. White or even a Marion Zimmer Bradley.

But this may be a case where the medium is more important than the message. The real achievement of Arthurian pop music is that it has internationalized the tradition to a degree greater than any of the other popular arts. Thanks to modern marketing and distribution methods, the world-wide audience for pop music is listening to Arthurian material being produced by singers and bands in Australia, Sweden, Brazil, Latvia and Italy. And the Arthurian images they present, however reshaped, will resonate with new audiences, and they, in turn, will respond by creating new Arthurian music, fiction, and films. And that, after all, is how a tradition works.

Notes

1. To cite a single example, the German rock group Blind Guardian describe themselves on their website as a "power-melodic-speed-fantasy-progressive-elf-Metal band."

2. A contemporary music critic, Robin Denslow, met Renbourn on a train where the guitarist was engrossed in the medieval romance. He told Denslow he intended to base an album on the poem, but this is the only song that appeared (Laing *et al.* 148).

3. The lyrics earned Coe a place in *The Oxford Book of English Traditional Verse* for his contributions to the corpus of Cheshire songs (Woods 349).

4. An acquaintance with a preference for music with a harder edge once

dismissed new age works as "music to receive massage therapy by"—an unkind judgment, I felt, until I discovered the song "Excalibur Returned" by the composer/performer Llewellyn in a collection, *Shiatsu* (1995), which was advertised as music to accompany massage.

5. This band's website reveals the somewhat disturbing fondness of the darker element of heavy metal music for the Arthurian legend. The site includes a report on Skrewdriver's participation in a 1991 event called "Return to Camelot," which consisted of three days of political lessons, speeches and music on "white power" themes.

6. Most subsequent recordings of the song have been jazz instrumentals, and although Jolson and Vincent Rose are credited as composers, they were subjected to one of the first lawsuits over pop music composition when Giacomo Puccini brought charges that the song's melody was taken from an aria in his *Tosca*. Jolson and Rose each paid Puccini $25,000.

Works Consulted

Campbell, Michael. *And the Beat Goes On: An Introduction to Popular Music in America 1840 to Today*. New York: Schirmer Books, 1996.

Clarke, Donald. *The Rise and Fall of Popular Music*. New York: St. Martin's Press, 1995.

Fisher, James. *Al Jolson: A Bio-bibliography*. Westport, Conn.: Greenwood Press, 1994.

Hamm, Charles. *Yesterdays: Popular Song in America*. New York: W.W. Norton, 1979.

Laing, Dave, Karl Dallas, Robin Denslow and Robert Shelton. *The Electric Muse: The Story of Folk into Rock*. London: Methuen, 1975.

Logan, Nick, and Bob Woffinden. *The Illustrated Encyclopedia of Rock*. New York: Harmony Books, 1977.

Rewa, Michael P. "The Matter of Britain in British and American Popular Music (1966–1990)." In Sally K. Slocum, ed. *Popular Arthurian Traditions*. Bowling Green, Ohio: Bowling Green State University Press, 1992: 104–110.

Taylor, Timothy Dean. *Global Pop: World Music, World Markets*. New York: Routledge, 1997.

Woods, Frederick, ed. *The Oxford Book of English Traditional Verse*. Oxford: Oxford University Press, 1983.

Information on the music cited is from the recordings themselves and Internet websites of record companies and musicians. Other useful websites have been Jerome V. Reel's "Arthurian Musical Theatre: A Listing" on the Camelot Project site (www.lib.rochester.edu/camelot/acbibs/reel.html), Keir J. Howell's "The Arthurian Music List" (www.geocities.com/SunsetStrip/Palladium/7195/arthur/arthur.html), The All Music Guide (www.allmusic.com), The Ultimate Band List (www.ubl.com), and various commercial sites.

Discography of Popular Arthurian Music (and Works with Titles Suggesting Arthurian Content/Inspiration)

The following list has been extracted from *The Arthurian Annals*, a work in progress by the author and Phillip C. Boardman in which more complete information is furnished. Descriptive terms in quotation marks are from the original sources. Unseen works are asterisked.

Individual Songs

Agnel, Henri. "Tristan et Yseult: Improvisation," *Italian Stamps of 14th Century* (1998), Al Sur. [France] "World music."*

Alexandrakis, Eric. "Sir Gawain and the Green Knight," *I.V. Catatonia* (2000), Y & T Music. [USA] "Experimental pop music."*

Alke, Bjorn. "Holy Grail" (comp. Lars Gullin), *Forever Lulu* (1995), Dragon Records. [Sweden] Jazz.*

Allen, Richard and Kirby Shelstad. "Merlin's Suite," *Peaceful Solutions* (1984), Love Circle Music, PS-327. [USA] New age instrumental.

Amon Düül. "Merlin," *Pyragony X* (1976). [Germany] "Progressive rock/Kraut rock."*

Amorphis. "Grails Mysteries" (comp. Esa Holopainen), *The Karelian Isthmus* (1992), Relapse Records. [Finland] "Melodic doom music."

An Triskell. "Tristan hag Isild" and "Viviana" (comp. H. Queffeleant), *Harpe Celtique* (1977), Le Chant du Monde, LDX 74640. [France] "Traditional/folk-inspired music."

Annegarn, Dick. "Lancelot," *The Best of Dick Annegarn* (1998), Poly. [France] Jazz.*

Anúna. "The Fisher King," *Deep Dead Blue* (1996), Claddagh Records. [Ireland] Contemporary folk/choral music.*

Aquarium. "Giniver" (comp. Boris Grebenshikov), *Triangle* (1994). [Russia] Rock music.*

Arkenstone, David. "Guinevere's Tears," *Wind and Reed* (1972), Narada Records. [USA] New age instrumental.*

_____. "The Dragon's Breath" and "The Quest of Culhwch," *The Celtic Book of Days* (1998), Windham Hill Records, 01934-11246-2. [USA] New age instrumental.

Aston, Michael. "Avalon SW 10," *Why Me Why This Why Now* (1995), Triple X Records. [UK] "Subdued rock music."*

Attila the Stockbroker. "Camelot by Numbers" (comp. John Baine), *The Siege of Shoreham* (c1992), Shellshock Records. [UK]*

Avalon. "Tintagel," *Second Sight* (1998), Avalon Records. [UK] "Celtic folk rock."*

Bad News. "Excalibur," *Bad News* (1989), Atlantic Records. [UK] "Musical parody."*

Baez, Joan. "Sweet Sir Galahad," *One Day at a Time* (1969), Vanguard Recording Society, VSD-79310. [USA] Contemporary folk music.

Ball, Patrick. "The Ram on Arthur's Mountain" (comp. Lawrence Davis), *Celtic Harp: From a Distant Time* (1983), Fortuna Records, 17011. [USA] Traditional folk music.

The Banded Geckos. "Ode to Camelot" (comps. Tim Taylor and Eveline Taylor), *Gecko Canyon* (2000). [USA] Contemporary folk music.*

Barone, Richard. "Guinevere," *Between Heaven and Cello* (1994). Re-released by Line, 1997. [Germany] Rock instrumental.*

Barrett, Ruth and Cyntia Smith. "Apples of Avalon," *The Heart Is the Only Nation* (1991). [USA] New age vocal.

Basho, Robbie. "The Grail and the Lotus," *The Grail and the Lotus* (1965), Takoma Records. [USA] Contemporary folk instrumental.*

Beck, Christophe. "Queen Guinevere," *Guinevere* (1999), RCA Victor, 63545. [USA] Instrumental from film soundtrack.

Beltane Fire. "Excalibur (I Believe)" and "King Arthur's Cave" (comp. Clint Bradley and Carlo Edwards), *Different Breed* (1985), CBS Records, 26582. [UK] Pop music.

Berry, Heidi. "Holy Grail," *Miracle* (1996), Warner Bros., 46020. [USA] Folk rock.*

Berry, Jay Scott. "Avalon," *Concept for a Dream* (1992), CSI, 2001. [USA] New age instrumental.

Berthelot, Jean-Luc Hervé. "The Flight of Merlin (from Killarous to Salisbury)," *Tales: Stonehenge for Eternity* (1997), Somewhere in Time Records. [France] New age music.

Bessler, Gerd. "Sir Galahad's Sunburn," *Under the Flying Violin* (c1997), Erden, M63646. [Germany] Progressive jazz.*

Big Fella. "Merlin," *Good to Go* (c1995). Rock music.*

Blackmore's Night. "Avalon" (comp. Ritchie Blackmore), *Under a Violet Moon* (1999), Platinum Entertainment, 15095-3741-2. [UK/USA] Contemporary folk music.

Blaspheme. "Excalibur," *Blaspheme* (1983). [France] Heavy metal music.*

Blind Guardian. "A Past and Future Secret," "The Script for My Requiem" and "Mordred's Song," *Imaginations from the Other Side* (1995), Virgin. [Germany] Heavy metal music.

Blitzkrieg. "The Legend" (comps. Brian Ross and Glenn S. Howes), *The Mists of Avalon* (1998), Neat Metal Records, NM032. [UK] Heavy metal music.

Blonker. "Merlin" (comp. Dieter Gieke), *Musik Für Die Seele* (1998), Poly. [Germany] New age music.*

Bogle, Eric. "Lancelot and Guinevere," *Singing the Spirit Home* (1986), Larriken Records, LRF 186. [Australia] Contemporary folk music.

Bok, Muir and Trickett. "Merlin's Waltz" (comp. Kathy De Francis), *Language of the Heart* (c1994). [USA] Popular vocal music.

Bond, Graham. "Return of Arthur," *Holy Magick* (1971), Mercury Records. [UK] Urban blues.

Braheny, Kevin and Tim Clark. "Merlin's Last Voyage," *The Spell* (1996), Hearts of Space, 11065-2. [USA] New age instrumental.

The Breeze Brass Band. "Excalibur (Sword of Justice)" (comp. Jan Van der Roost), *Excalibur* (c1998), Tokyo Kosei. [Japan] Band arrangement.*

Britt, Pat. "Tristan," *Starrsong* (1976), Catalyst Records, CAT-7612. [USA] "Jazz fusion music."

Broguière, Patrick. "King Arthur," *Icônes* (1996), Musea Records. [France] Progressive rock instrumental.*

Bruner, Karen. "Taliesin's Daughter," *Taliesin's Daughter* (1986), Songbird Unlimited. [USA] New age instrumental.

Bruntnell, Peter. "Camelot in Smithereens," *Camelot in Smithereens* (1997), Almos. [UK] "Alternate country rock."*

Burger, Jorg and Mike Ink. "Avalon," *Las Vegas* (1998), Matador Records. [USA] Rock music.*

Burmer, Richard. "Tristan and the Book," *Miramar Tea* (1996), Miramar Records, 23081. New age instrumental.*

Burning River Brass. "Of Kingdoms and Glory" (comp. Anthony Di Lorenzo), *Of Knights and Castles* (1999), Dorian Recordings. [USA] Five-movement band arrangement.*

Buskin, David and Robin Batteau. "Lancelot's Song," *Buskin and Batteau* (1988), Single Wing Records, CD 2012. Contemporary folk music.*

Byrd, Donald. "King Arthur," *Landmarks* (1998), 32 Jazz Records, 60412-32080-2. [USA] Jazz instrumental.

Caddick, Bill. "Gawain and Ragnell," *Reasons Briefely Set Down by Th'author to Perswade Every One to Sing* (1979), Highway Records, SHY 7006. [UK] Contemporary folk music.

California, Randy. "Camelot," *Restless* (1985), Vertigo 19. [USA] Folk rock.*

Calloway. "Sir Lancelot," *All the Way* (1989), Epic Records. [USA] "Urban dance music."*

"Camelot Rag" (comp. William Perry), *Mark Twain* (1994), Premier, 1012. [USA] Song from soundtrack album.*

"Camelounge" (wr. Gerard Alessandrini), *Forbidden Broadway: The Unoriginal Cast Recording, Vol. 3* (1994), DRG Records. [USA] Musical parody.*

Carlyle, Jackie. "You're the Sexiest Man Alive," *Souls in the Breeze* (1999). [USA] Popular vocal.

Carter, Dave and Tracy Grammer. "Lancelot," *When I Go* (1997). [USA] Contemporary folk music.

Carter, Jan. "Lament of Tristan," *Where Angels Fly* (1994), Larriken Records. [Australia] Traditional instrumental.*

Cement. "King Arthur," *Man with the Action Hair* (1994), Dutch East India Trading, DE 12038-2. [USA] Heavy metal music.

Cetera, Peter. "The End of Camelot," *One Clear Voice* (1995), River North, 1110. [USA] Popular vocal.

Cipelli, Roberto. "Morgana" and "Avalon," *Moona Moore* (1989), Splasc(h) Records, H 173. [Italy] Jazz instrumentals.*

Climax. "Merlin," *Climax* (1973), Rocky Road Records, RR-3506. [USA] "Soft rock."*

Cocteau Twins. "Grail Overfloweth" (comps. Robin Guthrie, Will Heggie and Elizabeth Fraser), *Garlands* (1982), Capitol Records, CDP-7-96415-2. [USA] "Art rock."

Coe, Peter and Chris Coe. "The Wizard of Alderley Edge," *Open the Door and Let Us In* (1972), Trailer Records, LER 2077. [UK] Folk music.

Commander. "Knights of the Round Table" (comps. Dave Macias and Jon Natisch), *High n' Mighty* (1987), Iron Works Records, IW 1028. [USA] Heavy metal music.

Cornerboys. "Rose of Avalon" (comp. Rob Currie), *Dukes of Granville: Live at the Split Cow* (1996), Motrad Music. [Canada] "Celtic traditional music."*

Council, Maggie. "Holy Grail," *Shaking the Hive* (c1995). [USA] Popular vocal.*

Court, Susan. "Sir Galahad," *High Relief* (1998), Fundeling Productions. [USA] "Folk-pop."

Cradle of Filth. "Haunted Shores," *Dusk and Her Embrace* (1997), Music for Nations. [UK] "Gothic romantic metal music."

Crosby, Stills and Nash. "Guinnevere" (comp. David Crosby), *Crosby, Stills and Nash* (1969), Atlantic Recording Corp., SD 19117. [USA] Folk rock.

Cross, Christopher. "Walking in Avalon," *Walking in Avalon* (1998), CMC International. [USA] Pop rock.

d.i.g. "Merlin's Muse," *Speakeasy* (1995), Polygram Records. [Australia] Jazz.*

Dagda. "Merlin's Cave" (comps. Reg Keating and Phillip O'Reilly), *Underworld* (2000), Paras Recording, 1104. [Ireland] New age music.*

Dale, Andrea D. "The Lady of Avalon," *A Step Out of Time* (1998), Merlyn Productions. [USA] New age music.

Dale, Heather. "The Prydwen Sails Again" and "The Trial of Lancelot," *Light of the North* (1996), Amphisbaena Music. [Canada] Contemporary folk music.

_____. "Culhwch and Olwen" and "Tristan and Isolt," *White Rose* (1997), [Canada] Contemporary folk music.

Darvill, Martin. "In Search of the Holy Grail," *The Greatest Show on Earth* (1999), Mystic Records, Pen 004. [UK] "Progressive rock."*

Deacon Brody. "Excalibur," *Songs from a City of Marigolds* (1998), Deacon Brody Music. [USA] Rock music.*

Dead Can Dance. "Tristan" (comp. Lisa Gerrard), *Toward the Within* (1994), 4AD Records, 45769-2. [USA] "Progressive art rock."

De Canck, Philippe. "Crusades and the Search for the Holy Grail," "Holy Grail" and "Knights of the Holy Grail," *Voyage of the Spirit* (1995), Madacy Records, 5658. [UK] New age instrumentals.*

Deep Purple. "Listen, Learn, Read On" (comps. Ritchie Blackmore, Jon Lord and Rod Evans), *The Book of Taliesyn* (1968), Tetragrammaton, 107. [UK] Rock music.

Distant Oaks. "Iseult of the Swallow's Hair" (comp. Deborah White), *Dance to Bright Steel* (1994), Northern Wind Recordings. [USA] Contemporary folk music.

Doan, John. "Castle Dinas Bran: Procession of the Holy Grail" and "St. Joseph Arrives in Avalon," *Wayfarer* (1999), Hearts of Space. [USA] New age instrumentals.

Donovan [Leitch]. "Guinevere," *Sunshine Superman* (1966), Pye Records, NLP 18181. [UK] Folk rock.

Douglas, Bill. "Lady of the Lake," *Songs of Earth and Sky* (1998), Hearts of Space. [USA] New age music.*

Drama. "Excalibur," *Drama* (1995). [France] Progressive rock.*

Duca, Curd. "Tristan," *Elevator* (1998), Mille Plateaux. [France] New age music.*

Dutch. "King Arthur" (comp. Sean T. Starbuck), *Brilliance for a Better Future* (1994), Silent Records, 9455. [USA] Song on a compilation album of "rave" dance music by various artists.*

Electrafixion. "Holy Grail," *Lowdown* (1995), Spacejunk Records, YZ977CD. [UK] "Alternative rock music."*

Eshuijs, Margriet. "Merlin," Shadow Dancing (c1995). [Netherlands] Popular vocal music.*

"Eternal Dream of Avalon," *A New Age in Relaxation* (1994). Uncredited New age music.*

Evans, Chris and David Hanselmann. "Glastonbury, Temple of the Stars" and "Cadbury Castle, King Arthur's Camelot," *Stonehenge* (1980), Warner Music. [Germany] "Symphonic rock."*

F.C.B. "Excalibur 2000 Radio Edit," "Merlinmelodic Song" and "Excalibur 2000" (comps. M. Christofori and C. Favilla), *Excalibur 2000* (1998), Colossal Records of Australia, COLCDS97. [Australia] "Techno-rock music."*

Farris, Gene. "Grail," *This Is My Religion* (2000), Soma Records. [USA] "Jazzy house music."

Fast Forward Music Project. "At the Round Table" (comp. Alexander Borodin, arr. Volker Barber), *Excalibur* (1993), Edel Company, EDL 2727-2. [Germany] Progressive rock.

Finn MacCool. "Glastonbury" (comps. Peter McGowan and Kathleen McGowan), *Sherdana's Hand* (1998). [USA] Celtic rock.*

Flynt, Clif, Carol Roper and Barb Riedel. "Sword in the Stone," *Let's Have a Filksing* (1995), Wail Songs, WS042. [USA] Contemporary folk music.

Fogerty, Tom. "Mystic Isle Avalon," *Zephyr National* (1974), Fantasy Records, F-9448. [USA] Rock music.*

Foster, Frank. "Square Knights of the Round Table," *Here & Now* (1976), Catalyst Records, CAT-7613. [USA] Jazz.*

Fripp, Robert. "A Connecticut Yankee in the Court of King Arthur," *Show of Hands* (1991), Editions. [USA] Progressive rock.

Froese, Edgar. "Sad Merlin's Sunday," *Goblin's Club* (1996), Castle Records. [Germany/USA] "Electronic orchestral pop music."*

Galahad Acoustic Quintet. "Sir Galahad," *Not All There* (1995), Avalon Records, GAQ1CD. [UK]*

Gilkyson, Eliza. "Key to Avalon," *Undressed* (1994), Revelizations. Contemporary folk music. [USA]*

Goggins. "Excalibur" (comp. Dan Lord), *Goggins* (1995). [USA] Rock music.*

Grave Digger. "Keeper of the Holy Grail," *Knights of the Cross* (1998), BMGG, M59669. [Germany] Heavy metal music.

Grebenshikov, Boris. "Death of King Arthur," *Radio Silence* (1989), CBS Records, 44364. [USA] Folk rock.

Grinder. "Mordred," *Nothing Is Sacred* (1991), Noise Records, N0165-2. [Germany] Heavy metal music.*

Guinevere. "Guinevere," *One Sailor Dies* (c1995), D&A Productions. [Netherlands] "English Nether folk music."*

"Guinevere Among the Grapefruit Peels" (comps. Mira J. Spektor and June Siegel), *The Housewives' Cantata* (1981), Original Cast Records. [USA] Song from soundtrack of musical review.

Gullin, Lars. "Merlin," *Late Summer 1945–55, Vol. 3* (1959), Dragon Records. [Sweden] Jazz.*

Habian, Cliff. "Merlin," *Tonal Paintings* (1988), Milestone Records, 9161. [USA] Jazz.

Happy the Man. "Merlin of the High Places" (comp. Frank Wyatt), *Death's Crown* (1999), Cuneiform Records, 55015. [USA] Progressive rock music.*

Harrison, Michael. "Bells from the Garden of Avalon," *From Ancient Worlds* (1993), New Albion Records. [USA] New age instrumental.*

Hayes, David. "Guns of Avalon," *Sunbathing in Leningrad* (1975), Gold Castle Records, 171-012-1. [USA] New age music.*

Heart. "Back to Avalon" (comps. Kit Hain, Ann Wilson and Nancy Wilson), *Desire Walks On* (1993), Capitol Records. [USA] Pop rock.

Hedgehog Pie. "Camlann's Battle," *Green Lady* (1975), Rubber Records, 014. [UK] Folk music.*

The Hellecasters. "King Arthur's Dream" (comp. Jerry Donahue), *Return of the Hellecasters* (1993), Pacific Arts Audio, PAAD-5055. [USA] Instrumental rock music.

Hollienea. "Vision of the Grail," *Vision of the Grail* (1996), Waterark Records, 0001-2. [USA] New age instrumental.

Hoppé, Michael. "Avalon," *Quiet Storms* (1988), Gaia/PolyGram Records, 13-9010-2. [USA] New age music.*

Hunters and Collectors. "Holy Grail" (comp. Mark Seymour), *Cut* (1993), BMG Records, M10625. [Australia] Rock music.

Idha [Övelius]. "Fields of Avalon," *Troublemaker* (1997), Creation Records, M33093. [UK/Sweden] Folk rock.*

If. "Merlin, the Magic Man" (comp. Cliff Davies), *Tea Break Is Over—Back on Your 'Eads* (1974), Capitol Records, ST-11344. [UK/USA] Progressive rock music.*

Innocent Nixon. "Camelot," *Relax and Enjoy an Evening with...* (c1995). [USA] Rock music.*

Jag Panzer. "The Moors" (comp. Harry Conklin), *The Age of Mastery* (1998), Century Media Records. [USA] Heavy metal music.

Joe and Bing. "Looking for Camelot" (comps. Joe Thomas and Bing Bingham), *Joe and Bing* (1974), RCA Victor, APL1-1499. [USA] Rock music.*

Johnson, Larry. "Queen Guinevere and Sir Lance," *The View of San Francisco* (1994), Salty Dog Records. [USA] Contemporary folk music.*

Jolson, Al. "Avalon" (comps. Al Jolson, Vincent Rose and B.G. De Sylva), Columbia Records, A-2995. [USA] Popular vocal music.

Jones, Brad. "Knights of the Round Table," *Live at Five* (1991), Flat Five Press, FFP-1111. [USA] Instrumental music.*

Joy, Greg. "Lady Guinevere," *Textures* (1986), Midsummer Music, MM130. [Canada] New age instrumental music.

Kadwaladyr. "Morgan," "Avalon" and "Blues evit Merlin," *The Last Hero* (1995), Musea Records, LC 9709. [France] Folk rock music.*

Kamelot. "Siege," *Siege Perilous* (1998), Noise Records, N0297-2. [Germany] "Fantasy metal music."*

Kamm, Paul and Eleanore MacDonald. "The Walls of Caerleon" and "The Lady of Shallot," *Unbroken Chain* (1989), Freewheel Records, FR102. [USA] Contemporary folk music.

Kamminga, Judy. "Secret Hearts" and "Isle of Avalon," *Visions of Freedom* (1998), [self-produced] JKCD1. Contemporary folk music.

Kane, Mancy A'lan. "Camelot," *Paper Moon* (1998), Alliance Music, 7927992. [UK] Popular vocal music.

Kaplansky, Lucy. "Guinevere" (comp. Robin Batteau), *The Tide* (1994), Red House Records, RHR 65. [USA] Contemporary folk music.

Karukas, Gregg. "Avalon," *You'll Know It's Me* (1995), Fahrenheit, 9510. [USA] Jazz.*

The Kiltie Band. "King Arthur's Quest," *The Kiltie Band* (c1997). [USA] Marching band music.*

Kissing Judas. "Guenevere," *Eternity* (1997), Baby Jane Records, BJ 89802-2. [USA] "Alternative rock music."

Koch, Greg. "Holy Grail," *Defenestrator* (1998). [USA] Progressive rock instrumental.*

Kokila. "Angels of Avalon" and "Merlin's Vision," *Celtic Angels* (1996), Astromusic. [USA] New age instrumental music.*

Kristianne, Krysia. "The Lady of Shalott," *Tyger and Other Tales: English Romantic Poetry Set to Music* (1996), Sentience Records, 70002. [USA] New age vocal music.

Lady Isadora. "Table Round," *Priestess of the Pentacle* (1990), Dance of Life Productions. [USA] New age music.*

Lauper, Cyndi. "Sisters of Avalon" (comps. Cyndi Lauper and Jan Pulsford), *Sisters of Avalon* (1997), Sony Music. [USA] Pop rock.

Legend. "Mordred," *Second Sight* (1993), Pagan Media, PMR CD/MC6. [UK] Rock music.*

Legion. "Merlin" (1986), Idlers Records, TI-1001. [USA] Single recording, rap music.

The Lemon Drops. "Guinevere," *Crystal Pure* (1985), Cicadelic Records, 984. [USA] "Psychedelic garage rock music."*

Lister, Anne. "La Folie Tristan," "The Lady of Shallott" and "Advent," *Spreading Rings* (1993), Hearthfire, HF002CD. [UK] Contemporary folk music.

_____. "A Flame in Avalon" and "Morte D'Arthur," *A Flame in Avalon* (1995), Hearthfire, HF003CD. [UK] Contemporary folk music.

Llewellyn. "Excalibur Returned," *Shiatsu* (1998), New World Music. [UK] New age instrumental music.*

_____. "Gawain and the Loathly Lady" and "Avalon—Place of Apples," *Celtic Legend* (1999), New World Music, NWC 472. [UK] New age music.

Loggins, Kenny. "Back to Avalon" (comps. Kenny Loggins, Peter Wolf and Nathan East), *Back to Avalon* (1988), Columbia Records, OC 40535. [USA] Pop rock.

Luke Slaters 7th plain. "Excalibur's Radar" (comp. Luke Slater), *My Yellow Wise Ring* (c1995). General Production Recordings. [USA] "Techno-rock music."*

Magical Strings. "Lament for Merlin" (comp. Pam Boulding), *Bell Off the Ledge* (1994), Flying Fish Records. [USA] "Folk, jazz and Celtic music."*

Mallett, David. "Arthur," *David Mallett* (1978), New World. [USA] Contemporary folk music.*

Malmsteen, Yngwie J. "Queen in Love," *Trilogy* (1986), Polydor. [UK/USA] "Heavy metal/classical rock music."

Manmademan and Tristan. "Purple Merlin," *Colours of Shiva/The Psychedelic T.I.P. Trip, Part 2* (c1998). [UK] Progressive rock on compilation album by various artists.*

Mansun. "The Holy Blood and the Holy Grail" (comp. Paul Draper), *She Makes My Nose Bleed* (1997), Parlophone, CDRS 6458. [UK] Rock music.*

Mantrawave. "Tower of Guinevere" (comps. Noel Boland and Fred Whitfield), *The Traveler* (1999), Aviator Records. [USA] Instrumental music.*

Marradi, Giovanni. "Lancelot," *Always* (c1995), Newcastle Entertainment. [USA] Popular instrumental music.*

Matheos, Jim and John Arch. "Fata Morgana," *Awaken the Guardian* (1986), Roadrunner Records. [USA] Heavy metal music.

McArthur, Doug and Garnet Rogers. "Merlin," *Doug McArthur with Garnett Rogers* (1989), Snow Goose Records, SGS 1116G. [Canada] Contemporary folk music.

McCain, Edwin. "Guinevere," *Honor Among Thieves* (1995), Atlantic Records, 92597. [USA] "Pop rock music."

The McCalmans. "Avalon" (comp. Nick Keir), *Ancestral Manoeuvres* (1984), MAC 003. [UK] Contemporary folk music.

McCloud, Brendan. "Lady of the Lake," *On the Edge of Time* (1999), Dream Time Records. [USA] Contemporary folk music.

McKane, Sumner. "Kansas to Camelot," *Pictures for Stories* (c1995).*

McKennitt, Loreena. "The Lady of Shalott," *The Visit* (1991), Warner Music Canada, WEA 17-51514. [Canada] Contemporary folk music.

Mecca Normal. "Excalibur" (comp. Jean Smith), *Who Shot Elvis?* (1997), Matador. [USA] Alternative rock music.

The Mekons. "King Arthur," *The Edge of the World* (1996), Quarterstick Records, QS 42. [UK/USA] "Punk rock music."

Micon. "Avalon" (comp. Marcus Reichard), *Dance of the Elves* (1997), Bluestar, 60042. [Germany] New age instrumental music.*

The Moody Blues. "Are You Sitting Comfortably?" (comps. Justin Hayward and Ray Thomas), *On the Threshold of a Dream* (1969), Deram, DES 18025. [UK] Orchestral rock music.

Mordred. "The Last Battle" (comps. Tim Ridley and Ed Lepper), *No Mortal Man* (1990). [UK] Rock music.*

Morgana Lefay. "Excalibur," *Knowing Just As I* (1993), Black Mark Records, 28. [Sweden] Heavy metal music.*

Morrison, Van. "Avalon of the Heart," *Enlightenment* (1990), Mercury Records, 847 100-2. [UK/USA] Pop rock.

Mortifee, Ann. "Merlin," *Born to Live* (1983), Jabula Records, 25 03361. [Canada] Popular vocal music.*

Motorpsycho. "Sonic Teenage Guinevere" (comp. Bent Sæther), *Blissard* (1996), Offaworld. [Norway] Alternative rock music.*

The New York Room. "The Mists of Avalon," *The New York Room: 1991–1995* (1996). [USA] "Gothic/ethereal music."

Nields, David and Nerissa. "Sweet Holy Grail," *Live at the Iron Horse Music Hall* (1993). [USA] Contemporary folk music.

Not Sensibles. "King Arthur," *Instant Punk Classics* (1994), Cherry Records. [UK] "Punk rock music."*

O'Connell, Maura. "Send the Whisper (to Avalon)" (comp. Thom Moore and Janie Cribbs), *Maura O'Connell* (1983), Ogham Records, BLB5007. [Ireland] Contemporary folk music.*

O'Connor, Frank. "Mystic Moon of Avalon" and "The Grail," *Mystic Moon of Avalon* (2000), New Earth Records. [USA] New age music.

Oldfield, Sally. "Merlin's Song," *Three Rings* (1994), BMG. [Germany] Contemporary folk music.*

Paradise, Danny, "Searching for the Holy Grail (Sail On)," *River of the Soul* (2000), V2 Records. [USA] Rock music.*

Parker, Sandra. "Guinevere's Lament," *Waters Wide* (1998), Parker Productions. [USA] Contemporary folk music.

Pavement. "Jackals, False Grails: The Lonesome Era" (comp. Stephen Malkmus), *Slanted and Enchanted* (1991), Matador Records. [USA] Art rock music.*

Pendragon. "Excalibur," *Fly High, Fall Far* (1984), EMI Records, ARRMP-001. [UK] Folk rock.*

Pentangle. "The Hunting Song," *Basket of Light* (1969), Transatlantic Records. [UK] Contemporary folk music.

Phantom. "Merlin," *Phantom's Divine Comedy* (1974), Capitol Records. [USA] Rock music.

Pillow, Charles. "The Trouble with Camelot," *Currents* (1998), Challenge, 73108. Jazz.*

Pine, Courtney. "Holy Grail, Pt. 1–3," *To the Eyes of Creation* (1992), Fourth and Broadway Records, 444054. [USA] Jazz.*

Pintar, Judith. "Bedd Taliesin" and "In Defense of Guenevere," *Celtic Harp: Secrets from the Stone* (1985), Sona Gaia Productions, 123. [Netherlands/USA] Contemporary folk music.

Plantastik. "Merlin Street Magic" (comp. B. Matthew), *London Electronica* (1997), Kickin, 31. [UK] Electronic rock music.*

Pluck Theatre. "Merlin" (comp. Doug Cowan), *Five Finger Disco* (c1995), Bad Habits Music. [USA] "Pop rock music."*

Powers, Laura. "My Avalon," *Legends of the Goddess* (1998), Punch Records. [USA] New age music.*

Pringle, Peter. "Merlin's Dance," *Rain Upon the Sea* (1981), A&M Records, SP 9054. [Canada] Rock music.*

Prophetess. "Avalon," *Prophetess* (1993), Cleopatra Records, 1592. [USA] Alternative rock music.*

Pur. "Merlin's Rock" (comps. Ingo Reidl and Hartmut Engler), *Pur* (1987), Intercord. [Germany] "Pop-rock music."*

Purple Shadow. "Excalibur" (comp. Han Uil), *Excalibur* (1998), Purple Shadow Records. [Netherlands] Folk rock.

Quartz. "Avalon," *Against All Odds* (1983), Heavy Metal, 9. [UK] "House rock music."*

Rakatan. "Song for Merlin," *Better Than That* (1990), Auriga Music, AU-19. [USA] Rock music.*

Raven. "Holy Grail" (comp. John Gallagher), *Everything Louder* (1997), WEA M28566. [Germany] Heavy metal music.*

Real Magic. "Arthur's Lullaby" and "Avalon Is Rising!" (comp. Isaac Bonewits), *Avalon Is Rising* (1992), Ar aDraíocht Féin, ADF 2. [USA] New age music.

Renaissance. "Island of Avalon" (comp. Michael Dunford), *Songs from Renaissance Days* (1997), HTD Records. [UK] Folk rock music.*

Renbourn, John. "Morgana," *Sir John Alot of Merrie Englandes Musyk Thyng and Ye Grene Knyghte* (1968), Transatlantic Records. [UK] Contemporary folk music.

Rong. "Lancelot in Vain" (comp. Timoth E. Gard), *Iceberg in the Hot Tub* (1999), Quilted Fish Records. [USA] Pop rock music.*

Roth, Uli Jon. "The Wings of Avalon," *Sky of Avalon: Prologue to the Symphonic Legends* (1996), Imprint. [Germany] Instrumental rock music.*

Roxy Music. "Avalon" (comp. Bryan Ferry), *Avalon* (1982), Warner Bros. Records, 23686-1. [USA/UK] Pop rock.

Ruby. "King Arthur's March," *Rock 'n' Roll Madness* (1978), PBR 7004. [USA] Rock music.*

Runnalls, Jana. "Spirit of Avalon," *Ancestral Dream* (1985), Stroppy Cow Records, SC300. [UK] New age music.

Ryan Kisor Quartet. "Sir Lancelot" (comp. Justin Kisor), *Point of Arrival* (2000), Criss Cross Jazz, 1180. [USA] Jazz.*

Scarymeanie Demons. "Merlin (Free the Stone)," *Dragon's Breath* (1998), RP Media, CDRPM0035. [UK] Pop rock.*

Schoof, Manfred and Paul Shigihara. "Tristan," *Stadtgarten Series, Vol. 7* (1993), Jazz Haus Musik. [Germany] Jazz.*

Seffer, Yochk'o. "Excalibur," *Rétrospective* (1997), Frémeaux & Associés, FA 070. [France] Jazz.*

Shimmer. "Holy Grail" (comp. Chris Gilmartin), *Credo* (1996), Jenn Records, 102. [USA] Rock music.

Skrewdriver. "Excalibur," *Warlord* (1988). [UK] Heavy metal music.*

Sky. "Tristan's Magic Garden," *Sky* (1979), Ariola Records. [UK] Instrumental rock music.*

Smashing Pumpkins. "To Sheila" (comp. Billy Corgan), *Adore* (1998), Virgin Records, CDHUT 51. [USA] Rock music.

Snuff. "Guinevere," *In the Fishtank* (1999), Konkurrent. [UK] "Punk rock music."

The Soil Bleeds Black. "Behold Thou My Crest," "The Charm of Making" and "He Shall Be King" (comps. Mike Riddick and Mark Riddick), *The Kingdom and Its Fey* (1996), Cruel Moon International. [USA/Sweden] Contemporary folk music.*

_____. "Gromer Somer Jour" (comps. Mike Riddick and Mark Riddick), *The Dark Ages* (1997), Arborlon Music. [Netherlands] Folk song on compilation album by various artists.*

_____. "Avalon (Shore and Sea)" and "The Temptation of Mordred" (comps. Mike Riddick and Mark Riddick), *March of the Infidels* (1997), Draenor Productions, DPR 002. [Netherlands] Contemporary folk music.*

_____. "Next Morning He Must Away," "A Song for Guinevere" and "Journey's End" (comps. Mike Riddick and Mark Riddick), *The Maiden, the Minstrel, and the Magician* (1998), Dark Age Productions, DAP 024. [USA] Contemporary folk music.*

_____. "Some Sweet Sorrow Act II (The Lady in the Lake)" (comps. Mike Riddick and Mark Riddick), *Baited Breath* (1999), Live Bait Recording Foundation. [USA] Folk song on compilation album by various artists.*

Somber Blessings. "Neath Mountain Sleep" (comp. Scott Randall), *Legend* (1998). [USA] "Traditional death metal music."*

South Shore Circus Concert Band. "Sir Galahad" (comp. Lawrence King), *Sounds of the Circus, Vol. 3* (1991). [USA] Band arrangement.*

Spielberg, Robin. "Return of a Knight," *Heal of the Hand* (1994), North Star Records, NS0065. [USA] New age instrumental music.

Spring. "Grail," *S/T* (1998), Reper. [Germany] Rock music.*

Springfield, Rick. "Guinevere," *Beautiful Feelings* (1984), Mercury Records, 824107-2. [USA] Pop rock.

Starcastle. "Lady of the Lake," *Starcastle* (1992), Sony. Progressive rock.*

Stewart, Al and Shot in the Dark. "Merlin's Time" (comp. Al Stewart and Peter White), *24 Carrots* (1980), Arista Records, AL 9520. [USA/UK] Pop rock.

Stonehenge. "King Arthur" and "Excalibur," *Tales of Old Britain* (1998), Hobgoblin Records. [Russia/Canada] "Folk metal music."

Stormwitch. "Excalibur," *Walpurgis Night* (1991), Laser Light. [Germany] Heavy metal music.*

The Strawbs. "The Vision of the Lady of the Lake" (comp. Dave Cousins), *Dragonfly* (1970), A&M Records. [UK] "Progressive folk rock."

Superdrag. "She Is a Holy Grail" (comp. John Davis), *Head Trip in Every Key* (1998), Elektra Entertainment. [USA] Rock music.*

Sweet. "Anthem (Lady of the Lake)," *Level Headed* (1978). [UK] Pop rock.*

The Tansads. "Camelot," *Up the Shirkers* (1993), Musicdisk S.A. [UK] "Folk punk orchestral music."*

Taxi Mauve. "Merlin's Time," *Far Off Fields* (1994), Keltia Musique. [France] Contemporary Celtic music.*

Taylor, Allan. "The Boy and the Mantle," *The Lady* (1971), United Artists, UAS 29275. [UK] Folk music.*

Thiel, Lisa. "Lady of the Lake," *Lady of the Lake* (1992), Ladyslipper Records, LR112. [USA] New age music.

Tingstad and Rumbel. "Guinevere's Lament" (comp. Nancy Rumbel), *Pastorale* (1997), Narada Records, 61061. [USA] New age instrumental music.

Too Much Joy. "Hey Merlin" (comp. Tim Quirk), *Gods & Sods* (1999), Sugar Fix Records. [USA] Rock music.

Totten, Lee. "Camelot," *Sleeping Alone* (1966), Ninibudu Music, NB4242. [USA] Contemporary folk music.

Tremor. "Avalon," *Ear Protection Required* (1995). [Netherlands] "Atmospheric metal music."*

Trisquel. "O Chapeu de Merlin" (comp. Carlos Corral), *O Chapeu de Merlin* (1992), Sonifolk, CDJ 1023. [Spain] Contemporary folk instrumental.

Troika. "Gwenhwyfar" (comp. David Arkenstone), *Goddess* (1996), Enso Records, ND-62804. [USA] New age instrumental music.

Tyrannosaurus Rex. "Stones for Avalon" (comp. Marc Bolan), *Unicorn* (1969), Regal Zonophone, SLRZ 1007. [UK] Folk rock.

Valgardena. "Avalon" (comp. Jeff Leonard), *Migration* (1997), Polygram, 534470. [USA] New age instrumental.*

Velvet Viper. "Merlin," "Perceval," "Parsifal" and "King Arthur," *Velvet Viper* (c1995). Rock music.*

Vollenweider, Andreas. "Song of Isolde" (comp. Eliza Gilkyson), *Eolian Minstrel* (1993), Capitol Records. [USA] Instrumental music.*

Wagner, Adrian. "Glastonbury Grail Meditations," *Ambient Collection, Vol. 1* (1992), The Music Suite, MS 114. [UK] New age instrumental.

Walton, Jake. "Tristan's Song," *Songs from the Gurdy-Man* (1979). Contemporary folk music.*

_____. "The Wanderer (Merlin's Exile)," *Sunlight and Shade* (1983), Folk Freak Records, FF 4012. [Germany] Contemporary folk music.

The Watersons. "King Arthur's Servants," *New Voices* (1965), Topic Records, 12T125. [UK] Folk music.*

Webb, Guire. "Merlin's Bride," *Tonight* (1995), Red Barn Records. [USA] Instrumental music.

White Animals. "Tristan's Woe," *White Animals* (1986), Dread Beat. [USA] Rock music.*

Wilson, Denise. "Chevaliers de la Table Ronde," *Souvenirs du Temps Passé* (1991), Marimac Recordings, 4007. Traditional folk music.

Wine Field. "Holy Grail" (comps. Shawn Tooley and Jimmy Landry), *Wine Field* (1998), Watchtower Records. [USA] Rock music.*

Wizards. "Memories of Avalon" (comp. Charles Dalla), *Beyond the Sight* (1998). [Brazil] "Melodic/progressive metal music."

Workman, Reggie. "Half of My Soul (Tristan's Love Theme)," *Cerebral Caverns* (1995), Postcards. Jazz.*

Zeltsman, Nancy. "Merlin I & II" (comp. Andrew Thomas), *Woodcuts* (1993), GM Recordings, GM2043. [USA] Instrumental music.

Albums

Alkæmy. *The Merlin Mystery* (comp. Julia Taylor Stanley), (1998), Earthtone Records, ETD-7803. [USA] New age music.

Ayreon. *The Final Experiment* (comp. Arjen Anthony Lucassen), (1995), Transmission Records, TM-110. [Netherlands] Rock opera.

_____. *Into the Electric Castle* (comp. Arjen Anthony Lucassen) (1998), Transmission Records, TM-014. [Netherlands] Rock music.

Blacklight Braille. *Zauzomank Castle* (comp. T. Owen Knight) (1984), LP 710. [USA] Narrative with "fringe rock music."*

_____. *The Carbonek Album* (comp. T. Owen Knight) (1991), LP 727. [USA] Rock music.*

_____. *Camelot Palace* (comp. T. Owen Knight) (1993), CD 605. [USA] Rock music.*

_____. *Carmarthen* (comp. T. Owen Knight) (1993), CD 603. [USA] Rock music.*

_____. *Avallon Tower* (comp. T. Owen Knight) (1997), CD 611. [USA] Rock music.*

Broguière, Patrick. *Brocéliande* (1994), Musea Records, MP 3018. [France] Instrumental music.

Calverley, Roger. *Avalon* (1992), Oasis Productions, OAS 1006. [Canada] Instrumental music.

Caudel, Stephen. *The Earth in Turquoise: Episodes in the Life of Arthur* (1996), Dark Sea Records, DSR1. [UK] "Rock symphony."

Clarke, Caroline Anne Marie. *Sir Gawain and the Green Knight* (1995), Over the Moon Productions, OTM 46. [UK] Narration with traditional music.

_____. *The Celtic Quest for the Grail* (1995), Over the Moon Productions, OTM 47. [UK] Narration with new age music.

Cooper, Simon. *Celtic Heart: The Story of Tristan and Iseult* (1996), Oreade Music, OMM 5441-2. [Netherlands] New age instrumental music.

Dale, Heather. *The Kingsword* (1997), Amphisbaena Music. [Canada] Contemporary folk music.

_____. *The Trial of Lancelot* (2000), Amphisbaena Music. [Canada] Contemporary folk music.

Dore, Valerie. *The Legend* (comps. Marco Tansinsi and Simona Zanini), (1986), EMI Italiana. [Italy] Vocals/urban dance music.

Edgecomb, Diane. *New Age Gawain & The Green Knight* (1995), Wilderwalks Productions. [USA] Satirical narration with music.

Enid. *Enid* (comp. Martin Wiese), (1997), Elven Witchcraft. [Latvia/Germany] "Epic, atmospheric, bombastic medieval/fantasy metal music."

The Enid. *In the Region of the Summer Stars* (1976), EMI/BUK. [UK] "Classical rock music."*

Fervant, Thierry. *Légends of Avalon* (1988), Real Music, RM 1831. [USA] New age instrumental music.*

Gardner, Kay. *Avalon* (1989), Ladyslipper Records, LRC 106. [USA] New age instrumental music.

Goodall, Medwyn. *Excalibur* (1990), New World Cassettes, NWC 199. [UK] New age instrumental music.

_____. *Merlin* (1990), New World Cassettes, NWC 196. [UK] New age instrumental music.

_____. *Tintagel, Castle of Arthur* (1995), Oreade Music, OMM 5220-2. [Netherlands] New age instrumental music.

_____. *The Grail Quest* (1996), Oreade Music, OMM 5432-2. [Netherlands] New age instrumental music.

_____. *The Gift of Excalibur* (1996), Oreade Music, OMM 5433-2. [Netherlands] New age instrumental music.

_____. *The Fair Queen Guinevere* (1996), Oreade Music, OMM 5415-2. [Netherlands] New age instrumental music.

_____. *The Round Table* (1998), Oreade Music, OMM 5451-2. [Netherlands] New age instrumental music.

Grave Digger. *Excalibur* (comps. Chris Boltendahl and Uwe Lulis), (1999), Gun Records, 184. [Germany] Heavy metal music.

Green, Chris. *Quest for the Grail* (1996), New World Music, NWCD411. [UK] New age instrumental music.

Halloween. *Merlin* (1994), Musea Records, FGBG 4084AR. [France] "Progressive/classical rock music."

Haskell, Patrick. *Avalon: The King Will Come Again* (1990). [USA] Folk rock.*

Johnson, Jeff and Brian Dunning. *Music of Celtic Legends: The Bard and the Warrior* (1997), Windham Hill Records, 01934-11181. [USA] New age instrumentals.

Kayak. *Merlin* (comps. Ton Scherpenzeel and Irene Linders), (1981), Phongram/Vertigo Records 6423-432. [Netherlands] Progressive rock music.

Kerr, John. *Knights* (1984), TBN Records, JKPCD 310493. [Netherlands] New age instrumentals.

La Nef. *Perceval: La Quête du Graal, Vol. 1* (comp. Sylvain Bergeron), (1999), Dorian Recordings. [Canada/USA] Contemporary/traditional folk music.

Lambert, Lane. *Tristan and Iseult: A Celtic Love Story* (1999), LL-3162-2. [USA] "Celtic rock opera."

Lind, Helena and Michael Taylor. *The Magic World of Avalon: The Sound of Eternity* (1991). [Germany] New age music.*

Lister, Anne. *Root, Seed, Thorn and Flower* (1997), Hearthfire, HF004CD. [UK] Contemporary folk music.

Lyonesse. *Tristan de Lyonesse* (comps. Pietro Bianchi and Bernard Sever), (1976), PUD, PLD A 606A. [France] Contemporary folk music.

Mark, Jon. *Land of Merlin* (1992), Celestial Harmonies, Kucknuck 11094-2. [Germany/USA] New age instrumentals.

Martin, Philip. *Visions of Avalon* (c1995). New age music.*

McCullough, L.E. and T.H. Gillespie. *The Healing Cup: Guinevere Seeks the Grail* (1997), Ethos Productions. [USA] Musical score from a ballet.

Merlin's Arthur (comps. Colin Rudd, Nick Hill and others), (1995), Brenin Productions, 50-30082. [UK] Contemporary folk music.

Otterlei, Alex. *Arthur* (1994), DM Music, DMCD 1031. [Belgium] Instrumental music.

Schiff, Artie. *The World of King Arthur* (1992), Hypnovision/Audiovision, TM1. [USA] Instrumental music.

Shirra, Fiona. *Arthur and Guinevere: The Epic Arthurian Musical* (1991), AD 500. [USA] Soundtrack album.*

Shulman, Richard. *Keeper of the Holy Grail* (1999), Rich Heart Music. [USA] New age instrumentals.*

Simmons, Mike. *Dreams of Avalon* (1996), Music from the Mountains. [UK] New age instrumentals.

Simon, Alan. *Excalibur, La Légende des Celtes* (1999), LTC Tristar Sony Music France/Isis Music, TSR 492713. [France] Folk and orchestral rock.

_____. *Excalibur: Le Concert Mythique* (2000), Sony Music/Epic, EPC 4977012. [France] Concert version.

The Soil Bleeds Black. *May the Blood of Many a Valiant Knight Be Avenged.* Daenor Productions, DPR 004. [Netherlands] Contemporary folk music.

Stivell, Alan. *The Mist of Avalon* (1991), Disques Dreyfus, 191-010-2. [France] Contemporary folk music.

Tropa de Shock. *In the Blade of the Wind* (1998). [Brazil] "Classical heavy metal music."*

Tyler, Nick. *Arthur: The Once and Future King* (1995), Kindeane Records. [UK] Contemporary folk music.

Wagner, Adrian. *The Holy Spirit and the Holy Grail* (1993), The Music Suite, MS 118. [UK] New age instrumental music.

_____. *Genesis of the Grail Kings* (1999), Media Quest Records. [UK] New age instrumentals.*

Wakeman, Rick. *The Myths and Legends of King Arthur and the Knights of the Round Table* (1975), A&M Records, SP-4515. [UK/USA] Orchestral rock music.

Wheater, Tim. *The Enchanter* (1986), New World Music, NWC 118. [UK] New age instrumentals.

Zeitler, William Wilde. *The Passionate Quest: A Romance of the Grail* (1998), Eris Records. [USA] Instrumental music.

Zuffanti, Fabio and Victoria Heward. *Merlin: The Rock Opera* (2000), Iridea records, 2000-6-2 AB. [Italy] Rock opera.

Camelot in Comics

Jason Tondro

In recent years talented writers and artists have produced comics adaptations of *Beowulf*, Wagner's Ring cycle, and the saga of the Trojan War. It is not surprising that Arthur, whose popular footprint is larger than any of these rivals, also has a significant presence in comics. This marriage of comics and Arthurian legend is not new—to the contrary, it stretches back many decades to the dynamic birth of the comic book form, and through the many ups and downs of the comic book industry Arthur has continued to be a reliable mechanism for storytellers who want to connect quickly and powerfully with the popular audience. In the analysis that follows, a non-exclusionary emphasis has been placed on works that are easily accessible to the audience. Many rare comics from the 1930s and 40s, for example, contain Arthurian references, but few people can afford the time and money required to locate and purchase them. This leaves us with reprints and titles published in the last two decades.

Arthur's presence in comics can be broadly divided into five categories.

The Traditional Tale: These comics are faithful to the conventions of Arthurian romance. Arthur is King in Camelot and surrounded by familiar figures. New characters, especially the knight errant, may be introduced, but superheroic elements are kept to a minimum.

The Arthurian Toybox: Arthurian characters, items and places often appear in otherwise unrelated comics as allies, enemies, victims or objects of quest. These elements are typically wielded with great energy and fun, but with little concern for their literary pedigree.

Arthur as Translator: These stories are the reverse of Arthur's use as "toybox." Instead of Arthurian elements appearing in the superhero world, the superhero is "translated" into an Arthurian context. This includes

"Connecticut Yankee" stories and also "alternate history" tales in which the superhero exists naturally within the context of Arthur's Britain.

Arthur as Silent Collaborator: Arthurian symbols and themes—such as the boy king, the sword in the stone and the round table—are often used in a subtle and unspoken way within superheroic tales. The similarity in genres makes this a natural and effective tactic in an art form where space is at a premium.

Arthur Transformed: The current trend in Arthurian comics is to take him out of his traditional setting. "Return of the king" tales and stories which pick up after the death of Arthur are particularly common.

The Traditional Tale

When William Randolph Hearst went looking for a new comic strip he turned to Hal Foster, a man who had already gained considerable attention writing and drawing *Tarzan* for Edgar Rice Burroughs. In searching for a new subject to please the publishing magnate, Foster followed the lead of one of his chief artistic inspirations: Howard Pyle. Foster researched the Arthurian legend for eighteen months before turning in *Derek, Prince of Thane*.[1] Quickly re-christened, *Prince Valiant* debuted on February 13, 1937. Thirty-four years later Foster turned the art chores over to John Cullen Murphy, continuing to write the story until 1980. *Prince Valiant* is still published today, drawn by John Cullen Murphy and written by his son, Cullen Murphy. Foster's entire run on the strip is available in handsome reprint volumes, each containing a single year of adventure "in the days of King Arthur."

Much has been written about the heroic Prince of Thule and *Prince Valiant* is surely the most famous Arthurian comic. Foster's extensive research and tours of Europe allowed him to craft a tale that satisfied Arthurian scholars. His mastery of the human figure and amazing facility with natural settings endeared him to the art critic. A conscious decision to focus on issues of home and family allowed the strip to resonate with the post-war American: Val married Queen Aleta of the Misty Isles in 1946 and became first a father and then a grandfather. While the story of *Prince Valiant* often intersected with major Arthurian events such as the Battle of Badon or the Quest for the Holy Grail, Foster was always ready to take his hero farther afield in search of adventure. When his son married the daughter of the wicked Mordred, Camelot's political crisis became a personal one and Val had more trouble dealing with his in-laws than he did negotiating peace with North American tribes or dueling Saxons with the Singing Sword.

Foster's storytelling techniques differ from nearly all other Arthurian comics in one important respect. The burden of comics storytelling is usually shared by both words in pictures; neither one alone can tell the tale. Foster, however, always relied on the words to tell his story while the art worked to enhance rather than narrate.[2] A reader who was willing to miss out on some breathtaking scenery could read *Prince Valiant* through captions alone, never requiring a single picture. This places *Valiant* at odds with the American comic tradition, but it contributes to the strip's appeal among scholars of Arthurian literature.

Although it is the quintessential example of the traditional Arthurian comic, *Prince Valiant* has many close relatives. The gifted Rafael Astarita wrote and drew twelve pages of "King Arthur" in *New Comics* a year before Hearst would summon Hal Foster to his office. Stan Lee created a Black Knight for Marvel in 1955 and, in the same year, influential artist Irv Novick helped to create the Silent Knight in *Brave and the Bold*. In recent years Caliber Press has released a series of self-contained traditional Arthurian tales titled *Legends of Camelot*. Some of the stories mentioned here use new characters while others are adaptations of older tales in the Arthurian "canon," but all share the Arthurian setting, and they are largely free of the superhero influence that otherwise dominates the American comic industry.

The Arthurian Toybox

The typical western comic is a work of great economy, in more than one sense. The writers and artists who work in comics have very strict limitations of space, time, and art. The average comic has 22 pages of story with half a dozen panels per page. It is produced in one month, passing from writer to penciller to inker to print with many steps along the way, constantly monitored by an editor; artistic style is often sacrificed to speed (during the early formative years of comics reproduction, technology was especially primitive). The net result of the factors is a remarkable pressure on comic creators. They must tell their story in as economical a manner as possible and one of the best ways to do that is with iconic symbols and recognizable names.

When the villainous Doctor Doom abducts the Fantastic Four in their fifth issue, he sends them back in time to recover "the lost stones of Merlin." By invoking Merlin, Lee was able to avoid detailing a lengthy origin for this particular object of quest. Merlin's iconic resonance as a great wizard is all the explanation needed. Merlin created the stones, so they are clearly very old and very powerful. Merlin does not appear in this story; in fact, it has no other Arthurian elements at all. The FF go back not to Camelot but to the era of Blackbeard the pirate, whose famous treasure happens to include the stones.

In this way Arthurian elements often appear in comics as objects of quest, allies, enemies, or victims. Merlin, for example, is on hand to grant Captain Britain an enchanted amulet, and Morgana Le Fay is tapped to become the archenemy of Marvel's first spin-off heroine, Spider-Woman. More recently Morgana allies with her nephew Mordred "the Evil" to conquer the world in the pages of *The Avengers*. Excalibur lends its famous name to an entire comic series, though there is only the most tenuous of connections between the content of the story and the legendary sword.[3] DC's *All-Star Squadron* explains why World War II superheroes had not simply stormed Berlin or Tokyo to end the conflict—Hitler possessed the Holy Grail and could use its power to turn heroes against each other or even to strip them of their powers.

Not all such uses of the Arthurian toybox are so superficial, however. DC's *The Chalice* is a self-contained Batman story published in hardcover and on high-quality paper using a combination of photography, medieval manuscript illustrations and watercolors. In it, Bruce Wayne becomes the next guardian of the Holy Grail. It is suggested that the Wayne patronym evolved from Gawaine, and Master Bruce is related to the Arthurian knight. Even as the Grail is pursued by thieves, self-appointed guardians, and megalomaniacs out to secure eternal life, writer Chuck Dixon introduces more subtle Arthurian elements into this tale (before Wayne is given the Grail, for example, he receives a crippling thigh wound that the chalice later heals; the Fisher King is never explicitly mentioned).

A common use of the Arthurian myth as toybox is to ground an original character in an Arthurian setting, from which he soon departs to carry on modern superheroic adventures. The earliest example of this technique may be DC's Shining Knight, a member of the Round Table who is accidentally frozen in ice after defeating a monstrous giant. He awakens at the outset of World War II in time to safeguard Winston Churchill from assassination and later join the heroic "7 Soldiers of Victory." Like many of the superheroic Arthurian characters invented in later comics, Sir Justin proved able to move back and forth between mythic Britain and the present day. Equipped with a winged steed and a sword that deflects bullets, he was always more of a superhero than a traditional Arthurian knight. Marvel's

Black Knight is a character cut from a similar cloth, his chief distinguishing feature being that unlike the Shining Knight he is still in use today.

When Jack Kirby, perhaps the single most influential creator in comics, delved into the Arthurian toybox in 1972 he did so with characteristic originality. Eschewing the usual invention of a previously unknown knight of the Round Table, Kirby's Merlin instead conjures forth a weird and threatening demon named Etrigan. Like the Shining Knight and other Arthurian superheroes, Etrigan is soon whisked to the 20th century, albeit in the unwitting form of occultist Jason Blood, who has no memory of the time that he spends as Etrigan the Demon. This Jeckyll-and-Hyde character lasted only 16 issues in his own comic but remains popular due in no small part to his status as a Kirby creation. Like most modern characters with Arthurian backgrounds he no longer has much thematic interaction with the legend that served as his origin, instead being used as an antihero who sometimes aids the cause of good and sometimes works hand in hand with the forces of Hell.[4]

Arthur as Translator

One method of tapping the myth while still keeping the superheroic elements of a character intact is to transport a protagonist back to Camelot. This can be done in two ways: Connecticut-Yankee style or the "alternate history" approach. In the first, a modern character is transported to an Arthurian setting with full knowledge of his home and identity. In the other, a hero such as Superman or Batman is placed within the context of Camelot and the Round Table as if he belonged there.

Although many characters have been cast adrift in time and space only to wash up on Arthur's shore,[5] perhaps the most memorable example of this story starred Marvel's Iron Man. Millionaire playboy Tony Stark battles crime and saves the world from within a suit of high-tech armor, and writers have never been shy when using the knight analogy with him.[6] But when he and the armored supervillain Doctor Doom are accidentally sent back to Camelot in "Knightmare," they quickly come face to face with more overt Arthurian elements, including the King himself and Morgana Le Fay. After amazing the king by magnetically levitating the throne, Tony is made welcome, but Doom chooses to ally himself with Morgana in exchange for instruction in the ways of magic. Marvel Comics has traditionally used Morgana as an evil sorceress and here she is in excellent form, raising an army of corpses to attack Camelot and even transforming her pet falcon

into an Iron Man–eating monster. Thanks to Tony, however, the out-
matched Round Table triumphs, and it is only by working together that
Stark and the evil Doctor are able to build a time machine that takes them
home. This story has spawned numerous sequels and was recently reprinted
in trade paperback form.

If the Connecticut Yankee story is familiar to Arthurian scholars, the
alternate history approach is somewhat more arcane. In these tales, writers and artists create new characters within the Arthurian setting who
nonetheless are based on their modern archetype. The superhero is "translated" into an Arthurian context. Perhaps the best way to illustrate this is
by example. Bob Layton returned to the Arthurian era with *Dark Knight of
the Round Table*, capitalizing on Batman's nickname "the Dark Knight" for
a two-issue story published in 1999. Bruce Wayne as we know him does not
exist in this tale, which is set in Arthurian England. Instead, Bruce is the
young scion of the Waynesmoor family, caught up in the May Babies incident (the mass murder of Malory's Arthur is here softened to exile). Initially antagonistic towards the King, Bruce is given magical arms and a
mount by Merlin and encounters medieval versions of Robin and the faithful Alfred. Following in the footsteps of many former enemies of Arthur,
however, he eventually joins the Round Table and figures prominently in
the struggle against Mordred and Morgana. Superheroic elements are particularly strong in this story, which draws heavily on Boorman's *Excalibur*
and relies on the novelty of Batman in armor to make up for uninspired
plotting.

Arthur as Silent Collaborator

A skilled creator can turn the tight space constraints of the comic
form into an asset by working a story on multiple levels, using artistic and
thematic elements that are subtle—perhaps even unspoken—yet which resonate with the reader. The depth to which Arthurian legend has perme-
ated our culture makes the king a natural subject for this sort of iconic
shorthand. Comics are full of round tables, boy kings, and swords drawn
out of stones; the trick comes in sifting the Arthurian elements from the
occasional parallel myth or outright coincidence. Academic interrogation
is particularly needed in this area, as the last 60 years have produced an
astounding number of comics, and multiple perspectives are required to
grant validity to any suspected Arthurian element.

When the greatest superheroes of the world gather together to organize their battle against injustice, they invariably do so at a round table. It would be easy to dismiss this as mere coincidence were there not so many other similarities between the knight errant and the superhero. They wear costumes instead of armor and wear modern symbols instead of heraldic devices, but they still work to preserve the status quo and even profess a mission of "might for right." When British writer Grant Morrison took over the scripting chores for the Justice League of America he expanded the membership to twelve, one of the traditional sizes for the Round Table. Like the sieges of the Round Table each seat is labelled for its occupant— in this case using symbols instead of golden letters—and in a gesture reminiscent of the Siege Perilous Morrison always ensured that there was at least one empty seat. Marvel's premier hero team, the Avengers, likewise boasts a large round table in the middle of their headquarters. Less prominent groups like the Fantastic Four and the X-Men, however, have no such table. It is reserved for "Earth's Mightiest Heroes!"[7]

Morrison has discussed these Arthurian influences on his own website:

> The JLA Round Table was indeed intended to invoke the Arthurian table and the "Rock of Ages" storyline [in issues 10–15] was constructed upon the Grail Quest template (the "worlogog" or Philosopher's Stone is the Grail, the Watchtower is Camelot, Dr. Alchemy appears briefly as Klingsor, Kyle Rayner retraces Sir Perceval's journey to the Grail Castle, the Wasteland appears as Darkseid's conquered, ravaged Earth and so on until you grow a third eyebrow just thinking about it).[8]

When Marvel Comics exploded into the industry in the 1960s, characters were debuted with terrific velocity and inspiration for them came from many sources, some more traditional than others. One example of a possible—though more problematic—Arthurian influence is found in *Journey into Mystery* #83: the origin story of the Mighty Thor. Stan Lee and Jack Kirby tell the tale of Doctor Donald Blake, who is vacationing in Norway when he is caught up in the attack of "the Stone Men from Saturn." Losing his cane, he seeks shelter within a cave where he comes upon a walking stick lying atop a round, flat, stone. Taking it as a replacement for his own cane, he finds that it transforms him into the mighty Norse god of thunder. Magic words are written upon the mallet: "Whosoever wields this hammer, if he be worthy, shall possess the power of Thor."

If that final line sounds familiar to readers of Malory there is a reason: magic words appeared on a very famous stone to read, "Whosoever draws this sword from this stone and anvil is rightwise king born of all

England." Arthur lost a sword (Kay's) instead of a cane, and in desperation drew a new weapon to discover that he was now lord of Britain. Stan Lee, of course, had written more traditional tales of Arthur's Britain in "Black Knight Comics."

Forty years after *Journey Into Mystery*, the sword in the stone motif is still vibrant. Jim Starlin and Chris Batista tapped the Arthurian myth in *Spaceknights*. This five part comic portrays an enlightened intersteller civilization waging war against a diabolical alien race. The two brothers who are heirs to the throne of this benevolent space kingdom are Princes Balin and Tristan, of note because although these names are instantly recognizable to Arthurian scholars, they mean nothing to someone whose sole awareness of the legend is through television and film. Balin is rash and aggressive, his every action seemingly doomed to failure. In order to prove his right to take the throne, Balin (the elder brother) attempts to draw Axadar, his dead father's personal sidearm, from out of a force field. He fails, and in the end the young Tristan performs the feat instead to become a boy king. Despite a singular reference to the princes' deceased father as "Artour," these Arthurian motifs are employed in a relatively subtle manner. Even the names of Balin and Tristan can be explained away in context, for the Queen of this empire is born of Earth and has an interest in the legends of her homeworld. It is debatable whether Starlin and Batista even intend the Arthurian symbols to be seen and recognized by the audience.

By the mid–1980s the tastes of comic readers had changed. Influenced by the postmodern approaches of titles like *The Dark Knight Returns* and *Watchmen*, the public now demanded "dark and gritty" tales much different from the science fantasy that had come before. Some characters did not survive the change. Aquaman went from one of the industry's most recognizable characters to a laughing stock whose power to talk to fish simply did not stack up to the more brutal approaches of characters like Batman or Wolverine. When DC Comics sought to revitalize Aquaman in the 1990s, writers turned to the Arthurian myth, and Aquaman is now arguably the King Arthur of DC Comics.

Born to an Atlantean mother and a human father, Aquaman is given the human name "Arthur Curry" but also stands to inherit the throne of Atlantis. This literal King Arthur works to unite the disparate remnants of Atlantean civilization in a memorable story arc by writer Peter David. David made free use of Arthurian motifs, such as when Arthur discovered he had a bastard son who eventually tried to usurp the throne. In *Aquaman #10* the hero has a dream sequence that reenacts Perceval's encounter with the

Holy Grail in Boorman's *Excalibur*. By issue twenty Arthur's best friend and comrade had begun a covert affair with Arthur's own lover. Even the legendary sword Excalibur had a sort of surrogate in the pages of this monthly comic. When Arthur loses his hand to a school of disobedient piranha in "A Crash of Symbols" he decides, "Symbols are *very* important. Superman has his 'S', Batman has his bats, Lantern has his ring, on and on. I need a symbol, too." His amputated hand is replaced with a golden harpoon, which he soon uses to duel Atlantean knights just as if it were a sword.

Peter David eventually left the comic but Arthurian themes remained. Dan Jurgens, a veteran of many projects from *Superman* to *Thor*, continued to stress Arthur's regal majesty and obligations throughout a 13-issue run. Alas, it was not enough. Even legendary trappings could not rescue this character from the piranhas of poor sales. Although DC's King Arthur continues to appear in a supporting role in comics such as *JLA*, his monthly series was cancelled with issue #75.

Arthur Transformed

In 1982 Mike Barr and Brian Bolland created one of the best-known Arthurian comics: *Camelot 3000*. Arthur and his knights are brought back from death to defend Earth against hostile aliens led by Morgana and Mordred. *Camelot 3000* symbolizes the fifth and perhaps most dynamic form of Arthurian comic—a tale that takes Arthurian characters out of their usual setting in order to tell new stories that pick up where the canon leaves off. Tales of Arthur Transformed are typically finite in length (as opposed to the ongoing monthly titles which dominate industry) and they allow the writers and artists to explore personal visions with comparatively little interference. Two themes are particularly common: "Return of the King" stories in which Arthur comes back from the dead, and the "Aftermath" tale that continues the saga in Arthurian Britain but after the king's death.

Close behind *Camelot 3000* in terms of recognizability and influence, Matt Wagner's *Mage* tells the story of Kevin Matchstick, a modern man who discovers that he is the Pendragon reborn. Originally conceived as a trilogy of stories (*The Hero Discovered*, *The Hero Defined*, *The Hero Denied*), only the first two 15-issue segments have so far seen print. *Mage* is a very personal creation; Wagner writes, draws, inks and letters the book himself. Kevin is physically modeled on the author and other characters resemble his friends and acquaintances. At the same time the series allows Wagner to explore issues of mythology and self-identity in the Joseph Campbell mode. Kevin encounters modern analogs of Merlin and the Lady of the

Lake, but he also meets Hercules, Roland and Beowulf. Even his own identity as a new King Arthur is eventually thrown into doubt.

Lady Pendragon is another example of a very personal Arthurian vision. It began as an "Aftermath" tale depicting Guenevere's struggle to hold the kingdom together after Arthur's death. Initial sales success, however, led creator Matt Hawkins to begin a marketing crusade that included action figures and t-shirts as well as a dozen more issues and a wildly expanded plot involving a modern-day reincarnation of Guenevere unleashing apocalyptic magic onto an unprepared Earth. Hawkins' unpredictability and clear social agenda makes Lady Pendragon an interesting read, though the blatant sexuality of a nubile Queen in gold chainmail stockings can be distracting to the analytical mind. Another recent-but-extinct Arthurian comic, Knewts of the Round Table, begins after Arthur's death when four knights are transformed by a wizard's curse into man-sized lizards. Knewts is a grim fantasy in black and white similar in tone to the rogue vision of Dave Sim's Cerebus. In it, Camelot has been taken over by criminal gangs and usurpers, but it appears we will never know the end of the story. The comic ceased publication after four issues.

These cancellations and disappearances are not unique. Over the last two decades the comic book industry has been particularly volatile, and it is difficult to foresee the future of the Arthurian comic. Prince Valiant may be an institution, but other traditional retellings of the legend are rare. Artists and writers will continue, however, to use Arthurian elements in superhero tales. The exploits of the Black Knight and the Demon will continue, but these adventures are of questionable interest to the Arthurian scholar looking for innovative interaction with the canon. For arcane reasons of editorial decree, time travel stories are currently out of vogue and we are more likely to see Wonder Woman or Spider-Man "translated" into an Arthurian context than we are to see them actually transported back to Camelot as Tony Stark was. Energy still seems to lie with comics that transform the myth, combining the Arthurian romance with elements of the superhero genre. The challenge in this approach lies in finding an audience and a spot on the highly competitive shelf of the comic book specialty store. Titles without prolonged financial backing (like Camelot 3000) or exceptional fan support (like Lady Pendragon) can wither and die regardless of the talent that lies behind the script and pencil work. Academics have a challenge posed to them as well—not only to find those comic specialty stores but to investigate the Arthur that lies within them. Arthurian themes and motifs run deep in comics and date back to the foundation of this literary form. To find them, we need many eyes and voices.

Notes

1. Steve Duin and Mike Richardson discuss Foster—and just about everyone else in the comics industry—in their admittedly biased encyclopedia *Comics Between the Panels.*

2. For a full discussion of the way in which words and pictures split the effort of comic narration see *Understanding Comics,* cited as further reading at the end of this article.

3. Marvel's superhero team Excalibur debuted at the popular height of the "X-Men" phenomenon. The team was based in London and largely made up of characters from the X-Men books. Without any substantial Arthurian theme or content, the series appears to have been christened "Excalibur" because the name would sound like the other X-Men titles and would also be recognizable to the audience. A recent relaunch of the characters appears to have a more clearly Arthurian theme.

4. The Demon was followed a few years later by Marvel's "Mordred the Mystic," a pupil of Merlin who found himself transported to the present (*Marvel Chillers*). Mordred did not enjoy Etrigan's success, however, and was soon made into a pawn of diabolical forces for "The Yesterday Quest" an oft-reprinted *Avengers* tale.

5. Two examples: "Sir Batman in King Arthur's Court." *Batman* #36 (1946), DC Comics and "A Green Arrow in King Arthur's Court." *Adventure Comics* #268 (1960), DC Comics.

6. Iron Man's "knight analogy" is often drawn even more explicitly to Arthurian myth. In the first issue of his current series he investigates a terrorist attack on the "Avalon Trading Company" and is referred to as "Sir Galahad."

7. This phrase is a catchphrase of the Avengers and has appeared on most issues of the comic over the last 40 years.

8. Morrison goes on to provide inspiration for investigation beyond this study: "The final volume of *The Invisibles* drips equally with Grail imagery and overt Arthurian references. It's an aspect of the story that's rarely commented on but the book included, among other things, my attempt to update and revitalise a number of 'Archetypal Themes and Patterns' from the Grail romances and their weird Celtic precursors."

Further Reading

McCloud, Scott. *Understanding Comics.* USA: Kitchen Sink Press, 1993.
     There is no better introduction to comic analysis. Scott McLoud's book discusses essential comic concepts like the depiction of motion and emotion, time and sound in comics around the world. The sequel, *Reinventing Comics,* dwells on the ramifications of the online revolution.

Eisner, Will. *Comics & Sequential Art* (expanded edition). USA: Poorhouse Press, 1985.
     Advanced students of comic storytelling techniques consult this book and its sequel, *Graphic Storytelling.* Both are by Will Eisner, one of the living legends of the comic community and a former instructor at New York's School of Visual Art.

Online Resources

Camelot in Four Colors. http://members.tripod.com/camelot4colors
   A broad, useful, and up-to-date survey of the Arthurian legend in comics maintained by Alan Stewart. "Camelot in Four Colors" includes many foreign titles and is also handsomely illustrated with cover and interior scans.

Camelot 3000 and Beyond. http://www.lib.rochester.edu/camelot/acpbibs/comicbib. htm
   Michael A. Toregrossa's annotated listing of over 200 Arthurian comics published in the US first saw print in the journal *Arthuriana* 9.1 (1999): 67–109. It is also valuable for its listing of scholarship on Arthurian comics.

Arthurian Comics Discussion List. http://home.att.net/~torregrossa/comichome.htm
   Arthur's influence and presence in comics are discussed regularly on this list maintained by Michael A. Torregrossa.

Works Cited

Astarita, Rafael (w,p,i). "King Arthur." *New Comics* #3–8 (1936), DC Comics.
Barr, Mike (w), Brian Bolland (p), Bruce D. Patterson, and Terry Austin (i). *Camelot 3000.* Eds. Len Wein and Richard Bruning. NY: DC Comics, 1988.
Busiek, Kurt (w), Sean Chen (p), Eric Cannon (i). "Looking Forward." *Iron Man* v3 #1 (Feb. 1998), Marvel Comics.
Busiek, Kurt (w), George Perez (p), and Al Vey (i). "Once an Avenger..." *The Avengers* v3 #1–3 (Feb.–Apr. 1998), Marvel Comics.
Claremont, Chris (w), and Herb Trimpe (p). *Captain Britain* v1 #1–39 (1976–1979), Marvel UK.
David, Peter (w), Martin Egeland (p), Brad Vancata, and Howard M. Shum (i). "A Crash of Symbols." *Aquaman* #0 (Oct. 1994), DC Comics.
Dixon, Chuck (w), John van Fleet (a). *Batman: The Chalice.* NY: DC Comics, 1999.
Duin, Steve, and Mike Richardson. *Comics Between the Panels.* Singapore: Dark Horse Comics, 1998.
Fitzgerald, Brian (w), and Nirut Chamsuwan (a). *Knewts of the Round Table* #1–4 (1998), Pan Entertainment.
Foster, Hal (w,a). *Prince Valiant,* vol. 1–40. Seattle: Fantagraphics Books.
Hawkins, Matt (w), and John Stinsman (a). *Lady Pendragon* v2 #1–3 (Nov. 1998–Jan. 1999), Image Comics.
Kanigher, Robert (w), and Irv Novick (a). *The Brave and the Bold* #1–22 (1955–1956), DC Comics.
Kirby, Jack (w,p). *The Demon* v1 #1–16 (1972–1973), DC Comics.
Layton, Bob (w,i), and Dick Giordano (p). *Dark Knight of the Round Table* #1–2 (1999), DC Comics.
Lee, Stan (w), Jack Kirby (p) and Joe Sinnott (i). "Meet ... Doctor Doom!" *The Essential Fantastic Four* vol. 1. Ed. Polly Watson. NY: Marvel Comics, 1998.
Lee, Stan, Lary Lieber (w), and Jack Kirby (p). "The Stone Men from Saturn!" *Origins of Marvel Comics Revised edition.* USA: Marvel Comics, 1997: 171–184.
Lee, Stan (w), and Joe Maneely (p). *Black Knight Comics* #1–5 (1955), Marvel Comics.

Martin, Joe (w), and Jose Trudel (a). "Excalibur." *Legends of Camelot* (1999), Caliber Comics.

Michelinie, David, Mark Greunwald, Steven Grant (w), John Byrne (p), Gene Day, Klaus Janson, and Dan Green (i). *Avengers: the Yesterday Quest*. Eds. Roger Stern and Matt Idelson. NY: Marvel Comics, 1994.

Michelinie, David (w), John Romita (p), and Bob Layton [plot and finished art] (i). "Knightmare." *Iron Man* v1 #150 (Sep. 1981), Marvel Comics Group.

Morrison, Grant (w), Howard Porter, Gary Frank, Greg Land (p), John Dell, and Bob McLeod (i). "Rock of Ages." *JLA* #5, 10–15 (Late Sep. 1997–Feb. 1998), DC Comics.

Starlin, Jim (w), Chris Batista (p), Charles Wallace, [Holdredge] and Eric Cannon (i). *Spaceknights* v1 #1–5 (Oct. 2000–Feb. 2001), Marvel Comics.

[Uncredited (p)] and Flesel, Craig (a). *Adventure Comics* #66 (1941), DC Comics.

Wagner, Matt (w,p,i), and Sam Kieth (i). *Mage–The Hero Discovered*, vol. 1–3. Eds. Kay Reynolds, Gerry Giovinco, Diana Schultz, et al. Norfolk: The Donning Company [Starblaze Graphics].

Wagner, Matt (w,p,i). *Mage* [The Hero Defined] #1–15 (Jul. 1997–Oct. 1999), Image Comics.

Waid, Mark, and Alex Ross. *Kingdom Come: Revelations*. NY: DC Comics, 1997.

Wolfman, Marv, Bill Mantlo (w), and Yong Montano (p). *Marvel Chillers* #1–2 (1975), Marvel Comics.

Knights of Imagination: Arthurian Games and Entertainments

PETER CORLESS

Introduction

King Arthur, Merlin, Excalibur, and the Round Table are icons deeply ingrained in general and specialized segments of contemporary popular culture. The gaming community and industry, in particular, are rich in Arthurian material: over thirty such games are currently on the market or internet-accessible.

After a brief introduction to game genres and the demographics of the gaming community, this essay will discuss the ways in which the themes, characters, and stories of the Matter of Arthur are integrated into gaming and related entertainments, with particular attention to the strategies used to adapt the legend to the interests of the target subculture.

Adventure Gaming

> "You know about transmigration of souls; do you know about transposition of epochs—and bodies?"
> —Mark Twain, "A Connecticut Yankee in King Arthur's Court"

Many different types of games exist in present popular culture, and an overview of their types and formats is useful before delving further into the topic of King Arthur. They range entirely from formal, structured rules systems and packaged formats to open-ended, loosely-organized experiences which are more properly considered general entertainments or amusements.

This essay focuses on a particular domain known broadly as "adventure games," which are defined by strong elements of subjective roleplaying and objective strategy and decision-making, and are set in a context of simulated and fantastic situations.

The meta-goal of all games is to sustain interest in the leisure activity associated with the game. In order to achieve this goal, the game must fulfill the psychological needs and interests of the individual players. Adventure gaming at its best is an active mentally challenging form of entertainment. It can be a social activity providing informal education, it can encourage development of problem-solving skills and artistic expression, and it can provide inspiration and motivation for personal development. It accomplishes all this through various combinations of four game elements: roleplaying, simulation, fantasy, and strategy.

Roleplaying is, simply put, acting and playing at "make-believe." It is psychologically subjective, personal, and imaginative. Players put aside their real-world schema and modify their personality and behavior to become immersed into a fantastic situation. In this way, they may experience various novel and very risky situations with no real personal or physical danger. They may also experiment with temporary adoptions of uncharacteristic psychology.

The projection of the player's own mentality and personality into a fictional situation permits experimentation with personal beliefs and behaviors. This activity can be called "avataristic." The fictional character is primarily and ultimately a projection of the player's own mentality and subject to their whims and desires. It is based on modern sensibilities, knowledge, personality traits, idioms of speech, etc., and these often predominate in the roleplayer's decisions.

Avataristic behavior can be detected in players who never speak or act "in-character" but break character and resort to:

- Exclusive use of third-person description ("My character thinks about it, then attacks the Saxon...")
- Anachronistic or dramatically inappropriate dialogue ("Kewl! Thanks King Arthur! You completely rock!"), or
- Uncharacteristic behavior (a supposedly chivalrous and pious knight attacks a defenseless monk for no reason, to steal his silver cross)

A second type of roleplaying, which is more akin to method acting, requires players to subsume or modify their normal, actual mentality by temporarily adopting the personal behaviors of a different character (whether fictional or real). In general, the more the character behaves in accord with the psychological or social schema of the adventure game setting or world, the stronger and more dramatic is the experience produced.

In reality, it is very difficult to remain "in-character" indefinitely in games. Instead, a synthesis of psychological contexts occurs, where a player might drop "in-character" and "out-of-character" depending on real-world and game situations, and also have their mental focus shift between "what do I want to do?" in a game as opposed to "what would my character want to do?" A player might ask the player sitting on the right, "Prithee, but wouldst thou pass unto me the set of dice in thy possession? For I wax wroth and would smite my annoying younger brother therewithal." Humor produced by the situation stems from the curious blend of in-character Arthurian speech patterns and real world out-of-character events and knowledge.

Simulations are games with mechanics and artistic content representational of actual or imagined events, beings, objects, and situations. The goal of simulation is to produce *verisimilitude*: the appearance of truth or realism. A simulation is a conceptual model, image, projection, or abstraction of an actual event, and should not be confused with the object or instance itself. Yet on an emotional, psychological or intellectual basis, simulated events are desired to be perceived as real or possible.

A simulation permits or encourages the creation or re-creation of behaviors and outcomes according to a defined, abstracted schematic interpretation. In other words, it conforms to expectations about how things should work. Since games are not purely predictive, but stochastic—relying upon player choices, statistics, and probabilities—most game simulations provide rules to encourage certain behavior and outcomes. These incentives or constraints encourage properly conforming activities based on the design expectations of the simulation designer. If well-designed, a simulation should accord with the players' sense of verisimilitude for those familiar with the topic of the simulation.

Adventure game simulations exist for a broad range of activities: warfare, economic and social changes, technical developments, and so on. Simulations may also be roleplaying games, if they are representational of realistic or highly believable behaviors, such as first-person combat simulation games or simulated environments or worlds (even fantasy worlds). In many simulations, the player is not represented by a direct first-person avatar, but is an abstracted, objective director of events.

The psychological goal of a simulation is to enjoy the choices and alternates possible when interacting with and controlling the simulated environment. In addition, pleasure derives from being able to feel immersed in the virtual environment, and having faith in the aesthetics and logic of the simulation's context and content. This pleasure is often greater when the simulated experience is particularly rare or involves high risk and reward or dangerous situations.

Fantasy is a central theme of all adventure games. Even if the game is based on actual and historical times and places, concerning real events and people, and is a very strict simulation of events, it will have an essence of the fantastic and fictional. If there is no way to change the actual outcome of the original event, why play the game? The fantastic premise of all adventure games is always the exploration of "what if?" This "what if?" is not just a mechanistic strategy. It extends to consider dramatic—emotional—ramifications in the roleplaying or simulation experience. For instance, losing pieces in a game where the object or goal is to keep one's pieces intact has direct effect on the outcome of the game. However, if each piece is also representative of an identified knight, then the fantasy of "what if?" may have emotional ramifications as well.

The goal of fantasy is to appeal to and please the subrational senses of mental curiosity and interest. It is a form of dream or wish fulfillment. The more irrational the vision, the higher the level of fantasy. Akin to simulation, fantasy requires an aesthetic of complementary fantasy components. The inverse—contrasting or clashing elements—can be considered dystopian or horrific.

Most Arthurian adventure games play up the fantastical, mystical and magical elements of the Arthurian legends. Merlin, Excalibur, the Holy Grail, the magic of the Ladies of the Lake and Morgan le Fay, and so on. Many games also use Arthurian elements to add into otherwise realistic situations.

Strategy games focus on mechanics and mathematics as internally integral systems, rather than in the subjective contexts and contents of their topics. Games of strategy are often competitive, rather than cooperative. Many strategy games exist which are not considered adventure games. For instance, a chess set modeled with Arthurian characters would not classify as an adventure game. It is definitely a strategy game, but it is not a fantasy game, nor a roleplaying game, nor a simulation. Generally, a strategy game would also need to have elements of roleplaying, fantasy, or simulation to be considered an adventure game.

Adventure Game Media and Formats

Every year the adventure gaming industry adopts the latest forms of communications media and mass-market commercial vehicles to produce new adventure gaming products. There is no single definitive classification of adventure game formats, but the following will serve as a brief survey of types broken out by media and format:

Traditional Gaming Formats
- Board Games: paper/stock board, components, cards, dice, etc.
- Card Games: including both set deck and collectible card game systems
- Dice Games: polymorphic dice games, collectible dice, etc.
- Miniatures: metal or plastic scale figurines played on tabletop topology
- Traditional Roleplaying: dice & paper rules books, character sheets, etc.
- Live Action Roleplaying (LARP): improvisation with rules and goals.

Computer Gaming Formats
- Computerized Tools: adventure gaming utilities and facilities
- Text-based Extended Games: Play-by-Email (PBEM), Bulletin Boards
- Text-based Real-Time Roleplaying: MUDs/MOOs/MUSHs, Chat Systems
- Graphical Virtual Worlds (2D, 2.5D, 3D Environments)
- Web Sites: adventure gaming resources & communities

Computer Game Media & Markets
- Console System Games—set-top game systems (Nintendo, Sega, etc.)
- PC Games—Windows and Macintosh platform
- Internet Games—Console or PC games with real-time connectivity
- Wireless/Hand-held Device Games—emergent/experimental market

Most of these game types have significant histories or mass-market presence, and are obvious to a participant in modern popular culture. Since the list of communications media and commercial formats continues to burgeon with every year, for the sake of brevity this essay will leave aside the exercise of trying to catalog all types of games in detail.

Live action roleplaying (LARP) games include costumed and noncostumed roleplaying events. Some use abstracted conflict resolution, such as with ability cards, gestures ("scissors-paper-rock"), or other game mechanics.

Others use light physical dueling (with mock or padded "boffer" weapons and armor). They are the least commercialized of traditional game types, often based on localized communities and highly reliant upon individuals or small groups of organizers.

They are not to be confused with reenactment societies. Re-enactment groups, such as medieval or renaissance organizations, do roleplay, but do so as improvisational acting, rather than as a directed game featuring structured rules and the objective of winning. Neither should they be confused with organizations which focus on mock combat as a sport or modern martial art, such as the Society for Creative Anachronism (SCA) or the Company of St. George. (See the essay by Brian Price in this volume.)

Computerized tools are often adjuncts of traditional printed or manufactured game systems. They are often aids in generating randomized or facilitated characters, settings (mapping) or graphics (character visualization and heraldry), as well as record-keeping utilities. They are not games of themselves, but are used to improve the experience of games.

Text-based extended games use non-real-time exchange mechanisms, such as email distribution or electronic bulletin boards or web sites to post updates of game events. These can be strategy games or roleplaying games. Text-based real-time roleplaying games are often called multi-user systems. There are a few primary types:

- Multi-User Dungeons (MUDs)—mostly combat-oriented systems, often derived from "Dungeons & Dragons"–like fantasy roleplaying mechanics.
- Multi-User Object-Oriented (MOOs)—a MUD, with more advanced game engine technology
- Multi-User Shared Hallucinations (MUSHs)—roleplaying-oriented systems; often more interested in social interaction than tactical combat.

These types of virtual environments have robust algorithmic mechanical engines. They provide structured grammars and command line interfaces for personal activities and social interactions: "attack [character]," "get [item]," and "tell [character] '[message].'" These highly-structured roleplaying environments are open-ended games, and often run on a constant basis. They are not as popular or as aesthetically appealing as full graphical user interface (GUI) virtual worlds, but are often far more engaging on a narrative basis. The textual log files of activities of these worlds often constitute a form of "living novel" of the character's activity. Many integrate illustrations or graphical element facilities such as maps of the environment. These services have limited numbers of users, but there are many small sites, each dedicated to specialized communities. It is rare for any of these text-based systems to exceed more than a few hundred or thousand concurrent players.

Chat services, because of their ubiquity, are used for very loosely-structured Internet roleplaying, or as an adjunct communication channel for other Internet adventure games. Chat, as a general umbrella, includes a broad-range of textual and even visual lightweight messaging services:

- Internet Relay Chat (IRC)
- Online community chat services (America Online and Yahoo Chat)
- Internet Messaging (IM) services (America Online, Yahoo IM)
- Avatar Chat (or "av chat")

These are often lacking utterly in algorithmic mechanical systems. But like MUDs/MOOs/MUSHs, their textual logs help build a historical narrative.

Graphical virtual worlds include objectively-controlled worlds (civilization development and strategy games), as well as first-person roleplaying. They include console and PC games, as well as Internet environments. Because of their highly interactive and complex real-time situations, it is often not possible to record fully the historical or narrative development of these games. One may at best snapshoot the game in progress: save the world in its current state or the state of one's character. The visual aesthetics of such games make them highly pleasing and engaging. Virtual communities of the most popular online games are now numbering in the tens of thousands of concurrent players on a worldwide basis—the equivalent of a small city of roleplayers.

Demographics of Arthurian Adventure Game Players

Before we turn to the instances and treatment of specific Arthurian games, let us consider just the influencing factors of demographics. Adventure gaming is and has been a predominantly Western phenomenon. Strategy games, especially toy soldiers, were popularized in Europe in the 1800s; these spread to North America and the rest of the world. Roleplaying games were invented and mass-marketed in the United States in the second half of the twentieth century and became a world-wide phenomenon. There are signal cultural exceptions, such as Japan, which produces a wide range of historical games, miniatures and models, as well as fantasy, science-fiction and other anime-oriented art. Australia and parts of Latin America are also viable markets. Yet for the most part, the adventure game market is dominated by North America and Western Europe.

Generally, adventure games are linked to levels of access to information, whether through education or communications infrastructure. Common language also helps adventure games propagate through popular culture. Unlike true abstract strategy games, such as chess or card games, there are often extensive rules or communications requiring fluency or literacy.

The Arthurian subject matter is also historically sourced from Western Europe, and has appeal in North America and Australia because of the English language and cultural heritage. There is also a nominal popularization of Arthurian myth in Japanese culture.

In theory, Arthurian interest and adventure game markets should coincide strongly. Consider the popular appeal of Arthurian content in general mass-market media and entertainment: modern fiction, literature and mythological studies, movies, television shows, comic books, and so on. The adventure game market, which often relies heavily upon a cross-media pull from these mass-media consumers, would seem to be a natural market for a popular line of products. And yet success with strictly Arthurian adventure games has proven as elusive as the Holy Grail.

The mass-market appeal and commercial success of Arthurian myth is limited compared to, say, *Star Trek* or *Star Wars*, which have developed quite successful adventure game brands. Even compared to other fantasy adventure games, such as Dungeons & Dragons or The Lord of the Rings, the Arthurian myths have a very small overall market presence. Is this because of something inherent in the subject matter, the proclivity of adventure gamers, or some mismatch between the two? According to a market study of 65,000 households prepared in February 2000 by Wizards of the Coast, now a division of Hasbro, adventure game consumers in the United States are generally considered to have the following attributes:

- Ages range from 12 to 35. (Though there are a significant number of players who are age 35 or older, they are not part of the Wizards of the Coast targeted market; they have often already been recruited into the market, and therefore have a different sustaining marketing interest.) Age brackets were broken down as follows:

Young Adult	ages 12–15	~25% of market
High School	ages 16–18	~17%
College Age	ages 19–24	~24%
Adult	ages 25–35	~34%

- Educational breakdown was as follows:

Grades 6–8	~27% of market
High School	~37%
College	~31%
Post Graduate	~ 5%

- Traditional adventure gamers are roughly 80% male and 20% female.
- Most gamers have a favorite format of game, whether computer game, board game, traditional roleplaying or card game. Very few play many different types of games regularly.
- 63% use Windows PCs, 9% Macintosh. The ~28% remaining either have some other form of computer or no computer at home.
- 75% use the Internet at least once a week, but only 63% have access from home.
- The amount of investment per consumer varies widely. Many purchase as little as $7 of materials a month, or play free Internet games. Others spend upwards of $4,000 on gaming materials (even aside from computing equipment) including miniatures, books, game materials, and so on, over their consumer lifespan.

There has been a generally strong Eurocentric ethnicity to both the adventure game and Arthurian market demographic groups.

Arthurian Adventure Gaming

The adventure gaming industry covers many topics of popular culture. Within this broad context exists the small industry and niche of Arthurian adventure games.

The Arthurian Matter of Britain comprises a very small percentage of the overall adventure game market, estimated at less than $500,000 annually. Even considering the larger context of medieval-based roleplaying games (but excluding high fantasy games), this is a small percentage of the overall market, probably less than 1%. *Dungeons & Dragons*, published by Wizards of the Coast/Hasbro, is the leading brand of original fantasy roleplaying games, with millions of players. It sells hundreds of thousands of new books every year. In contrast, *King Arthur Pendragon*, published by

Green Knight Publishing, the most popular Arthurian roleplaying game, has had tens of thousands of consumer purchasers over its history and sells a few thousand copies annually. Though it has been credited as an artistic achievement, as well as a faithful adaptation of the Arthurian myths to an innovative game design, it has not succeeded commercially to the same degree as other fantasy roleplaying games.

While some Arthurian-based games may treat the Matter of Britain as sacrosanct, it is far more common for an Arthurian game to lift or incorporate names, symbols, characters, or other elements of the Arthurian legends into a different topic or setting than to wholeheartedly focus on the Arthurian legend as the central focus of an adventure game. King Arthur, Merlin, Morgan le Fay, Excalibur, Camelot, the Holy Grail, and other names and symbols of the Arthurian legends are commonly found in adventure games. At the lowest level, their application is used to capture attention or interest. Sometimes they are applied archetypically or iconographically and are not deeply or faithfully related to their original sources. One could encounter a Camelot that King Arthur, if he ever walked out of history, myth or literature, would never recognize.

The issue of "generalized" use versus "canonical" use has often been debated. A certain balance of generalized, adapted, and original materials is required to provide novelty and interest to players. A low barrier to entry is needed to adopt Arthuriana to modern idioms, cultural expectations, and other requirements for mass-marketing. There is also a need for novelty to make the old materials topically interesting and relevant to new audiences.

At the same time, fidelity to the history, mythology, and literature of the Arthurian matter are required to appeal to the knowledgeable player's sense of nostalgia—comfort in the familiar—as well as provide verisimilitude and suspension of disbelief.

In summary, these are the types of Arthurian adventure games:

- Generic: Nominal, iconographic, archetypical or other symbolic or cultural reference to Arthurian elements; no strict reliance upon corpus; often found in abstract strategy games.
- General: Faithful reference to corpus, but peripheral to other game design goals, such as mechanics, content or context; Arthurian subelements not primary focus; often found in roleplaying games.
- Adaptive: Modified use of Arthurian elements; some reliance upon corpus, but often used to underlie novel, original materials; often basis for original fantasy games.

- Authentic: Faithful reliance upon one or more versions of the original Arthurian corpus for "simulations" of historical scenarios or to comply with themes or plots of literary or mythological sources.

A Survey of Arthurian Adventure Games

Card Games

Quest for the Grail (Stone Ring). http://www.ccsi.com/~graball/quest/.

In 1997, Stone Ring Games produced a visually stunning collectible card game, with 280 cards based on the legends of King Arthur. It uses many traditional and original artworks, with illustrations from N.C. Wyeth, Arthur Rackham, and many other sources. The game is aesthetically faithful to the Arthurian tradition. As a card game, it should be considered an abstract strategy game. The point is to build out Dominions (territories of Britain), assemble a collection of Knights of the Round Table, and play cards representing various objects and events associated with Arthurian tradition to score points. Game play involves use of dice for resolution. It was considered a poor game, and the market for collectible card games was saturated at the time of its release. The game did not fare well commercially.

Quest for the Grail (Review). http://www.geocities.com/TimesSquare/Cavern/7378/questfhg.html.

Quests of the Round Table (Gamewrights, Inc.). http://www.gamewright.com/games/quests.html.

Published in 1995, this is a simple card game for 2 to 4 players. It has a "fixed" deck of 165 cards. It is a general and rather authentic adaptation of the Arthurian legend to a card game. Players can take part in quests and sponsor tournaments to earn "shields." The first person to get enough can be admitted to the Round Table, winning the game. It has a good background on Arthurian legends, and a short bibliography for younger players who might become more interested in Arthurian subject matter as a result of playing.

Board Games

Round Table Chess. http://www.chessvariants.com/large.dir/contest/rtc-rules.html.

Round Table chess is a variant of chess invented by Richard G. Van-

Deventer and played on a special circular board. According to the inventor's research, a form of round chess board was popularized in the Byzantine empire around 1100 AD and achieved some interest over the centuries. However, other than the name "Round Table," this game has no Arthurian content or relation to the subject matter.

Britannia (Gibson Games, Avalon Hill, Multiman Publishing). http://www.multimanpublishing.com/store/prod03.htm.

The authoritative game on British cultural history, subtitled "Game of the Birth of Britain," this game spans the period from the Roman invasion of Britain to the dramatic invasions of 1066. This is a strategic simulation game. Each of the 16 turns of the game represents a fixed historic period. Hengist arrives on Turn 6 (410–485 AD). King Arthur appears Turn 7 (485–560 AD). Leaders are only used temporarily, and are removed on the turn following their appearance. Arthur only gets to lead existing Roman units, which become converted to Romano-British cavalry and infantry.

The game has a long history. Originally designed by Lewis Pulsipher and published in Britain by Gibson Games in 1986, it was published in a 1987 edition by The Avalon Hill Game Company, and when Hasbro acquired Avalon Hill the remaining inventory and sales rights were licensed out to Multiman Publishing (MMP). The game is playable by 3 to 5 players in about 4 to 6 hours.

There is a Play-by-Email site for Britannia, including rules and clarifications:

Britannia PbEM Page. http://britannia.ralnet.net.

Roleplaying Games

King Arthur Pendragon (Chaosium, Green Knight). http://www.green knight.com/products/rpg/.

The premiere roleplaying game for Arthurian fans, Pendragon was created in 1985 by Greg Stafford and originally published by Chaosium, Inc. It was innovative for its use of "Traits" and "Passions" which represented a schema for the dramatic interpretation and definition of personality. Rules for chivalric, religious, romantic and other cultural ideal behaviors and virtues separated it from games that placed little emphasis on characterization and more on combat simulation.

The game is based primarily upon Sir Thomas Malory's *Le Morte D'Arthur*, and incorporates material from Geoffrey of Monmouth, the

French Vulgate Lancelot-Grail cycle, Chrétien de Troyes, the Welsh legends and other Arthurian literature.

There are currently a dozen titles available for the game system, including adventure books, campaign supplements, and guides to lands and peoples of Arthur's Britain, and also extends to Beowulf's Scandinavia and mythic Ireland.

The game system can be daunting. At 350 pages, the physical and intellectual weight of the subject matter and the main rules book can intimidate newcomers to roleplaying, or to the Matter of Britain.

The Book of Knights, released in November 2000, is a 48-page entry-level game more appropriate to newcomers to adventure games and to Arthur's Britain.

Pendragon Reviews. http://www.gamers.com/game/274688/reviews.

Pendragon LARP: The King of the Woods (Neil Laughlin, Green Knight).

Neil Laughlin designed this Live Action Roleplaying (LARP) adventure game in 1999 for Green Knight. It is unpublished commercially, but has been hosted as a special event in the US, Ireland, and England. Designed for a cast of up to 25 players, it allows players to roleplay Knights of the Round Table, queens and ladies of Britain, and other characters at a mysterious and magical tournament.

Prince Valiant: The Storytelling Game (Chaosium, Inc.).

Published in 1989, Prince Valiant was an interpretation of Hal Foster's perennial comic book, designed for entry-level roleplaying. It was designed by Greg Stafford, who had created Pendragon. The game was modestly received, discontinued and is now out of print.

Prince Valiant (Reviews). http://www.io.com/~sos/rpg/princval.html; http://www.pensee.com/dunham/reviews/pv.html.

GURPS Camelot (Steve Jackson Games). http://www.sjgames.com/gurps/books/Camelot.

GURPS is the Generic Universal Roleplaying System, a roleplaying gaming rules and mechanic system devised by Steve Jackson Games to be applied to practically every genre and setting imaginable. King Arthur and crew get their treatment in this supplement.

Miniatures

Miniature figures are a staple of adventure games. Thunderbolt Mountain makes "canonical" Arthurian figures, including Arthur, Guenevere,

Merlin, Morgan le Fay, Knights of the Round Table, Sir Turquine, the Green Knight, and so on. Lance & Laser makes figures licensed for use with the Pendragon roleplaying game. Other companies produce various lines of historical Dark Ages and fantasy figures appropriate for Arthurian wargames or roleplaying games.

L'Morte d'Arthur, Legendary King Arthur (Thunderbolt Mountain). http://home.fuse.net/tbolt/arthur.html.

Pendragon Miniatures (Lance & Laser Models, Inc.). http://www.lance-and-laser.com.

Late Romans and Arthurians (Wargames Foundry). http://www.p-o-p.demon.co.uk/shop/foundry/wf_later.htm.

Pendraken Miniatures: Dark Ages Miniatures. http://members.tripod.co.uk/pendraken/.

Gripping Beast Miniatures: Dark Ages Miniatures. http://bath.ac.uk/~ccspgo/bodygripping.html.

Warhammer Brettonians (Games Workshop). http://www.games-workshop.co.uk.

Computer Games: Desktop and Console Games

Many Arthurian games have been developed for personal computers over the years. The largest problem with cataloging these is the fact that they tend to come into and go out of print rather rapidly, and the technical standards to run them change every three to five years. If there was ever such a thing as a "digital Dark Ages," these rapidly changing times would qualify.

Monty Python & the Quest of the Holy Grail (7th Level, 1996). http://www.game-revolution.com/games/pc/adventure/grail.htm.
A wonderfully silly game that follows the movie's plot and tone. Mostly multimedia clips with a few abstract strategy and puzzle-solving games, such as a Tetris-like game of "Bring Out Your Dead," a bawdy "Spank the Virgin," and an opportunity to shoot down coconut-laden swallows.

Quest for Camelot (Titus for Nintendo). http://www.nintendo.com/gb/quest_for_camelot.
Based on the Warner Bros. movie, this is a GameBoy product with little Arthurian content. A prime example of a generic abstract adventure

game, where you wander around looking for 8 pieces of a scroll to thwart the evil Sir Ruber.

Computer Games: Internet

Avalon Multiplayer Gameworld. http://www.avalon-rpg.com.

Avalon borrows little from Arthurian legend but the name of the mythical Isle of Apples. Another example of a generic use of Arthurian nomenclature applied to a fantasy roleplaying game. Play knights, sorcerers, bards, and other roles.

Dark Age of Camelot (Mythic Entertainment). http://www.darkageof camelot.com.

Currently under beta testing, will be a 3D virtual world set after the fall of King Arthur. In this post–Arthurian Britain, players take the role of various warriors or magical characters. A world exploration and tactical combat simulation, similar to EverQuest. Unknown how much Arthurian content will be included in game implementation.

In the Lists:
The Arthurian Influence
in Modern Tournaments
of Chivalry

Brian R. Price

*"...there are some whose physical strength, skill and agility enable them
to perform so well that they achieve in this activity such great renown
for their fine exploits ... and because they often engage in it, their renown
and their fame increases."*
Geoffroi de Charny, 14th c. [Kaueper & Kennedy 87]

In a park on a quiet Saturday afternoon, against a lush green backdrop and families enjoying one another's company, a shining glint lures
the eye to an unlikely sight: a fully-armored knight makes his away across
the close towards a fenced list surrounded by brightly clad ladies, brilliant
heraldic displays, and squires running to and fro, helping the knights prepare for combat.

The knights might be competing in a *béhourd*—a medieval form of
tournament fought with bâtons—or in a *pas d'armes* with rebated (blunted)
weapons. All manner of medieval weapons are employed, and the casual
observer might notice that some combatants wear the white belts and spurs
of a knight. Some of the ladies sport coronets. As the day progresses, combatants meet in earnest combat, striving one against the other for the honor
of their consorts and for their own renown.

Such tournaments are common in the United States, Europe, and

Australia, where every weekend some ten thousand or more enthusiasts compete and observe tournaments on an unprecedented scale. Who are these "knights," and why are they engaged in an activity that has been essentially extinct for five hundred years?

The answer lies in a surprising place. The tournament survives because the rich corpus of Arthurian literature has carried the powerful images of the knightly ideals forward, ideals that have been adapted—some would say co-opted—by writers and visionaries creating powerful and important landmarks in literature and its newest extension, film.

Christian Tobler in his armor used for combats within his Order of the Selohaar, a group that follows medieval Round Table formats in a spiritual variant on the tournament company model. Members of tournament and reenactment societies press craftsmen for ever-improving authenticity in harness and raiment; such equipment is critical in connecting to the medieval reality that created the Arthurian romances. Armor by Christian Fletcher.

The magic of the Arthurian mythos is bound up with the images of the tournament, with knighthood, and with romantic ideals. We see this mythos evinced in the most modern iterations of the chivalric pantheon, from Robin Hood to Star Wars. Surrounded by the Arthurian mythos, it is perhaps less of a surprise that the tournament has survived the demise of the knightly station to be reestablished by passionate enthusiasts who approach it from a variety of perspectives: romantic historian, combat enthusiast, martial artist. It is a mixture of martial expression and romantic pageantry, a rich alloy that seems to entrance us as it has entranced audiences since the establishment of the tournament in the 11th century.

The Tournament in History

The earliest tournaments seem to have been training for war, a theme that was stated plainly by William of Newburgh about Richard I's 1194 tournament license decree:

> The famous King Richard, observing that the extra training and instruction of the French made them correspondingly fiercer in war, wished that the knights of his kingdom should train in their own lands, so that they could learn from tourneying the art and custom of war and so that the French could not insult the English knights for being crude and less skilled [Barber & Barker 25].

Early tournaments were barely distinguishable from war. Casualties were frequent, the shedding of blood an expected feature and the destruction of property a common occurrence. The church made valiant but largely ineffective efforts to curtail them, but the knights by and large ignored their pleas, in part because the tournament by this time fulfilled an economic as well as a military purpose, particularly insofar as second sons often used it to make their fortunes (Duby 42). The softening of the "simulacra of battle" that came later was due in part to the dangers posed to the knights themselves in this barely constrained contest of mounted companies. Informal regulatory customs emerged to reduce the danger: these seldom survive in written form but are often alluded to in various chronicles.[1]

A significant development came about through the influence of the romances—particularly Arthurian—on the ladies at court, under whose patronage a vast body of exceptionally powerful images would be generated, images that would over time completely alter the form of the tournament. In the words of tournament scholar Juliet Barker:

> Chivalric literature no doubt reflected the preoccupations of knightly life in the twelfth century by featuring the tournament so prominently (often to the detriment of the story-line) but on the other hand the glorification of chivalric virtues so often displayed in literary tournaments increased the prestige of tourneying in real life and inspired

knights to perform great feats of arms modeled on those of the romantic heroes [Barker 6].

Edward I, in his efforts to reinvigorate his English chivalry and bind
the knights of England together into a more cohesive subculture, engaged
on a series of "round table" tournaments that consciously reflected popular Arthurian literature (Sandoz).

> The Round Table ... was especially popular in the reigns of Edward I
> and Edward III. The particular form of the tournament was marked
> by unusual pageantry and feasting; the presence of ladies was an impor-
> tant feature of the Round Table and ensured that singing and danc-
> ing were continued long into the night after the sport had ended ...
> the Arthurian origins and overtones were frequently exploited to the
> full, with knights taking on the names and even the characters of
> Arthurian heroes and thus identifying themselves with the ideology
> and supremecy of Arthur's court. Round Tables therefore became inex-
> tricably involved with Arthurian propaganda which was cultivated by
> English kings in answer to the French cult of Charlemagne [Barker
> 13].

While the Round Table was perhaps more pageant than competition,
the record does include some martial contests alongside the interludes with
Arthurian pseudo-plots. While the round-table festivals usually incorporated the familiar jousts, they often included, in addition, a new form of
competition, somewhat safer, fought with bâtons of ash or whalebone and
armor of cloth or *cuirboille*, hardened leather. Throughout the 13th–15th
centuries, this form of combat sometimes replaced more dangerous (and
prestigious) encounters with the rebated sword or lance (Price 2001, 154;
Contents: 297–310).

At the close of the 14th century and surviving well into the 15th, the
pas d'armes was a more competitive form of tournament conducted both *à
plaisance* and *à outrance*. A challenge format, defenders—the *tenans*—would
declare their intention to hold a particular place at a particular time against
all comers—the *venans*. Consciously modeled on passages from literary
romance, the spectacles became increasingly elaborate during the 15th century, as illustrated in fine illuminations of descriptive passages by King
René d'Anjou and Olivier de la Marche. Although the tournament itself
fell out of favor at the close of the 15th century, the imagery has survived
both in the rich iconographic record and in the descriptions that inspired
tourneyers of the high Middle Ages.

The Knightly Order

Alongside the early development of the tournament, the knightly order also sprouted, seemingly fully formed, from the pages of Arthurian literature. The first knightly order seems to have been created not in England or in France but in Hungary. King Károly (Charles) founded the Society of Saint George in 1325–6. This confraternal community pursued what seems to have been religiously inspired support for God & crown. Alongside devotional and feudal obligations, fraternal members also participated in tournaments sponsored by the King:

> ...by the time Károly inherited a claim to the throne of Hungary, the tournament and its associated games and rituals had come to function as a festival of chivalry, at which most of the qualities associated to the ideal knight—prowess, courtesy, franchise and largesse—could be both cultivated and displayed. Károly probably required the members of the Society to follow his lead in all such exercises because he hoped that, within the controlled environment of the tournament, they would serve as models of knightly behavior which the other knights present would be moved, by envy or admiration, to emulate as closely as possible [Boulton 44].

It is unclear whether Edward III was aware of the society's existence, but it seems likely. In his own quest to secure his position in a turbulent succession and in wars with Scotland and France, he seems to have followed his grandfather's lead, binding his regime closely to the prestige of the Arthurian ideology.

Much has been written on Edward's efforts, ranging from the cynical (purely political) to the rhapsodic (purely romantic), but the truth of his efforts probably lies somewhere in between. Upon concluding successful campaigns in Scotland and France, he held a series of successful jousts and round tables throughout England, building both popular and chivalric support.

In 1344, following his successful campaign in Brittany, it appears that Edward founded a "Round Table" tourneying society. Many scholars confuse this date with that of the later Order of the Garter, which appears to have followed the Calais campaign of 1347. Froissart, in his recounting of the founding, also appears to confuse the Round Table Society with the OG, but probably does successfully capture the essence of the eventual Garter foundation:

> At this time Edward, King of England, resolved to rebuild the great castle of Windsor, formerly built and founded by King Arthur, and

where was first set up and established the noble Round Table, from whence so many valiant men and knights had issued forth to perform feats of arms and prowess throughout the world. And the said king created an order of knights, to consist of himself, his children, and the bravest in the land. They were to be forty in number, and were to be called the knights of the blue Garter; their feast was to be kept and solemnized annually on St. George's Day. And in order to institute the festival, the King of England assembled earls, barons and knights from his whole realm, and signified to them his purpose and great desire to found the same. In this they joyfully concurred, for it appeared to them to be an honorable undertaking, and calculated to nourish affection among them. Then were elected forty knights known and celebrated as the bravest of them all, and they bound themselves to their king, under their seals, by oath and fealty, to obey the ordinances which should be devised. And the king caused a chapel of St. George to be built within the castle of Windsor, established canons therein for the service of God, and provided and endowed them with a good and liberal revenue. And in order that the said feast might be promulgated in all countries, the King of England sent his heralds to publish and proclaim the same in France, Scotland, Burgundy, Hainault, Flanders, Brabant and the German Empire, granting safe-conduct until fifteen days after the feast. And there was to be held a feast a joust by forty knights, against all comers, and also by forty squires. And this feast was to be celebrated on the following St. George's Day, which would be in the year of grace one thousand, three hundred, and forty-four, at Windsor Castle. And the Queen of England, accompanied by three hundred ladies and damsels, all noble and gentle women, all dressed alike, were to be present [Boulton 102–3].

This conscious invocation of the Arthurian model quickly spread beyond England, where the Garter became an order composed both of English princes and renowned princes from abroad. Similar orders were also immediately founded in Burgundy with the Order of the Golden Fleece and in France with Jean de Valois' Order of the Star, philosophically lead by that hero of 14th century French chivalry, Geoffrey de Charnay.

Although these orders drew obvious organizational cues from the monastic orders and the religious orders of knighthood, especially the Templars and Hospitalers, the imagery of the Knights of the Round Table resonated firmly in the minds of the chivalric community raised on the romances of Chrétien de Troyes and his followers.

In Germany, societies of tourneyers bound themselves together for reasons of business or politics and possibly for more idealistic reasons. These 14th century tournament societies, led by bands of tournament knights, seem to have sponsored and participated in tournaments and were not affiliated with a monarch as were the more famous orders mentioned above.

During the 15th century, combats *à plaisance* (for pleasure) quickly dominated in the rich festivals held throughout Europe, hosted by rich princes such as the Dukes of Burgundy and King René d'Anjou. Like their 14th century Royal predecessors, rich princes of the late 15th century continued the traditions both of membership in knightly orders and in the sponsorships of grand festivals of arms. The pageantry of the Dukes of Burgundy and René d'Anjou provided a fitting climax for the traditions of the knightly order and the pas d'armes.

Modern Tournament Societies

During the 1960s, small groups—steeped in the 19th century medieval revival and popular Arthurian culture—sprouted up, reviving the tournament as a martial sport. The founders of these groups attempted to re-create the chivalric tone they found in medieval and revival literature, building whole societies based on their interpretation of the chivalric ideals, tempered by the ethics of the day.[2]

With little recent research material available, the form of these tournaments generally took a rather modern shape. The combats were conducted with béhourd-style bâtons of rattan in a double-elimination format reminiscent of a 20th century martial arts or fencing tournament tree. Such trees were used in the 16th century for jousting cheques. Fights were—and are—largely conducted on foot, partially owing to animal protection legislation and partially owing to the expense entailed for any equestrian activity.

Fighting with bâtons over the three and a half decades following the foundation of these groups has become a Western martial art in its own right. It is highly competitive, usually full contact, and features armored combatants pressing one another as far as safety allows but relying on the inherent safety of the rattan weapons and slightly over-heavy armor to provide protection against off-target blows or the occasional foul blow. Some groups fight either with very padded weapons known as "boffers," or, at the other end of the spectrum, rebated weapons. Rebated fighting is generally much more constricted owing to the inherent danger of the weapons, the accompanying risk and the expense.

Each of these systems can be strongly differentiated from modern fencing or tournament martial arts by their most important quality: their expectation of "chivalric" conduct by the combatants, represented chiefly in their responsibility for calling the blows that land upon them. Combatants who

Combats fight à plaisance at the barrier with poleaxes before an appreciative gallery. Modern tournaments of chivalry are oriented more for participation than for demonstration: both combatants and gallery members alike participate in the drama as the stage is set for knightly deeds.

are successful at this earn renown both for their virtue and for their prowess. The minority of combatants who choose to cheat suffer infamy for their choices, and their renown suffers as their opponents and the gallery make decisions about their character under the magnifying glass that is the tournament field. Precisely the same mechanism seems to have been present within the medieval lists and in Arthurian literature, as knights errant strove forth boldly to win praise and earn renown within the lists.

These informal groups quickly expanded as individuals flocked to the color and quasi-medieval interpretations of medieval fiction. Social structures quickly evolved in which "Kings" and "Queens" "ruled" over geographic regions known as kingdoms, served in their temporary reigns by knights, squires, lords and ladies representing the prosperous townsmen and nobility of a stylized medieval court. These elaborate social structures strove to reinforce chivalric conduct and rewarded physical prowess, artistic ability and service, all revolving around the central activity—the tournament.

The Society for Creative Anachronism (SCA) was to become the largest of these romantic societies, but others were founded in the United States at about the same time. Markland, Ltd., based on the east coast, still survives today. A host of other smaller groups have either perished or sprouted from the SCA's fold, and although the founders frequently deny prior SCA affiliation, a quick examination of the rules, combat and tournament forms, and social structures reveals the dominant influence of the SCA.

None of these groups can be called reenactment societies, generally small groups fascinated with highly accurate portrayals of historical life merging both intensive research with field experimentation. The most successful combat societies have few mechanisms for enforcing the level of authenticity required by organizations such as the American Civil War groups, nor are they particularly adept at rewarding those who strive towards reenactment objectives. Like the medieval tournament patrons who sponsored tournaments celebrating a particular event or era in history, modern combat societies have very loose interpretations for what is historical, but are adept at creating a tone that encourages chivalric conduct and martial prowess.

For the SCA, for example, the framework is between 650 A.D. and 1600 A.D., and yet you will commonly see at large events Roman Centurions (some of whom are painfully accurate in their portrayal), Greek Hoplites, Cavaliers, Samurai, and even the odd Aztec warrior clothed in faux Jaguar "armour." This loose framework is at once the large combat society's best strength and most damaging weakness. Generally not well thought of in reenactment or scholarly circles, which consider the SCA an invitation for many an odd sword-toting misfit to set up camp, this vast umbrella allows thousands of people annually to review dozens of different tournaments and sparks healthy debate concerning the practical exercise of chivalric skills within the lists. Under the aegis of the SCA, the Empire of Chivalry and Steel, and the Adrian Empire, more than 30,000 individuals are organized into countless subgroups, each playing the common game a different way, yet each generally upholding the chivalric commonality that binds members together—a true mixture of American democratic heritage with medieval and medieval-revival ideology.

Out of these groups have sprung scholars, reenactors and enthusiasts who have delved more deeply into the history and literature of the Middle Ages. Led by the American Company of Saint George, some individuals have organized themselves into small 'tournament companies' that work

Combatant Michael Plotts readies himself in a modern pas d'armes conducted as a béhourd. Members of tournament societies have organized themselves around the confraternal model and seek to demonstrate, exercise and celebrate the complete spectrum of chivalric virtues. Armor by Brian R. Price.

in more focused historical bands, doing a great deal of research into the medieval tournament, the chivalric ideals, and knighthood as a model for an unreachable but noble ideal. They have also championed the infusion of new medieval martial arts knowledge being extracted from medieval *fechtbuchen* (fighting manuals), integrating it into their derivative combat forms to work toward continual improvement of the accuracy of their tournament portrayals.

In trying to reproduce the medieval formats, tournament companies are a blend of the German tournament society and the monarchical confraternities exemplified by the Order of the Garter. Governing themselves through charters sealed by all members, these companies consciously reflect the same "round table" organization of their Arthurian and monarchical inspiration.

Tournaments, whether modern or medieval, have a two-fold purpose: on one hand to improve knightly prowess by testing physical technique and on the other hand to provide a stage upon which knightly deeds are demonstrated for an appreciative gallery. The tournament is a celebration of the knightly virtues, enjoyed by both participants and spectators alike. Modern feats of arms sponsored by these societies take the form of medieval

Round Tables, *pas d'armes*, and in the new millennium with jousts as well. Familiar combat systems are generally employed beside historical models for the feat of arms; those inspired by the events are, by design, "through envy or admiration" enjoined to renew their pursuit of the chivalric ideals.

In the late 1990s, the limited availability of medieval *fechtbuchen* inspired the growth of a different sort of combat society, modern schools of "historical" swordsmanship. Coming from the perspective of the traditional martial arts community, these schools have raised awareness of the *fechtbuchen* and medieval technique within both the combat society and the reenactment community. The Historical Armed Combat Association (HACA)—initially led the movement, though at the very end of the decade other organizations such as the Academy of European Medieval Martial Arts (AEMMA) and the Swordplay Symposium International have served alongside museums, notably the Higgens Armoury in Worchester, MA, and the Royal Armouries at Leeds, to build the community.

As the new millennium dawns, these initiatives have resulted in the desire for the reestablishment of an international tournament circuit, both to test the reconstructed techniques and to exercise the whole spectrum of chivalric virtues. Tournaments of ever-increasing authenticity and impact await those who would follow the modern chivalric pilgrimage. The four main communities—romantic, reenactment, tournament and *fechtbuch* societies—are coming together with a renewed vigor to exercise themselves not only in prowess, but in pursuit of the virtues extolled by that most influential of chivalric reform writers, Ramon Llull: prowess, loyalty, courage, faith, humility, courtesy, fidelity, largesse and franchise. Truly, Arthurian inspiration is alive and well in more than just literature.

Notes

1. There are many such citations in Froissart, Jean le Bel and Olivier de la Marche. For a notable exception see the tournament regulations of the *Statuta Armorum*, reproduced in Cripps-Day Appendix 3.

2. Conversations with Andrew Smith, early participant in the Society for Creative Anachronism, 12/2000.

Works Cited

Barber, Richard, and Juliet Barker. *Tournaments: Jousts, Chivalry & Pageants in the Middle Ages.* Weidenfield & Nicholson, 1989.
Barker, Juliet R.V. *The Tournament in England, 1100–1400.* Boydell & Brewer, 1986.

Bel, Jean de. Eds. J. Viard & Bernard Prost. *Chronique.* 2 vols. 1904.

Bennett, Elizabeth. *King René's Tournament Book.* Unpublished translation, 1992.

Bornstein, Diane. *Mirrors of Courtesy.* Archon, 1975.

Boulton, D'Arcy J. *The Knights of the Crown: The Monarchical Orders of Knighthood in Later Medieval Europe, 1325–1520.* St. Martins Press, 1987.

Cline, Ruth Huff. "The Influence of the Romances on Tournaments of the Middle Ages." *Speculum,* 1945.

"Copy of a Roll of Purchases for a Tournament at Windsor Park in the Sixth Year of Edward I." Ed. S. Lysons. *Archaeologia* 17 (1819): 297–310.

Cripps-Day, Francis. *The History of the Tournament.* Bernard Quaritich, 1918.

D'Anjou, René. *Traité de la Forme et Devis d'un Tournoi.* Verve, 1946.

Duby, Georges. Trans. Richard Howard. *William Marshal: Flower of Chivalry.* Pantheon Books, 1985.

Froissart, Jean. *Oeuvres.* Ed. Kervyn de Lettenhove. 25 vols. 1867–77.

Kaeuper, Richard W., and Elspeth Kennedy. *The Book of Chivalry of Geoffroi de Charny.* University of Pennsylvania Press, 1996.

Keen, Maurice. *Chivalry.* Yale University Press, 1984.

Loomis, Roger Sherman. "Chivalric & Dramatic Imitations of Arthurian Romance." *Medieval Studies in the Memory of A.K. Porter,* 1939.

_____. "Edward I: Arthurian Enthusiast." *Speculum,* 1953.

Neste, Évelyne van den. *Tournois, Joutes, Pas d'Armes dans les Villes de Flandre à la Fin du Moyen Age (1300–1486).* École de Chartres, 1996.

Price, Brian. *The Book of the Tournament.* Chivalry Bookshelf, 1996.

_____. *Pas d'Armes & Roundtables: Reenacting Medieval Feats of Armes.* Chivalry Bookshelf, 2001.

_____. *Ramon Llull's Book of Knighthood & Chivalry: A Translation.* Chivalry Bookshelf, 1997.

_____. *Techniques of Medieval Armour Reproduction.* Paladin Press, 2000.

Sandoz, Eduoard. "Tourneys in the Arthurian Tradition." *Speculum.* October, 1944.

Vale, Malcom. *War & Chivalry: Warfare and Aristocratic Culture in England, France and Burgundy and the End of the Middle Ages.* University of Georgia Press, 1981.

King of the World (Wide Web): Arthur on the Internet

JOHN J. DOHERTY

I am thinking of a great cathedral, where Saxon, Norman, Gothic, Renaissance, and Georgian elements all co-exist, and all grow together into something strange and admirable which none of its successive builders intended or foresaw.

C.S. Lewis

It is hard to overestimate the influence of the Internet in contemporary culture. The Internet is everywhere, from television advertisements to academic endeavors. It entertains, communicates, sells, buys, informs, and educates. In short, it is an interesting reflection of the times. The Internet is also an unforeseen (if very interesting) addition to what C.S. Lewis called the "great cathedral" of the Arthurian Legend.

Arthuriana has been the domain of print through most of its history. For most of this history, however, it has changed with the times, adapting to various mediums and genres. In no small measure this is due to the legend's popularity in whatever age it has appeared. Indeed, Richard Barber comments that much of the enchantment of Arthur as hero has "stemmed from his ability to shift his shape in accordance with the mood of the age" (Barber). The Arthurian Legend has easily crossed over into other media, especially film and the Internet, in recent times; it was somewhere on the Internet before the Internet became the monster it is today.

The use of the Internet to disseminate academic information in the humanities has been somewhat controversial. For academic disciplines focused on print media it has been an especially difficult transition to the electronic medium. Articles have discussed the globalization of the humanities through the use of the Internet (Liu), and how the Internet affects the quality of information retrieval in literature (Anderson). All of this ignores a simple fact—the majority of today's Internet users are not academics. The change in the Internet's audience is something that the academy has not really paid much attention to but which, in Arthurian Studies, is something that has probably begun to attract more students to the field than any other form of course advertising.

Academic Sites

Initially, booklists dominated Arthurian Internet resources. These ranged from basic core collection guides to extensive readings. Quite a few of these are still available, while others are being developed in conjunction with new Internet sites, school or university courses, and "Frequently Asked Questions" resource lists (for examples, see the end of this chapter). A 1995 survey of Arthurian Internet resources presented mostly academic resources (Callery). In the main, these were book lists, journal indexes, and some electronic texts (texts, pre-prints of articles, original research). Many of these sites are in surprisingly good shape.

All of the electronic texts are still available, most through the Web (thus doing away with the need for anonymous FTP, Gopher, Archie, and other early Internet technologies). The availability of electronic texts has grown with the Internet. Not only are the texts more readily available, but more texts are coming online every day. The University of Virginia E-Text Center (http://etext.lib.virginia.edu/uvaonline.html), mentioned by Callery, now boasts 51,000 texts and 350,000 related images. It provides access to fourteen languages, from English to Apache and Tibetan. Project Gutenberg (http://www.promo.net/pg/), arguably the prototype of all e-text services, began making non-copyrighted material available electronically in 1971 (History and Philosophy).

> However, for the person who wants an "authoritative edition" we will have to wait some time until this becomes more feasible. We do, however, intend to release many editions of Shakespeare and the other classics for the comparative study on a scholarly level, before the end of the year 2001, when we are scheduled to complete our 10,000 book Project Gutenberg Electronic Public Library [History and Philosophy].

The E-Text Center and Project Gutenberg have produced many com-petitors and some sites of special Arthurian interest (see the end of the chapter). By far the most comprehensive Arthurian e-text site is the Uni-versity of Rochester's *The Camelot Project* (http://www.lib.rochester.edu/camelot/cphome.stm). This resource provides access to Arthurian texts, images, bibliographies and some basic information. Begun in 1995, the web site is still very much in development. For example, there are some categories in the "Knights and Ladies of Arthur's Realm" section that have waited for six years to be completed (and are still waiting). That said, this service fulfills some of the basic requirements for a quality Internet resource: good authority (Alan Lupack and Barbara Tepa Lupack of the University of Rochester are the primary editors), ease of use, and currency (the site is being constantly updated).

Electronic texts are not the only academic resources on the Internet to survive the advent of the commercial web site. Of the remaining cate-gories listed by Callery (Articles and References, Bibliographies, Discussion Lists, Audio-Visual Media, The Labyrinth), most of the sites are still pre-sent and functioning. In many instances, they have developed into some-thing larger than could have been predicted in 1995. The main focus of these sites was academic. The post-military, early Internet was driven by academic institutions that could afford to host services such as FTP and Gopher. With the advent of the graphical Web browser (first Mosaic and then Netscape) the Internet spread its wings. Also, as potential authors learned the ease of Hypertext Markup Language (HTML) and, later, HTML editors, content expanded exponentially.

The only Web site mentioned in Callery's 1995 survey was *The Labyrinth* (http://labyrinth.georgetown.edu/). At the time, this site was indica-tive of the academic side of the Internet: a quality resource that had under-gone some form of scrutiny before "publication." However, the information available on today's Web does not have such quality control. It can range from the most current copies of government reports to the latest ravings of Australian neo–Nazis. The United States' Government Printing Office, for example, is now presenting a great deal of its publications on the Web; state governments are following suit. Many traditional resources, such as academic journals and encyclopedias, are also publishing versions of their print runs on the Web, though usually through a subscription service.

Two Arthurian-related journals now have a home on the Internet: *Arthuriana*, the journal of the North American Branch of the International Arthurian Society (http://dc.smu.edu/Arthuriana/), and *The Heroic Age*, an online journal dedicated to the study of early medieval Northwestern

Europe with some Arthurian content (http://members.aol.com/heroicage1/
homepage.html). Supplementing these journals are various forums such as
the ArthurNet e-mail discussion group.

Academic journals are not the only serials available—the Internet is
the home for many popular magazines. The online magazine *Britannia*
(http://www.britannia.com/) has had a section on King Arthur and the Early
British Kingdoms since 1996. The section is one of the magazines most popular. It includes biographies of the legends' characters, a subsection on the
basics for those new to Arthuriana, and much more. For a time Arthurian
scholar Geoffrey Ashe was an editor for this section of the magazine
(http://www.britannia.com/history/h12.html).

Quality vs. Quantity

Academe is no longer the Internet's driving force. Since 1995, *Time*'s
"Year of the Internet," the commercial world has discovered the many uses
of the Internet. Today, .com websites dominate; they outnumber .edu, .gov
and the many other domains that make up the Internet. This makes the
Internet a very useful information resource for the careful and cautious
researcher who is aware that not all sources are either reliable or valuable.
The hype surrounding the Internet suggests that it is the ultimate research
tool, that it is the font of all knowledge. The reality is that anyone can publish almost anything on the Internet, usually without the intervention of
any form of quality control.

A search on any of the Web's indexing tools reveals that the Arthurian
Legend is a prime example of this reality. *Google*, for example, returns about
135,000 hits for a phrase search on King Arthur. A word search for
Arthurian returns only 43,400 hits. The same searches on *Alta Vista*
returned 89,338 and 40,677 respectively. *Northern Light* was slightly smaller,
with 68,915 for King Arthur and 27,852 for Arthurian.[1] These three utilities are ranked in the top five of the Internet's largest search engines (Notes).

It can be hard for the typical Internet user to determine the quality
of such a huge number of Web sites. While scholars abound on the Internet (more so than during the early days of academic control), finding their
work is like looking for the proverbial needle in a haystack. To the novice
researcher, it can seem like everything on the Internet has been touched
by King Arthur. For example, of the first ten web sites listed by the *Google*
King Arthur search, seven are personal pages; one is an online magazine
(*Britannia*); one is the only "authorised Web site of King Arthur Uther

Pendragon, The Once And Future King" dedicated to "the living, breathing, People's King, not the myth of legend" (King Arthur Pendragon); and the last is a link to "King Arthur Flour." Of the "personal" pages listed there is a great deal of information collated on the Arthurian history, legend, and mythology. From most of these sites the general researcher can cull many answers to the basic questions usually asked.

Questions to Ask

Most Arthurian researchers on the Internet are either looking for information to satisfy an interest piqued or to fulfill a basic research assignment (a school report or a basic-level literature/history college class.)[2] Of these, the school assignment is the major reason. Researchers are usually looking for information on whether or not King Arthur actually lived, where Camelot is located, a photograph of Lancelot, and so on. Most of them come to the Arthurian Legend through some form of entertainment, such as an episode of *Hercules: The Legendary Journals*; a movie, such as *First Knight*; or a book that mentions Merlin, such as the "Harry Potter" series. Their interest has been piqued, and they want to find out more. And if they can also complete an assignment or two while they are at it, so much the better.

The promise of the Internet is that it offers the answer to most, if not all, of life's questions and concerns. Newswires such as Reuters print their reports directly to the Web, making it one of the most accessed news resources of recent times. WebMD (http://www.webmd.com) offers services that previously were sought from a healthcare practitioner. Users can buy cars, shop for books, seek mortgages and other bank loans, and pay their bills through the Internet. Services such as Ask Jeeves (http://www.ask jeeves.com/) market themselves as research tools for the savy Internet user.

Interesting Web Sites[3]

The novice researcher, however, does not realize that the Internet is a virtual version of London's Hyde Park corner: anyone with the knowledge, skill, and a little courage can present any information on any topic. The information provided in a book or journal goes through some form of quality control before it has been published. On the Internet, however, anyone with access to a Web server and an HTML editor can publish his

or her theories on the origins, current existence, or mythology of the Holy
Grail, King Arthur, and the Knights of the Round Table without any quality control or review.

For example, the Web site *Templar Knights and Grail* has collated a
number of articles on the theories that attach the medieval order of the
Knights Templar to the Grail legend. Most of the articles echo the premise
of *The Holy Blood and the Holy Grail* (a work thoroughly debunked by scholars and critics alike) that the Templars discovered the Grail in the Temple
at Jerusalem and brought it back to Europe with them. The author of the
Web site, Mariano Tomatis, states unequivocally that "the knights who
guard the Holy Grail, the Grail castle, and the Grail family [in Wolfram
von Eschenback's *Parzifal*] are Templars." The source for this statement is
attributed to *The Holy Blood and the Holy Grail*, although Tomatis does not
"have the space to go fully into this here."

The Templar Research Institute.Org sounds much more official, noble
and academic. This web site proclaims that:

> [The Institute] has as its goal the harmonization of the world's Cul-
> tural and Spiritual Traditions through a rigorous program of unbiased
> research. And, as with the medieval Order of the Temple, TRI repre-
> sents but the outer activity of a Spiritual Core which animates it.

Areas where this research is conducted include the Homeless, Battered
Women, Drug Addiction, Chivalry Workshops, and Spiritual Healing
through Prayer or Visualization. What is missing from the Web site are the
"prices" to be paid to participate in these research programs.

These Web sites are prime examples of the sort of information easily
found on the Internet. Using Web search engines to look for information
can sometimes lead the unwary down interesting and unusual paths. *King
Arthur Pendragon*, for example, is the official Web site of "the third reincarnation of Arthur Pendragon." To some, that might seem like a wild
claim. Arthur, however, thinks differently:

> The current Queen [Elizabeth II] is forced down people's throats. She's
> the queen because the population of the country are told she's the
> Queen. Me, I'm Arthur Pendragon and if people want to believe I'm
> some nutter who thinks he's the reincarnation of King Arthur that's
> their choice.

The Web site exists to promote Arthur's "ideals of truth, justice and the
conservation of the planet for our children." It also provides some useful
links to other Arthurian Web resources and lists.

The name of a Web site can be very misleading, and that is usually all a user sees in a search engine list. While the name might seem to be informational or appropriate, it can sometimes be otherwise. Seeing a Web site called *The Ultimate King Arthur Web Guide* leads one to expect just that. Instead, it is a Web site about "Scotland's King Arthur," and comes complete with "evidence" to support the theory of Arthur's Scottish (as opposed to English or Welsh) origins. Tidbits offered include Merlin's Grave, Arthur's Grave, Camelot, Sir Lancelot the Pict, and much more.

The Internet has been used to promote information and theories that usually don't see the light in more traditional resources. This is what makes it such a unique and, at times, fun resource. However, somewhere between the "interesting" and the scholarly lies a much more moderate realm of Internet resources developed by enthusiasts whose sole goal is to share their love of something particular. Sometimes these resources turn up in traditional media. For example, the print press has been known to get scooped by so-called "fan sites" or "official" Web services where companies can control information being released to the public. For example, the normally secretive Lucasfilm is using the Internet to great success to keep a lid on Internet rumors that spread about its ongoing projects. The company releases just enough hints through its official Star Wars Web site (http://www.starwars.com) to maintain control of the rumor mill. That it is also an effective marketing tool has not been lost on them and other companies.

Enthusiasts put a lot of time and effort into their Web sites. The Arthurian Legend attracts more than its fair share of enthusiastic researchers, most of whom try hard to be objective in presenting their information to the world. One Web site that is comprehensive in its coverage is David Nash Ford's *King Arthur*. While this site has not been updated for a few years, it still has a lot of good information that assists the novice researcher in finding out the basics. It collates information from an extensive bibliography (also listed on the Web site) that gives some excellent overviews on topics like Popular Arthur, Early References to a Real Arthur, Arthur and Archaeology, and Aspects of the Arthurian Legend.

A worthy competitor to Ford's site is *Legends*, a web resource edited by Paula Katherine Marmor. The site honestly proclaims itself to be a "personal journey" through "the worlds of Robin Hood, King Arthur, D'Artagnan, and other swashbuckling characters of balladry, fiction, and film." The section on Arthur provides links to some of the better Arthurian resources on the Internet. Unlike some other, similar resources, these links are categorized in sections such as History & Archaeology, Malory, and

Elaine of Astolat. Also, it is much more current than Ford's site, and most of the links listed actually work.

One of the newer Arthurian Web sites, *King Arthur: A Man for the Ages*, which is not yet indexed on some of the major search engines, examines the historical and legendary aspects of the legendary King of Britain. Many characters, objects and aspects are covered, including Merlin, Guinevere, Lancelot, and the Sword in the Stone. The author also provides some details on medieval and modern authors, including a relatively up-to-date list of current Arthurian authors. This site also provides a FAQ or "Frequently Asked Questions" section, which gives a hint of some of the questions the site receives. They range from "Was Arthur a king or just a battle commander?" to "Was Guinevere really an adulteress?" and "Was Lancelot the greatest knight of them all?"

This Web site also includes links to some travel companies that provide guided tours of Arthurian sites in Britain, including *Britannia Travel* and *King Arthur Day Tour*. These are prime examples of travel sites that are proliferating across the Internet, providing an Arthurian twist to a hugely popular industry—the educational vacation.

Conclusion

Any survey of the Internet is going to produce a list that becomes dated almost from the moment it is put on paper. The Internet's contribution to popular culture has been unique. However, attempts at capturing this contribution can only be a snapshot at best, a list of dead links at worst. The Internet allows anyone to publish an article, a bibliography, or any other resource. Unlike print, however, it is not a static medium. Anything available on the Internet can be updated, changed, deleted, or just forgotten by the author or whoever might have access to the Web site.

The Arthurian Legend, however, has been well served by those who have put their work on the Internet. It is unusual to attribute staying power to so many resources for such a narrow field of study. But, as can be seen from Callery's 1995 survey, a lot of Arthuriana has survived six very tumultuous years of Internet history.

The popularity of King Arthur in other ages has come down into the twenty-first century. The legend began as oral tales in the valleys and mountains of early medieval Wales; crossed over into the chivalric literature of the France and Germany of the Crusades; returned to England and into printed books; came into the twentieth-century as novels, poems, plays, pseudo-histories, libretti and operas; crossed over into all visual media (film, video, television and CD-ROMs); and is now to be found all across the Internet, the medium that is defining communication and culture at the turn of the century. King Arthur might not be the current King of England, in spite of some claims, but it is difficult to find another pseudo-historical figure who dominates the Internet so.

A common element runs through a lot of "personal page" Web sites (those created and maintained by individuals): Arthur as a Dark Age Warrior destined to greatness. This Arthur is not the Arthur of fact, classical literature, or, in most instances, legend and myth. This is the Arthur of modern fantasy literature, the Arthur of Mary Stewart, Marion Bradley and Stephen Lawhead. The increasingly popular fantasy genre is producing Arthurian works at an ever-increasing pace (a tabulation of publication dates on some of the booklists on the Internet is enough evidence of this). This serves to bring more and more students to Arthurian Studies, either in formal or informal settings. The Internet is the most informal of them all—and it is where Arthur rules.

To borrow a phrase, he is the King of the World ... Wide Web.

Notes

1. All searches completed on March 12, 2001. A phrase search placed the phrase within quotes (""), while a keyword search did not use quotes. Also, where possible, only the utility's basic search engine was used. Web addresses for search engines are: www.google.com; www.altavista.com; www.northernlight.com.
2. The author receives about 10–15 questions a month through his Web site, "Arthurian Resources on the Internet." The statistics quoted here are a compilation of the questions he receives.
3. The addresses for all of the following Web Sites can be found in Appendix. The addresses were current as of February 22, 2001.

Recommended Web Sites for Electronic Arthurian Texts

The Camelot Project. http://www.lib.rochester.edu/camelot/cphome.stm
The Charette Project. http://www.princeton.edu/~lancelot/
Penn State's Electronic Classics Series Sir Thomas Malory Page. http://www.hn.psu.edu/faculty/jmanis/malory.htm
TEAMS Middle English Texts. http://www.lib.rochester.edu/camelot/teams/tmsmenu.htm
Textes de Français Ancien. http://www.lib.uchicago.edu/efts/ARTFL/projects/TLA/
Welsh Authors. http://jade.ccccd.edu/grooms/ydcm.htm

Some Interesting Arthurian Web Sites

Anthologies of Short Stories [with Arthurian Characters and Themes]. http://www.
    ugf.edu/english/courses/ENG226/226stories.htm
The Arthurian Legend: A Core Collection Bibliography. http://jan.ucc.nau.edu/~jjd23/
    corecoll/corecoll.html
The Arthuriana/Camelot Project Bibliographies. http://www.lib.rochester.edu/camelot/
    acpbibs/bibhome.stm
Bibliography of Novels with Arthurian Characters and Themes. http://www.ugf.edu/
    english/courses/ENG226/226novel.htm
Britannia Travel. http://britannia.com/travel/
King Arthur. http://freespace.virgin.net/david.ford2/arthur.html
King Arthur: A Man for the Ages. http://www.geocities.com/CapitolHill/4186/Arthur/
    htmlpages/kingarthur.html
King Arthur Day Tour. http://www.astraltravels.co.uk/king_arthur_tour.htm
King Arthur Pendragon. http://arthurpendragon.ukonline.co.uk/contents.html
Legends. http://www.legends.dm.net/index.html
Templar Knights and Grail. http://www.geocities.com/Athens/Delphi/3636/templar.htm
Templar Research Institute .org. http://www.templar-research-inst.org/
The Ultimate King Arthur Web Guide. http://www.magicdragon.com/Wallace/arthur.
    html

Works Cited

Anderson, Byron. "The World Wide Web and the Humanities." *Humanities Col-
    lections* 1:1 (1998): 25–40.
Baigent, Michael, Richard Leigh and Henry Lincoln. *The Holy Blood and the Holy
    Grail.* London: Cape, 1982.
Barber, Richard. *The Figure of Arthur.* Cambridge: D.S. Brewer, 1972.
Callery, Anne. "A Brief Guide to Arthurian Resources on the Internet." *Arthuri-
    ana* 4:2 (Summer 1994): 196–199.
"History and Philosophy of Project Gutenberg." *Project Gutenberg.* Aug. 1992. Feb.
    20, 2001. http://promo.net/pg/history.html.
King Arthur Pendragon. UK Online. Feb. 20, 2001. http://arthurpendragon.ukonline.
    co.uk/
Lewis, C.S. "The English Prose MORTE," *Essays on Malory.* Ed. J.A.W. Bennett
    (Oxford: Clarendon, 1963): 25.
Liu, Alan. "Globalizing the Humanities: 'Voice of the Shuttle: Web Page for
    Humanities Research.'" *Humanities Collections* 1:1 (1998): 41–56.
Notess, Greg R. "Search Engine Statistics: Database Total Size Estimates." *Search
    Engine Showdown.* Oct. 9, 2000. Feb. 20, 2001. http://searchengineshowdown.
    com/stats/sizeest.shtml.

Merlin in the
Public Domain

PETER H. GOODRICH

The figure of Merlin has long since entered the nonverbal space of consciousness that is the spawning ground of new creations with perceived archetypal underpinnings. His very name—and its associated images of grimoire, crystal ball, magic wand, shooting stars, long white beard and hair, flowing robe and conical cap emblazoned with astronomical images—is now so instantly recognizable that it is no longer even necessary to identify him as Arthurian or to explain his signification. That ubiquity was brought home to me recently by a long and highly technical legal article by legal scholar Michael Saks, titled "Merlin and Solomon: Lessons from the Law's Formative Encounters with Forensic Identification Science." Forensic identification science involves expert scene-of-the-crime observation and techniques such as fingerprinting and DNA analysis to help investigators divine the unseen facts of a crime. Yet the only reference to Merlin or Solomon in the entire 72-page article was the title. Saks knew his audience of legal experts would immediately understand that Merlin referred to the forensic scientists and technicians, and Solomon to the legal representatives empowered to make judgments based upon their testimony. And his point was that given the legal profession's historically credulous attitude towards this testimony and the sciences underlying it, the experts might just as well be magicians. That credulity, it seems to me, is willingly granted, and has always remained a wellspring of Merlin's iconic status within western culture.

Before testing that hypothesis, we should examine how deeply the figure of Merlin permeates our public consciousness, and ask how and why

219

it does so. Elizabeth Sklar's "Marketing Arthur: The Commodification of Arthurian Legend," first published in 1993, addresses this task by proposing that present-day Arthurian images are intended to reveal things about us, not about the Middle Ages. In general, the legend is still invoked as a romantic "fairy tale" about elite cultural experience, but promotes contemporary and largely material means of obtaining its mystical cachet. The name Merlin in particular "signifies the quick fix, the cure for what ails you" (Sklar 69), and therefore finds expression in the names of music boxes, liquor stores, pubs, pharmacies, businesses like Merlin's Magic Muffler & Brake, and high-tech devices like AT&T's Merlin business phone system, Varitronic's Merlin lettering machine, and the University of Michigan Library's Mirlyn computerized catalog. Not only are these varieties of "Merlin" still in existence, but they may also be discovered on the Internet and in many cases have been continually improved and updated. Nor are these always the only devices of their kind to bear the magic moniker. To append just one example to Sklar's list, the Mirlyn catalog has been emulated by the Missouri Education Research Libraries Information Network (MERLIN, http://www.merlin.missouri.edu/) at the Universities of Missouri and Saint Louis, and the Managing Effective Research across the Library Information Network system (MERLIN, http://www.merlin.lib.gla.ac.uk/) at Glasgow University in Scotland. Sklar finds a general fascination with the "glamour" of Arthurian legend, its characters, talismans, and themes; this article supplies many more instances of the legend's strangest and most powerful character. Merlin's longevity and distribution through such a variety of applications testifies to his remarkable effectiveness as a marketing agent in our commodity-obsessed society and to an equally strong but suppressed desire to transcend commodities altogether.

Sklar persuasively demonstrates that these commodifications are instrumental as "cultural currency" (79). They perform effective visual and verbal acts, like the allusive title of Sak's legal essay about forensic science, because they are conveniently intertextual and instantly recognizable, capable of summoning up whole narratives and networks of nonverbal associations in a single image. Like all good art or advertising, they are not intended only (or even primarily) for rationalization. In fact, their allusive effectiveness derives largely from their ability to elude rationality and appeal to what transcends it, establishing a type of validity that even normally discriminating people would rather invoke than test.

Merlin is the best example of this nonverbal space of consciousness in which magic rules and its validity is instantaneously granted. The magical technology of the Internet now permits us to expand Sklar's examples exponentially. This is the most public of all domains, and the most problematic for scholars. A number of websites including pages on Merlin are maintained by scholars or groups with trustworthy academic affiliations, chief among them Alan Lupack's *The Camelot Project* at the University of Rochester (http://www.lib.rochester.edu/camelot/). Other sites, especially those designed for popular audiences or from a New Age or mystical perspective, may look authoritative and contain substantially factual information, but may also include fanciful or speculative data and source citations (http://www.britannia.com/history/biographies/merlin.html, http://www.eliki.com/ancient/myth/camelot/merlin/). And by far the greatest number simply employ the figure's notoriety for their own nonacademic purposes.

Onomastic searching under the three main variant spellings *Merlin*, *Myrddin*, and *Merlyn* in *AltaVista* in April 2000 turned up over 300,000 hits—the numbers change each time you try—and a title search query modifier limited the results to 26,584. A visual image search in *AltaVista* at the same time turned up 1,495 images for *Merlin*, 13 for *Myrddin*, and 75 for *Merlyn*. In February 2001 there were 260,804 pages on *Alta Vista* and 1,437 images for the three names, not including buttons or banners (which raised the total to 1,810). On the same day over 1,300 items were listed for sale under these names on the *Ebay* auction site. By comparison, a similar search for *King and Arthur* returned 354,664 pages. These are World Wide Web pages only; a Web-based search of Yellow Pages directories would produce a considerably higher number. Moreover, since even the largest search engines only index about 25% of what is on the Web, the actual volume of Merlin references there is undoubtedly greater still. Given the dynamic evolution of the Internet, these numbers fluctuate constantly, but are powerful testimony to the wizard's popularity, even as measured against King Arthur himself.

While the Internet is a marvelously helpful tool for research, it is far from perfect. The keyword needs only appear somewhere in the HTML description, regardless of context. Consequently, many of the results for Merlin are not Arthurian allusions at all, but simply onomastic coincidences and dead ends such as irrelevant or defunct sites and multiple pages of the same sites. In some cases, such as the Merlin Metalworks bicycle company (http://www.merlinbike.com/), Merlin Open Systems electronic publishing software (http://www.merlin-os.co.uk/), and a number of online photographic images, the allusion is clearly not to the magician but to the species of hawk. In others, such as the Merlyn Formula Three and Formula Ford open-wheeled racecars of the 1960s and 70s (http://www.rensel.com/

merlyn.cfm) and the Merlin Medical Relief International humanitarian organization (http://www.merlin.org.uk/), it is ambiguous, with no obvious verbal or visual Arthurian cue.

The legendary Merlin's repertoire of expertise has become so vast that usually some plausible if tenuous association with him can nevertheless be postulated (the race car with his ability to travel great distances very rapidly, the humanitarian agency with his medical knowledge). Many other hits are simply personal names. In these cases also we may have difficulty determining whether any Arthurian reference was intended—although sometimes it does seem tantalizingly appropriate, as with the long-lived, 19-year-old black cat Merlin listed on http://www.petloss.com/, a website playing a continuous synthesized audio loop of "Can You Feel the Love Tonight" to memorialize deceased pets. It can be tempting also to construe an Arthurian connection for individuals like travel guide John Merlin Fisher, the two Merlin Stones who have published books about the Great Goddess and customer relationship marketing, the Merlin R. Carothers who has produced a raft of books on the power of praise and positive thinking, the equally prolific chiropterist, or bat expert, Merlin D. Tuttle, and many others with Merlinesque occupations and subjects. Yet precisely because Merlin has developed into a signifier for any special knowledge, the Arthurian allusion depends as much on the mind of the beholder as on the person or object beheld.

With all its drawbacks, the Internet does provide conclusive evidence that the Arthurian Merlin and its variant spellings is still a name to conjure with, even in places with no obvious connection to the Arthurian legend. The most convincing proof of this ubiquity is that it appears referenced to all of his primary roles in Arthurian literature: as wild man, half-human, prophet, poet, counselor, wizard, and lover.[1] These roles usefully demonstrate the widely distributed images of the mage in cyberspace.

To begin with, Bill Worthington's Merlin as a reclusive madman is available in poster form (http://www.crissiam.demon.co.uk/b3-8.html). Kikki's Celtic Landscape page (http://www.celticatlanta.com/kikki/a›alenau/applegrove.htm) includes a description of her plans for "Myrddin's Affalenau Apple Grove"—a reference to the Welsh "Yr Afallennau" or "Apple Tree Stanzas" in the *Black Book of Carmarthen* (1250) in which Merlin remembers the sixth-century battle of Arfderydd where he went mad.[2] Since this Merlin lives with (and like) animals and perches in trees, it is appropriate that you can order the Merlin Species Watcher by Ian Patton and D.W. Lloyd, a "powerful database system for birders and other naturalists" that can operate in different languages (http://www.hyperscribe.org/

merlin/). A poor soul under the name Lord Myrddin has posted on a website devoted to "the worst movies on earth," describing himself disconso-
lately as "a dork with no life who watches stupid horror films and posts
about them on [sic] here" (http://www.ohthehumanity.com/ur/158.html). The
medieval Merlin in the guise of a forest wild man or churl was fond of playing jokes; Brian Westley, *aka* Merlyn LeRoy, has collaborated with the comedy troupe Firesign Theatre (http://www.visi.com/~westley/). Author Ken
Kesey even regrouped his Merry Pranksters for "The Search for Merlin"
tour in the summer of 1999, during which he scheduled a pageant to "summon the spirit of the ancient wizzard [sic] Merlin" at the Minack Theatre
near Penzance, Cornwall (http://www.hazardous.com/merlin/). One could
also classify here a sidesplitting pseudo–Masonic website that must be a
deliberate spoof (on the Internet, many sites are unintentionally self-paro-
dic, so it can be hard to tell): the Merlin Foundation for Psychic Freedom,
self-proclaimed "Luddites for Jesus" and "Guerilla Warriors dedicated to
the pursuit of Psychic Freedom from the Tyranny of Computers and their
Digital Menace and the Insane Mind-Control Machinations of the C.I.A."
(http://www.merlin.org/).

Then there is Merlin as a half-human sired by a spirit or incubus. To
many New Age philosophers and neopagan cults, Merlin is indeed an
immortal spirit or deity who manifests himself through psychic communication and avatars, both individually and working in consort with some
form of the Great Goddess.[3] An example of many such claims is Robert L.
Thompson's website, where you learn that "Merlin is best described as a
'Demigod' although that term may not be fully accurate[...]. Usually in
spirit form, he has been to many people a mentor[...]. For instance, Merlin was greatly responsible for developing the U.S. Constitution. You never
see this in any history book, but Merlin whispered in the ears of the men
who wrote the Constitution and Bill of Rights" (http://www.ruidomain.com/
amulet/merlin.htm). Myrddin is even accorded full divinity on The Page of
the Archmage, generated from the four primary elements plus a fifth:
"Water and Air and Earth and Fire, and most importantly Light" (http://
homepages.go.com/~archmage15/). The close correspondence of the mage's
wild man affinity for nature and his own semi-divine nature is echoed by
several mystical groups such as the Ionian Druid Brotherhood (http://www.
ioniandruidbrotherhood.homestead.com/) and the Society of Celtic Sha-
mans, whose "Faery Apprenticeship Program" is accessed through Merlin's
Enclosure (http://www.faeryshaman.org/joinencl.htm). Latter-day mystics
like to link him not only to the woods, Wales, Avalon, and the Holy Grail,
but also to the mysteries of ancient Egypt, as in David Austen IV's "The

Order of Merlin" on The Official Temple of Set World Wide Web Site (http://www.exeper.org/pub/tos/orders/MER-ST.htm) and a series of remarkably imaginative postings concerning the "Thoth-Merlin Connection/Orion-gin Grail Genetics" in which the Egyptian god of wisdom is described as "one of the five souls of Merlin" (http://www.danwinter.com/buehler/merlin.html). And the Unidentified Flying Object contingent is represented by Ambassador Merlyn Merlin II, an "Alien Emissary in Human Form" (http://ufomind.com/area51/people/merlin/).

As a demigod, Merlin has even become a convenient way to personify computer servers and networks like Merlin Internet Services in NSW Australia (http://www.mis.net.au/), Merlin Information Services, a public records and access provider in Kalispell, Montana (http://www.merlin-data.com/), and the Mississippi Executive Resource Library and Information Network (MERLIN), an IBM software package developed to give state officials instant access to mostly financial data that will rationalize their cost-benefit analyses (http://www.mmrs.state.ms.us/Merlin-HP.htm). Moreover, Merlin may rule entire artificial worlds. A Swedish graphic artist and "level designer" for three-dimensional computer video games call himself Myrddin (http://www.10.torget.se/myrddin/). And Cyberspace Studios has been developing a three-dimensional computer environment called Merlyn's Castle, "a place so isolated from Man and metropolis that it would serve as the sorceror's [sic] final retreat," where is hidden "the secret of Merlyn's magical powers!" (http://www.cyberspacestudios.com/merlyn.html).

Naturally, the mage's prophetic function is not overlooked in such avatars and environments, as Kevin Myers' crystal ball image from Cyberspace Studios indicates (http://www.cyberspacestudios.com/gallery/merlyn.jpg). The future-oriented technology of computers is particularly appropriate to the role of seer, and his more mystifying prophecies find a contemporary counterpart in computer code—an opaque form of language understood by most of us as requiring adepthood to write or interpret. Computer geeks and hackers often see themselves in this light: for example, the self-proclaimed legendary programmer Randall L. Schwartz, coauthor of the Perl computer code, operates Stonehenge Consulting Services and carries the email moniker of Merlyn (http://www.stonehenge.com/). Merlin's Cavern is the name of an Internet page maintained by Pascal programmer Bill Catambay (http://www.pascal-central.com/merlin.html). In reaction to the surfeit of high technology, the seer's reputation is also embodied not only in the mystical sites previously mentioned, but in a website devoted to the seventeenth-century astrologer William Lilly, who issued a series of pamphlets under Merlin's name (http://www.skyhook.co.

uk/merlin/) and products like *The Merlin Tarot* of Neo-Celtic guru R.J. Stewart and artist Miranda Gray and *The Way of Merlyn: The Male Path in Wicca,* a "cookbook" of spells by Ly Warren Clarke and Kathyrn Matthews (both available from online booksellers). Just above an advertisement for 24-hour online psychic readings, The Enchanted Garden Web page on Merlin neatly sums up the esoteric view of him as "a multi-faceted figure—Druid, shaman, monk, bard, necromancer, magician, astronomer, youth and old sage. He was also known as a seer and a prophet, and his predictions always came true" (http://www.busywitch.com/wizards.htm).

The related function of bard or poet also applies to today's Merlin-sighting. Musicians range from the traditionally oriented Merlin singers of Carmarthen, Wales (http://www.btinternet.com/~dylan.jones/) to New Age meditation-music specialists Merlin's Magic whose works are available from many online music retailers, to the techno artist Merlyn (http://www.air-force-technology.com/projects/merlin/), and even to Merlin, a "brutal death ... grind core" Russian heavy metal rock band (http://www.geocities.com/Sun setStrip/Backstage/4032). The consumer electronics industry has entered the act, too, producing Bobby Palkovic's Merlin loudspeaker systems whose logo used to feature a bearded wizard's head and which still deliver "that old black magic" (http://www.merlinmusic.com/), Dusan Klimo's Merlin preamplifiers designed around the venerable technology of vacuum tubes, which many audiophiles consider to make "magical" sound (http://www.klimo.com/), and Camelot Technology's Merlin Compact Disc transport mechanism (http://www.camelot-tech.com/). An acknowledgment of the mage's mastery of language is *Merlyn's Pen,* a nationally distributed magazine of writing by American teenagers (http://www.merlynspen.com/).

Merlin's supernatural insight and mastery of language also make him the most effective tutor, strategist, and statesman in Arthurian legend. This counseling role is closely connected to the mage's prophetic and bardic skills, and expressed in many New Age resources such as Merlin's Tarot Readings (http://www.members.aol.com/ hta/merlinscards/) and pseudo-psychoanalytical works like *Merlin's Message* (2000) by Marelin the Magician (the daughter of an English professor) which "unlocks the secrets to creation that are being reawakened from our past and remembered from our future" (http://www.wizardwonderland.com/about_book.htm). Merlyn's Grove, the website of a Vancouver-based coven, offers correspondence courses in Wicca (http://www.geocities.com/Athens/Ithaca/8293/), Merlin's Academy of Alchemy provides computerized education in chemistry (http://www.synapses.co.uk/alchemy/), and the Merlin Flight School teaches hang-gliding (http://www.merlinflightschool.com/).

As you might expect, given the traditional past-future range of Merlin's knowledge, the all-knowing mage as master planner and trainer has become ubiquitous in both the publishing and computer industries, such as Belgium's Merlin Global Publishing Service (http://www.merlin.be/expo/) and Merlin's Library of Game Programming (http://geocities.com/Silicon-Valley/Bay/2535/). In addition to the examples mentioned in the categories above, you can observe a mighty proliferation of small business marketing and support companies like Myrddin Technologies, in Wales (http://www.myrddin.co.uk/) and Merlin Software Systems, "home of software magic" (http://www.merlyn.net/). The website of Ontario, Canada's Merlyn Communications states its rationale for adopting the magician quite simply: "Merlyn's magic was the very effective use of advanced knowledge" (http://www.merlyn.on.ca/name.html). This advanced knowledge is put to use in a wide variety of high tech devices. One of the most powerful and complicated of these is the EH 101 Merlin HC Mk 3, a military helicopter jointly developed by Great Britain and Italy for a wide variety of "quick response" support missions, which reflects the mage's medieval role as military strategist and logistical genius—the last resort of statecraft (http://www.airforce-technology.com/projects/merlin/merlin8.html).

Such examples of Merlin's all-encompassing expertise overlap the most prolific category of all: that of wizard, through which the figure of Merlin has historically accreted new knowledge and skills as they are discovered. Feats of magic may be just for show, transforming the mage or shaman himself in what E.M. Butler calls "manifestations of power," or they may operate on others through what she calls "practical functions" because they "ensure the prosperity" of those whom the wizard favors (Butler 5). In the first group are demonstrations of insight and physical power for their own sake, as in oracular divination, levitation and telekinesis, invisibility, and shape-shifting. These are invoked, often simultaneously, by the amazing universality and transportability of Merlin images, the invisibility of such things as the codes residing in your personal DNA, computer or telecommunications devices, and the metamorphosis implicit in designating one's self (or any object, for that matter) as Merlin. It is impossible to give more than a sample of these manifestations of power and practicality, with their correspondences to the legend. For example, the ultra-light, ultra-fast Merlin sailboat built in 1976 by Bill Lee's Wizard Yachts (http://www.north-country.com/sailing/merlin) and Merlin hot air balloons (http://www.merlin-balloons.co.uk/) recall Merlin's magical ability to transport himself, and his spirit-like affinity with the wind. They appear to have been developed as proof of what technology can achieve in concert with nature, and for sheer pleasure. Sometimes manifestations of power take the shape of scientific instruments like the sophisticated star-gazing products of the Merlin Controls Corporation (http://www.merlin.com/) and the Multi-Element Radio Linked Interferometer Network (MERLIN)—six United Kingdom observatories that together form a computer-controlled telescope with an aperture of more than 217 kilometers (http://www.jb.man.ac.uk/merlin). And the Merlin neurofibromatosis 2 tumor suppressor protein, a naturally occurring mutated gene product, signifies the mage's medical expertise by helping to combat some types of tumors which damage the human nervous system (http://www.hum-molgen.de/documents/abstracts/0045.html).

The practical group offers innumerable instances of applied wizardry; they exist less to exemplify our capabilities and extend our knowledge than to benefit our lives by accomplishing some specific and utilitarian task. It includes the obvious references to entertaining magic tricks and illusions, like Merlin's Magic Set from Natural Science Industries (http://www.toys-mart.com/) and role-playing game characters like the Myrddin who is profiled as a "Strong Sorceror all stats maxed out" (http://www.fanware.sim-plenet.com/dcd/sorcerer/myrddin.htm). More significant sorts of illusion-making activity is represented by the online, interactive *Merlin's Quest* game (http://www.shockwave.com/content/merlin/), Merlin Productions multimedia video company in California (http://www.merlinvideo.com/), and Ireland's Merlin Films Group, created by *Excalibur* director John Boorman (http://www.merlinfilms.com). Innumerable Merlin figurines suggest incantatory powers, like the Merlin incense smoker from the Camelot series of Germany's Steinbach Company (http://www.kurtadler.com/steinbach/retired/r830.html). A spell for summoning the mage's "shade" is available on the Internet (http://www.moonmuses.com/charge.html). I can't get him to manifest that way, but perhaps my Welsh pronunciation is imperfect. Merlin can represent very old technology for shaping reality, like the iconic narrative of amulets: "An amulet is a piece of jewelry that has a special meaning to the individual that wears it. Each piece I make holds and idea, expression, or story" (http://www.amuletsbymerlin.com/). He can also ease chores through such ancient means as Merlin's Wand, from the "makers of fine wands since 362 B.C." (http://www.thewandshop.com/), through more recently outdated technology like the Merlin industrial shunting steam engine (http://johnmetcalfe.btinternet.co.uk/museum/museumpage14.htm), or through fully up-to-date technology like Stenor's Merlin vulcanizer for repairing fire hoses (http://www.stenor.article7.co.uk/) and the automatic Merlin toilet flush system (http://www.parish-supply.com/merlin.htm). The Merlin metal detector will help you to unearth buried treasure, and Britain's

Merlin Fireworks provides "the ultimate in firework entertainment" (http://www.merlin-fireworks.co.uk/), exemplifying the mage's mastery over combustibles.

As we've seen, Merlin provides a convenient icon not only for computerized operational systems but for such varied computer software as the Ask Merlin web-search engine (http://askmerlin.8m.com/), Web Merlin Marketing for Internet promotional strategies (http://www.bidness.com/merlin/), Hyland Software's Merlin program, which "does for mathematics what the word processor and spell checker do for writing" (http://www.hyland-software.com/Tour.htm), the cleverly monikered Knozall Systems' NLMerlin 3 automation software for networks (http://www.knozall.com/nlmerlin.html), and the Merlin Feis Economic Information System from Czechoslovakia (http://www.merlin.cz), which underlines the wizard's international cachet. For more everyday needs, there are sites like Merlin Interiors for office furniture (http://www.merlin-interiors.co.uk/), and for special events you could call upon Merlyn Custom Costuming (http://www.merlyncc.com/) and the catering expertise of Merlin's Kitchen (http://www.venturabiz.com/merlins/). If you missed the Merry Pranksters' Search for Merlin tour but want an enchanting travel experience, there are agencies like Merlin's Tours Spiritual Travel in Somerset, England, whose motto is "Get Carried Away—To another Time & another Place" (http://www.merlintours.co.uk). The website features a photo of your genial host, suitably robed. The caption identifies him as "Healer, Teacher, Tourguide, Chieftain of the Loyal Arthurian Warriors."

Finally, we come to the mage's erotic role. The problematical eroticism of the mage's engendering, together with the conflict between his dominant popular image as a wise, benevolent old man and our cultural fixation on youth, complicate his potential uses for the sorcery of sex. This may even be seen in the redressing of doll icons Ken and Barbie as Merlin and Morgan Le Fay, recommended for postpubertal ages fourteen years and up (http://www.anythinggoesinc.net). They make quite a fashion statement, with Ken "wearing a robe of royal blue and matching hat both with golden accents, and has his long golden staff," and a raven-haired Barbie "is wearing a beautiful flowing burgandy [sic] and bronze toned gown and cape and a gloden [sic] chain with charms" (http://www.service.mattel.com).[4] Images of his seduction by Nimue/Vivien may be found at the previously mentioned Camelot Project. Even his sex has become open to question (which it never was in medieval romance); "Merlin's Studio" is the portfolio of St. Louis artist Marilyn D. Brown (http://webusers.anet-stl.com/~mdbrown/). His adoption by males and as the masculine persona of

Wiccan feminist occultism has not prevented female as well as male seers from assuming his name. One of these women states in her website, Myrddin's Cave, "Yeah, I know that all of the legends say I'm a guy[...]. Gimme a break!"—and appends a man-snaring love spell to be spoken "in your most witchy voice" (http://www.lunarace.com/rmyrdd.html).

Merlin is even to be found in the contemporary (under)world of sex. Whatever other erotic roles the mage may play in the private or public domain, he does have some experience in literary tradition as a perceiver of others' lusts and a matchmaker. Appropriate to this voyeurism, and adjunct of his all-seeing abilities, are Steve Merlin's Episodic Sites on the Web, for followers of soap operas and other episodic series (http://home.earthlink.net/~merlin200/), the dirty jokes available on Myrddin's Menagerie of Humor (http://www.myrddinsnet.com/), and the pornographic Merlin Adult Entertainment Gallery (http://freehost.crazyhost.com/yamade/west/hun02.htm) linked to that "one-stop adult entertainment center," Venezuela's Merlin Casino, http://www.merlincasino.com/). X-rated sites are notoriously the most ubiquitous yet ephemeral ones on the Internet: for example, the French sex site Fun Merlin (http://www.merlin.be/1001/), and the kinky Merlin's Dungeon, which advertises "hard to find sex toys at the lowest prices" and a meeting place for "swinging singles, couples, lesbians, gays and bi's" (http://www.mybdsm.com/pages/merlin/), are no longer available for visiting. Darn.

Even this brief survey makes apparent that Merlin's reputation as both a polymath and polymorph is not only undiminished, but further empowered by commodification and contemporary popular culture. In fact, Merlin has always been more a figure of popular culture than of high art, an elusive and adaptive icon that slides easily among contexts. In the parlance of chaos theory, he is less an individual literary character than a complex dynamic "system" with nonlinear, even fractal behavior in that apparently random, unpredictable developments in his use exhibit a "sensitive dependence" on his initial characteristics in the Arthurian legend. We need a set of tools to make sense of this behavior—but how much do we really want them?

This question returns us to the conundrum of forensic identification science and the law with which I began. Even to the experts in any given field, the science of another is often indistinguishable from magic. As Michael Saks tells us (1128),

> This area of law is riddled with contradiction, confusion, and chaos. Here is an area of law typified by uninformed acceptance or rejection

(usually the former) of empirical claims that courts rarely made any effort to try to understand [...] and by abdication of the intellectual and institutional duty to decide, in deference to the 'authority' of the very witness whose offerings were to be evaluated[...]. How can this potentially most lucid of evidence have been treated as if it were mere magic—impenetrable, calling for acts of faith rather than reason[...]?

Like empirical forensic divination, the figure of Merlin reveals the unseen, the hidden way the world works—yet we who live in it and evaluate what he reveals to us do not always want the assumptions and evidence underlying our beliefs to be questioned or made plain. Even professionals often fear logical procedures and distrust their ability to follow forms of expertise other than their own that seem increasingly difficult and arcane. Like the courts, we sense that those challenges and complications would lay upon us a burden greater than we can bear. Whereas "science evolved as a means of taking the mystery out of our understandings of the way the world works" (Saks 1128), the way of Merlin leaves the mystery in, amazing us with the gift of authoritative but privileged insights safely unavailable to the layperson. That is the way we like it best, most of the time.

Merlin is indeed a "quick fix" as Sklar says, and a semiotic shortcut to rationalize any type of specialized knowledge that we do not possess ourselves. Yet he also represents an often unacknowledged yearning for something even more fundamental than that. In acronymic terms, MERLIN could be said to signify the Multiplicity of Esoteric Realities that Link Interests and Needs. The very frequency of his name's acronymic applications suggests that his figure is a chirographic node of infinite possibilities and transformations. From earliest infancy, we humans relate to nothing more instinctively than another human form, and Merlin gives concrete human form to shifting conceptualities, making them instantaneously more accessible. As he absorbs them and gives them shape, we consume him and through him those concepts and their applications. In this way we, too, become masters, or summon the services of those who are. As master mage, master trope, and commodity his image extends a magic wand to the mundane, not just reassuring us with acts of reason, but also renewing our faith in the imagination, the irrational, and most of all the infinite possibilities of creation only waiting to unfold.

Notes

1. These roles or functions, in which he mediates opposing forces or concepts that are fundamental to culture and human psychology, were initially anatomized

in my 1983 Ph.D. dissertation *Merlin: The Figure of the Wizard in English Literature* (U of Michigan).

2. A Welsh edition of this important manuscript is A.O.H. Jarman, *Llyr Du Caerfyrddin* (Cardiff: U of Wales P, 1982), and a recent translation may be found in John K. Bollard, "Myrddin in Early Welsh Tradition," *The Romance of Merlin*, ed. Peter Goodrich (New York: Garland Publishing, 1990): 22–24.

3. For a more complete discussion of these esoteric enthusiasts, see Goodrich, "The New Age Mage: Merlin as Contemporary Occult Icon," *Journal of the Fantastic in the Arts* (1992) 5.1: 42–73.

4. Several medieval French narratives—the Vulgate (1215–35) and Post-Vulgate (1230–40) romances and the *Prophécies de Merlin* (ca. 1270)—and the Middle English alliterative poem *Sir Gawain and the Green Knight* (ca. 1390) allude to their romantic and even sexual involvement, though it is not always clear who seduces whom. For a thorough discussion of their bisexual forces and relationship, see Anne Berthelot, "Merlin and the Ladies of the Lake," *Arthuriana* 10.1 (Spring 2000): 55–81.

Works Cited

Boorman, John, dir. *Excalibur*. Perf. Gabriel Byrne, Helen Mirren, Nicol Williamson. Orion, 1981.

Butler, E.M. *The Myth of the Magus*. Cambridge: Cambridge UP, 1948; rpt. 1979.

"Characters: Name: Myrddin." 9 March 2000. http://www.fanware.Simplenet.com/dcd/sorcerer/myrddin.htm.

CYBERspace Studios. "Merlyn." 5 June 2001. http://www.cyberspacestudios.com/merlyn.html.

Hyland Software. "The Merlyn Tour." 7 April 2000. http://www.hylandsoftware.com/Tour.htm.

Lord Myrddin. Rev. of *Jack Frost*. 5 June 2001. http://www.ohthehumanity.com/ur/158.html.

Maia. "Merlin Masters of the Mound." E-mail to William Buehler. *Thoth-Merlin Connection/Orion-gin Grail Genetics*. 24 November 2000. http://www.danwinter.com/buehler/merlin.html.

Marelin the Magician. "*Merlin's Message*: About the Book." 5 June 2001. http://.www.wizardwonderland.com/about_book.htm.

Mattel, Inc. "Ken Doll and Barbie Doll as Merlin and Morgan Le Fay." 3 June 2001. http://www.service.mattel.com.

Merlin. "Amulets by Merlin." 3 June 2001. http://www.amuletsbymerlin.com/.

"Merlin—Brutal Death Metal Band." 16 April 2000. http://www.geocities.com/SunsetStrip/Backstage/4032.

Merlin Fireworks, Ltd. "Merlin Fireworks." 5 February 2001. http://www.merlin-fireworsk.co.uk.

"The Merlin Foundation for Psychic Freedom." 10 February 2001. http://www.merlin.org/.

"Merlin Music Systems. Inc." 24 November 2000. http:.www.merlinmusic.com/.

"Merlin Species Watcher." 5 February 2000. http://www.hyperscribe.org/merlin/.

Merlin's Tours. "Merlin Tours Spiritual Travel in Britain, Cornwall, Wales, Ireland and Scotland." 17 April, 2000. http://www.merlintours.co.uk.

Merlyn Communications, Inc. "Merlyn: What's in a Name?" 10 March 2001. http:.www.merlyn.on.ca/name.html.
"Merry Pranksters Journey Further to U.K." 17 April 2000. http://www.hazardous.com/merlin/.
Myrddin. "Myrddin's Cave." 5 February 2001. http://www.lunarace.com/rmyrdd.html.
"The Page of the Archmage." 5 April 2000. http://www.homepages.go.com/~archmage15/.
Thompson, Robert L. "Merlin: Who, What and Why?" 6 April 2000. http://www.ruidomain.com/amulet/merlin.htm.
Saks, Michael J. "Merlin and Solomon: Lessons from the Law's Formative Encounters with Forensic Identification Science." Hastings Law Journal 49 (April 1998): 1069–1141.
Sklar, Elizabeth. "Marketing Arthur: The Commodification of Arthurian Legend." Platte Valley Review 21.1 (Winter 1993): 61–82.
Stewart, R.J, and Miranda Gray. The Merlin Tarot. London: Aquarian Press, 1988.
The Wand Shop. "Wizard Wands." 5 February 2001. http://www.thewandshop.com/TraditionalWands.htm.
Warren-Clarke, Ly, and Kathryn Matthews. The Way of Merlyn: The Male Path in Wicca. Garden City Park, NY: Prism Press, 1990.
"Wizards, Medieval Merlin." 2 February 2001. http://www.busywitch.com/wizards.htm.

Arthurian Legend in Tarot

EMILY AUGER

Arthurian legends have always been subject to redefinition and reinterpretation through the mediums of story-telling, literature, and the visual
arts. Most recently, meditation and Tarot decks have been added to the
mediums in which Arthuriana is represented. About a dozen such decks,
all revised in accordance with the characters, events, and ideals of Arthurian
and Celtic legend, were published between 1988 and 1999, three of which
emphasize Arthuriana. Anna-Marie Ferguson's *Legend: The Arthurian Tarot*
(1995), which she both designed and wrote the guidebook for, is the most
devoted to representing the details of Arthurian legend as they are known
through historical literary sources such as Geoffrey of Monmouth's *History
of the Kings of Britain* (c 1136) and Sir Thomas Malory's *Le Morte D'Arthur*
(c 1485). Caitlin and John Matthew's *The Arthurian Tarot* (1990), with artwork by Miranda Gray, is also based on historical literary sources, but places
greater emphasis on the "archetypal" nature of the deck content. R.J. Stewart's *The Merlin Tarot* (1992), also with artwork by Miranda Gray, reinter-
prets the life of Merlin as known from Geoffrey of Monmouth's *Vita Merlini*
(1136–38). In this paper, I will contextualize these three "Arthurian" decks
within the Tarot "genre" and discuss their varied approaches to the representation of Arthuriana.

Tarot originated as a game in Italy in the later fourteenth or early
fifteenth century and has subsequently been reproduced in hundreds of
variations, enjoying a particular florescence of popularity in the final
decades of the twentieth century. Contemporary Tarot decks may be
regarded as a specialized type of "meditation" deck, distinguishable by their
conventionalized number of cards, card imagery, order of cards, and division of the deck into a major and minor "arcana." Like the more variable

233

and less conventionalized meditation deck, the Tarot deck is supposed to have particular spiritual or psychological import for, or effect upon, the user during visualization, meditation, or divinatory exercises. These exercises typically involve laying out the cards in "spreads" or patterns and interpreting them in accordance with the card explanations provided in various pamphlets and guidebooks.

The majority of the hundreds of Tarot decks invented and published in this century for a popular market composed of collectors, game players, and enthusiasts of anything with mystical, occult, or artistic associations are based on the now traditional *Rider-Waite* deck, first published in London in 1909 by William Rider and Son, reissued in 1910, and available through U.S. Games Systems since the early 1970s.[1] Arthur Waite, who researched and directed the creation of this deck, was then the leader of the British Hermetic Order of the Golden Dawn, an order founded in 1888 which became one of the most prestigious and influential organizations involved in the teaching and practice of western esotericism. It attracted the membership of such individuals as W.B. Yeats, Aleister Crowley, and Pamela Smith, the artist who actually made the *Rider-Waite* card paintings. Some of the medieval forms and labels of earlier decks, such as are found on the many variations of the still popular French *Tarot of Marseilles* (1700s), were revised in the *Rider-Waite* deck according to Rosicrucian, Kabbalistic, Christian, and other esoteric interests of the Golden Dawn and Arthur Waite. Like the *Rider-Waite* deck, most new Tarot decks have 78 cards; 22 of which belong to the "major arcana" and 56 to the "minor arcana." The major arcana consists of cards representing various forms of medieval hierarchical authority such as The Hierophant, The Emperor, The Empress, and so forth. The minor arcana has four suits (pentacles, cups, swords, wands) and four court cards (King, Queen, Knight, and Page) and 10 numbered cards in each. In most pre–twentieth-century Tarot decks only the major arcana cards are illustrated; however, the late fifteenth-century Italian *Sola-Busca* deck provided a precedent for the illustration of the minor arcana cards, as well as some of the specific images on those cards, in the *Rider-Waite* and many subsequent decks (Kaplan II: 1–45).

The various instructional pamphlets and guidebooks for the Arthurian Tarot decks, like those accompanying many other late twentieth-century decks, often explain and justify the authors' exegesis of Tarot through references to the "archetypal" nature and content of the cards. Although not invented by Carl Jung, Jung's early twentieth-century work establishing the definition and manifestations of the archetype has been widely influential in popular culture. Jung's work was based on his understanding of the unconscious mind as composed of forgotten events, people and places, of everything perceived without conscious awareness, and of whatever may be about to surface in the conscious mind, as well as what he believed to be unchanging and collectively inherited archetypes which are also represented in dreams and mythology. Jung defined the archetype as an essentially empty form from which the individual must derive his or her own meaning and experience: "the archetype in itself is empty and purely formal." Until such time as its content is determined, or filled out, by the conscious mind, it is simply "a possibility of representation which is given a priori" and it is the empty form of the archetype which is inherited, not the content. Jung believed he had proven that "archetypes are not disseminated only by tradition, language, and migration, but that they can rearise spontaneously, at any time, at any place, and without outside influence" (Jung 79). He also thought that the collective unconscious is the source of the archetypal images in mythology and that mythology provides a kind of vocabulary which allows the world of the unconscious to be transmitted and understood by others on a verbal level.

Waite, like Jung, engaged in extensive research which brought him to a realization of the many parallels in the symbolism of different cultures and religions. In his book on the Grail legend, *The Holy Grail: The Galahad Quest in the Arthurian Literature* (1933), he recognizes the similarity between the "hallows" of that legend: the cup, lance, dish, and sword, and the suits of common playing cards which also serve as the minor arcana symbols of the Tarot. Unfortunately, he did not further develop this realization in his well-known *The Pictorial Key to the Tarot* (1910), in which he provides interpretations of his Tarot deck for its users.

Joseph Campbell, whose mid-to-late twentieth-century work is Jungian based, believed that the primary myth of the contemporary world is that of King Arthur because it provides the first and primary articulation of the fulfillment of one's individuality through "amor," the love of one individual for another, and of the "quest" for individuality itself. Drawing on Jung's work, Campbell wrote "Symbolism of the Marseilles Deck," an essay which provides a concise summary of the origins of the Tarot images. In this essay, he points out that the four suits relate to the four estates or social classes of fourteenth- and fifteenth-century Europe: Swords (nobility), Cups (clergy; the chalice being that of catholic mass), Coins (merchants, townsmen, burghers), and Staves (churls, peasants, and servants). The court cards represent the nobility according to increasing power: Knave, Knight, Queen, and King (Campbell 9–11).

Given Campbell's more or less "Jungian" outlook, it is not surprising to learn that he understood the Tarot deck, as he understood Arthurian legend, in terms of a quest for what Jung called "individuation." In the "major arcana" of the original deck, the emphasis is, Campbell believed, on spiritual life. The Fool is not numbered and functions outside of the sequence to indicate the freedom to roam. The first card is the Magician, who is invariably shown in complete control of the symbols of the four estates. Campbell arranged the next twenty cards "in five ascending rows of four cards each, to suggest the graded stages of an ideal life, lived virtuously according to the knightly codes of the Middle Ages" (11). Column one represents the concerns of youth, column two those of maturity, column three those of age, and column four those of pure spirit. The first row shows the social aspects of human life and the row above it "their informing virtues." The third row shows "a testing and transition to higher, visionary spheres of understanding and fulfillment; and here, too, the imagery falls naturally into a lifetime-sequence of four stages" (15). The fourth row, beginning with the Temperance card, "is the first of the supernatural series," and the last and uppermost row is "where the highest revelations appear of those ultimate spiritual forces of which the figures of the lower ranges have been the graded reflections" (18). The reformulation of Arthurian traditions in Tarot appears to owe a great deal to Campbell, both in terms of philosophical interpretation and marketability. The authors of these decks describe the Tarot as a doorway and the study and use of the Tarot deck as a journey toward greater awareness and understanding of one's self, one's society, and the cosmos.

Historians have considered the possibility that illustrations to Arthurian legends directly influenced the imagery on the earlier Tarot cards. One of the earliest extant Tarot decks is the *Visconti-Sforza* deck, which was painted for Francesco Sforza around 1450 when he became the first Sforza to be Duke of Milan (Dummett 11). It has been speculated that an artist named Boniface Bembo, and more recently that an artist named Francesco Zavattari, produced this Tarot deck and also illustrated a 1446 manuscript written by Zuliano de Anzoli in Italian vernacular about "the chivalrous adventures of Tristan, Lancelot and Perceval of the court of King Arthur." This manuscript includes "289 illustrations of different sizes, drawn in pen over pencil sketches, and probably not intended to be painted since the shading is detailed. The pictures feature court life, nobility, tournaments, hunting scenes, alcoves and gardens, castles and landscapes, battle scenes and boats" (Kaplan II: 123).

Regardless of the name of the artist who completed them, there are some noteworthy similarities between the figures in the *Visconti-Sforza* deck, such as those of the Fool and the Hermit, and those in the scene in which Lancelot mourns for the supposedly dead Tristan in the *Lancelot* manuscript (Dummett 12). It is apparent, however, that Tarot did not originate in Arthurian legend or visa versa, but rather the origins of the Tarot figures and those of Arthurian legend have common roots in medieval society and cultural beliefs. The similarities in the figures of the *Visconti-Sforza* deck and the *Lancelot* manuscript are probably due not only to a common creative hand but also to the widespread artistic practice of using the same figure sketches in the composition of a variety of art works. The Tarot cards, like common playing cards, show us something of the Medieval world with its rulers, popes, knights, and castles. The artistic practice of making multiple uses of single sketches merely served to enhance the visual similarity of social forms that would have been easily recognizable even without this particular convention of artistry. Something of this practice continues in the frequent use of the *Rider-Waite* deck as a kind of template by later Tarot artists. In addition, the study of Tarot cards of almost every period and type heightens the user's awareness of the hierarchical structure of western society; thus it is not surprising that authors who associate Tarot with personal development should affirm the general tendency to grade levels of consciousness and self-awareness in a coinciding manner.

Many twentieth-century Tarot decks reinterpret the original Tarot as it is represented in the *Rider-Waite* deck by expanding its range of association into a modern or other cultural or symbolic context. All twentieth-century Tarot decks may be considered exegetical in that they explain or interpret Tarot by expanding its range of association into a modern or other cultural or symbolic context. There are two basic types of exegesis on Tarot represented in the imagery of the new decks: *Annotative* and *Discursive*, each of which has three subtypes (Auger, 1997). In brief, Annotative decks more or less follow the pattern of the *Rider-Waite* deck and may include references or allusions to some other symbolic system. They usually incorporate relatively minor, simple and consistent variations on, additions to, or substitutions for the familiar Tarot compositions, characters, labels, suits, court cards, etc., with the resulting cards remaining easily recognizable relative to those of the traditional Tarot. Annotative Types One, Two and Three are primarily distinguished by their increasing complexity in the stylistic elaboration of the Tarot images. Discursive decks, on the other hand, show a clear and deliberate integration of one or more symbolic systems. Most cultural Tarot decks are Discursive Type One, whereas multi-cultural Tarot decks are Discursive Type Two. Decks in which the symbolic references are extremely diverse and the deviation from the *Rider-Waite* template such that they approach the more general category of Meditation deck are Discursive Type three. As will be discussed at greater length below, *The Merlin Tarot* is an Annotative Type One deck, while *The Arthurian Tarot* and *Legend: The Arthurian Tarot* are Discursive Type One decks.

Legend: The Arthurian Tarot

Legend: The Arthurian Tarot[2] is a Discursive Type One deck since its references to Arthurian legend are fully apparent in both labels and images, as chart 1 shows. All cards, major and minor arcana, are identified with specific individuals and events derived from Arthurian or Celtic legend. In the handbook accompanying the deck, each card is discussed in relation to "meaning," "reversed" meaning, and "description and symbolism," and a synopsis of the relevant legend is provided.

Ferguson devotes five of the major arcana cards specifically to the life

Chart 1
Major Arcana Tarot Card Labels

	Rider-Waite Tarot	Arthurian Tarot	Legend: Arthurian Tarot
0	The Fool	The Seeker	Percivale
I	The Magician	Merlin	Merlin
II	The High Priestess	The Lady of the Lake	Nimue
III	The Empress	Guinevere	Guenevere
IV	The Emperor	Arthur	Arthur
V	The Hierophant	Taliesin	Taliesin
VI	The Lovers	The White Hart	Gareth & Lyones
VII	The Chariot	Prydwen	Battle of Mount Badon
VIII	Strength	Gawain	Percivale's Vision
IX	The Hermit	The Grail Hermit	Lancelot in Exile
X	Wheel of Fortune	The Round Table	Arthur's Dream
XI	Justice	Sovereignty	Lady of the Lake
XII	The Hanged Man	The Wounded King	Castle Perilous
XIII	Death	The Washer at the Ford	Gwyn ab Nudd & Wild Hunt
XIV	Temperance	The Cauldron	The Cauldron of Annwn
XV	The Devil	The Green Knight	Cernunnos
XVI	The Tower	The Spiral Tower	Vortigern's Fortress
XVII	The Star	The Star	The Firedrake
XVIII	The Moon	The Moon	Morgan le Fay
XIX	The Sun	The Sun	Lleu
XX	Judgment	The Sleeping Lord	Avalon
XXI	The World	The Flowering of Logres	The Giant's Dance

of King Arthur and a sixth to a significant historical event popularly interpreted as one leading to Arthur's eventual ascension to the throne. This later card is Card 16, The Tower, which shows, as does the *Rider-Waite* version of the card, a tower being toppled by lightning; but Ferguson adds the battling red and white dragons which Merlin told Vortigern were the cause of the repeated collapse of his new castle. Merlin also told Vortigern that his throne would be taken, as it was, by Uther Pendragon. Uther, with the assistance of Merlin's magic, not only takes the throne, but begets Arthur on his rival's wife Igraine. The child is raised by Merlin, who is here associated with card 1, the *Rider-Waite* Magician, and shown accompanied by a wolf in his retreat at a sacred spring near his mountain cave. After Arthur grows up, Merlin returns him to his people, whom he serves as a great leader.

Ferguson presents the arrival of Excaliber, with which Arthur worked his bravest deeds, from The Lady of the Lake in card 11, given in the *Rider-Waite* deck as Justice, but often assigned to Strength by other Tarot scholars. She transforms Waite's card 7, The Chariot, into the Battle of Mount Badon, in which Arthur led his troops to defeat the Saxons. Arthur appears as the traditional Emperor in Card 4 enthroned inside his castle, but unlike the *Rider-Waite* Emperor, he is in profile, rather than frontal view and he has a red dragon emblem on his throne.

Card 10, The Wheel of Fortune, is revised to show Arthur's dream on the eve of his final battle with Mordred. The card shows two women about to turn a wheel and thus topple Arthur from his position at its top. Ferguson's design for this wheel suggests the Winchester Table, first mentioned in literary sources around 1450 and claimed by more than a few British Kings as Arthur's original Round Table. This object is an 18-

16 THE TOWER

VORTIGERN'S FORTRESS

"Card 16, The Tower, Vortigern's Fortress." Illustration by Anna-Marie Ferguson. *Legend: The Arthurian Tarot* [deck]. St. Paul, Minnesota: Llewellyn Worldwide, 1995.

Left: "Card 4, The Emperor." Arthur Waite (writer) and Pamela Colman Smith (artist). *Rider-Waite Tarot.* 1910; Rpt. U.S. Games Systems, 1971. *Right:* "Card 4, The Emperor, Arthur." Illustration by Anna-Marie Ferguson. *Legend: The Arthurian Tarot* [deck]. St. Paul, Minnesota: Llewellyn Worldwide, 1995.

foot-diameter oak table top that once had legs and was, according to medievalists Roger Sherman Loomis and Laura Hibbard Loomis, made for Henry VII probably "for one of those festivities, supposedly held in imitation of the high feasts of King Arthur, and called Round Tables, at which knights distinguished themselves both in the *bohort* and at the board." The surface is painted with twenty-four spokes in alternating Tudor colours of green and white, each with the name of one of Arthur's knights, as recorded by Malory. The image of Arthur holding his sword and sitting on a throne appears in the segment that extends upward from the central Tudor rose (Loomis and Loomis 40–41). Ferguson's card 20, the traditional Judgment card, becomes Avalon and on it we see the magical boat carrying Arthur away after his battle with Mordred.

The next most important Arthurian character in Ferguson's major arcana is, not surprisingly, Percivale, to whom she devotes two cards. Percivale, as Ferguson tells us in the guidebook to her deck, was the young man who sought acceptance at Arthur's court and actually witnessed the procession of the grail, but because he suppresses his curiosity in the name of politeness he fails on his first attempt in the grail quest. Ferguson shows Percivale on the Fool card contemplating Camelot where the emblem of Arthur's Round Table of Knights is hanging over the gatehouse. Ferguson transforms card 8, the *Rider-Waite* Strength card, into Percivale's Vision, with images of a young woman riding a lion and an old woman on a serpent. Ferguson explains that this card is taken from Percivale's encounter with a lion and a serpent while on his quest for the grail. He decides to kill the serpent and thus wins the friendship of the lion, but in a dream that night a maiden riding a lion warns him about a battle he must fight the next day and a crone riding a serpent threatens him with a poor future love life because the serpent he killed was hers.

"Card 10, Wheel of Fortune, Arthur's Dream." Illustration by Anna-Marie Ferguson. *Legend: The Arthurian Tarot* [deck]. St. Paul, Minnesota: Llewellyn Worldwide, 1995.

Ferguson's major arcana includes several of the important female characters in Arthurian legend. Guinevere is represented on card 3, the card of the Empress, and Nimue on card 2, that of the High Priestess. Both women are shown enthroned in static frontal poses; but Guinevere is inside a building and Nimue is in a forest, suggesting the worldly and magical realms of their respective power. On card 11, Arthur kneels before The Lady of the Lake, who rises with outstretched arms drawing her swords from the water. She also is in a frontal pose.

On card 18, which corresponds to the *Rider-Waite* Moon card, Morgan Le Fay appears, like Nimue, in the woods, but unlike Nimue she is not enthroned but merely seated in a partial three-quarter position. She raises her arms, as does "The Lady of the Lake, but, unlike The Lady of the Lake, she does not rise directly from the water, she merely rests her feet in a pool reflecting the full moon rising in the night sky. Through her application of conventional artistic indications of power, Ferguson represents Morgan Le Fay as subordinate to both Nimue and The Lady of the Lake.

In all of Ferguson's major arcana representations of women, her interpretations of their respective sources and realms of power is made quite plain: Guinevere rules the secular world, Nimue that of nature, The Lady of the Lake controls and delivers destiny and justice, and Morgan Le Fay is empowered by the unconscious and unknown. By comparison, the representations of men in this deck tend to emphasize action rather than positions of power. Percival stands looking at the castle with his back to the viewer. Arthur is enthroned, but is shown in profile rather than in the more assertive frontal position. Merlin stands accompanied by his animal assistant, but he looks over his shoulder at the viewer as he walks away into the forest. The entire deck, however, shows Ferguson's commitment to demonstrating the most specific and individualized articulation of the Tarot archetypes in Arthurian legend possible.

The Arthurian Tarot

The Arthurian Tarot[3] is also a Discursive Type One deck, but with a slightly greater emphasis on the general, or archetypal, nature of the cards rather than on the specific people and events preferred by Ferguson. Most of the Arthurian major arcana cards identify specific events and people from Arthurian or Celtic legend, whereas all of the Legend cards make such a connection (see chart). This tendency is more pronounced in the minor arcana cards, all of which are fully illustrated in both decks, and is also apparent in the discussion of the cards provided in the deck guidebooks. In the Arthurian handbook each card is treated under the headings "description," "background," "archetypal meaning," and "divinatory meaning." The scholarship in the Matthews' books, like Ferguson's, is above the average for Tarot handbooks, but it is clear that Ferguson is more interested in the legends and their direct translation into the Tarot context, while the Matthews elaborate on the "archetypal" nature of each card. Only the Legend Tarot handbook provides a synopsis of the specific legends relevant to each card.

In the Arthurian deck five major arcana cards are specifically associated with Arthur, but six, including 11 Sovereignty, 14 Cauldron, 16 Tower, 17 Star, 18 Moon, and 19 Sun, are presented more "archetypally," without specific references to Arthurian legend in the card labels, although such interpretations can be filled in by knowledgeable users, and some are suggested in the deck guidebook. For example, the Matthews' card The Tower shows a single spiraling blue cone rising from a blue hilltop being struck by lightning from both sides rather than a specific identification with Vortigern's Fortress, as in Ferguson's card. But the Matthews do include Vortigern's Fortress and the battling dragons in the background of the Magician card, which they, like Ferguson, name after Merlin. The *Rider-Waite* Magician card shows a figure in red and white robes with a uroboros belt, his right arm raised, and the sign of infinity over his head, standing before a table holding the symbols of the four Tarot suits: a sword, a wand, a cup, and a pentacle. The *Arthurian* Merlin sits before a table holding a map of Britain and the four Hallows: sword, spear, grail, and stone chessboard. The dragons who battled beneath Vortigern's fortress, shown to Merlin's right, entwine in a symbolic infinity symbol above his head. The fortress to his left is said by the deck authors to be his otherworldly dwelling.

Like Ferguson, the Matthews identify card 4, the Emperor, with Arthur; but while the *Rider-Waite* Emperor faces the viewer directly and *Ferguson's* Arthur sits in profile, the *Arthurian* King sits in three-quarter view. This positioning suggests that the Matthews understand the King's power as subordinate to that of Merlin. The *Arthurian* card also differs in showing Arthur out of doors with a "draco" standard flying beside his throne, a red dragon emblem on his throne, Excalibur across his knees, a stream at his feet, and a bird nearby.

Where Ferguson identifies the *Rider-Waite* card 7, The Chariot, with Arthur's battle at Mount Badon, the Matthews transform it into Arthur's ship Prydwen tossed about in a storm. Card 10, the traditional Wheel of Fortune, which Ferguson identifies with Arthur's dream of the outcome of his battle with Mordred, is again associated with the round table, but in an abstract design evoking the more idealistic archetypal possibilities of the notions of roundness, ritual, and fellowship. The card shows Stonehenge, which Merlin is said to have transported from Ireland to Salisbury, with a circle of swords inside, a round table above, and above that a circle of stars with a crystal cup, or grail, inside. The grail is an important symbol in the overall conception of this deck. The *Arthurian* Tarot Fool is associated with Percivale in the guidebook, but there is no indication of this on the card itself, apparently because the authors wish to emphasize that every "Seeker," meaning Tarot user, is potentially a grail winner.

Left: "Card 4, Arthur." Caitlin and John Matthews (writers) and Miranda Gray (artist). *The Arthurian Tarot.* Wellingborough, Northamptonshire, England: The Aquarian Press, 1990. *Right:* "Card 10, The Round Table." Caitlin and John Matthews (writers) and Miranda Gray (artist). *The Arthurian Tarot.* Wellingborough, Northamptonshire, England: The Aquarian Press, 1990.

Rather than emphasizing Arthur's dream before his battle with Mordred as Ferguson does, the Matthews show Arthur after that battle as The Wounded King, in a poignant articulation of card 12, The Hanged Man. The *Rider-Waite* version of this card simply shows a figure, clothed in red and blue with a yellow nimbus, hanging with his right foot tied to a tree branch set at right angles to the trunk, along which the figure's body falls. There are no background details whatever. Ferguson adopts the more literal translation of this card as The Castle Perilous, where Gareth and Linet discover the bodies of the forty knights hanging from trees, all of whom had preceded them on a quest to free Lady Lyones from captivity. Like Ferguson, however, the Matthews associate card 20, Judgment, with Arthur's potential return in that they show him not dead but as the invisible Sleeping Lord who may one day awake and lead his people again.

Only two of the major arcana cards of the *Arthurian* Tarot are titled after female characters, and these two are Guinevere and the Lady of the Lake. Guinevere appears on the card of the Empress, but she is not enthroned as a queen as she is in the *Legend* Tarot. She is shown kneeling in three-quarter view with a spindle in a meadow, while a horned bull eyes her from the distance. The Lady of the Lake, on the other hand, appears enthroned as the High Priestess before a lake and beneath a canopy of leafless trees, holding Excaliber in her right hand and a book on her lap.

The Justice card, which becomes The Lady of the Lake in the *Legend* Tarot, also shows a woman in the *Arthurian* deck, but this woman sits in a frontal position in a woods beside a stream, holding what the

"Card 12, The Wounded King." Caitlin and John Matthews (writers) and Miranda Gray (artist). *The Arthurian Tarot.* Wellingborough, Northampton, England: The Aquarian Press, 1990.

deck authors describe as the "four-sided cup of truth," and is identified simply as Sovereignty. The authors say that this woman determines who will receive the gift of royalty, and they consider the various women in Arthurian legend, including Guinevere, Morgan Le Fay, and the Lady of the Lake, to be manifestations of her being. Likewise, the Matthews regard the female Washer at the Ford, shown on their Death card, as both a general figure of death known in many forms in the Celtic tradition and as one of Morgan Le Fay's aspects. The generalized treatment of women in the Arthurian deck is indicative of the authors' greater tendency to emphasize the archetypal rather than the individualized manifestations of Arthurian legend in Tarot.

The Merlin Tarot

The Merlin Tarot is an Annotative Type One deck. Although the author R.J. Stewart has rearranged the numerical order of the major arcana cards according to his own theory regarding the groupings of the card characters, they are recognizably similar to the Rider-Waite cards, with no overt Arthurian references in the labels and few in the images. Stewart's arrangement involves groups of three cards as follows: "The Three Worlds" includes 1, The Moon; 2, The Sun; and 3, The Star. "The Three Wheels" includes 4, Fortune; 5, Justice; and 6, Judgement. "The Three Enlighteners" includes 7, The Fool; 8, The Magician; and 9, The Chariot. "The Three Liberators" includes 10, The Guardian; 11, The Blasted Tower; and 12, Death. "The Three Redeemers" includes 13, The Hanged Man; 14, The Hermit; and 15, The Innocent. "The Three Givers" includes 16, Temperance; 17, The Emperor; and 18, Strength. "The Three Sharers" includes 19, The Empress; 20, The Lovers; and 21, The Priestess. The last card, 22, The Universe, is called the "One Manifest Reality." All of the labels remain similar or identical to those of the Rider-Waite deck except The Devil card, which Stewart labels The Guardian, and The Hierophant card, which he calls The Innocent.

The minor arcana cards of this deck are decorated with stylized motifs representing the suits, which are transformed into fish, beasts, serpents, and birds, and single words suggesting divinatory meanings. Only the Court cards and Aces have full color pictures in the same style as the major arcana cards. The deck guidebook treats each card very briefly, in keyword fashion, under the headings "World," "Wheel," "Beings," "Consciousness," "Partner Trumps," "Spheres and Planets," "Attributes," "Gods and Goddess Forms," "Key Phrases," "Merlin Texts," "Divinatory Meaning," and "Related Card Numbers." The references to Arthurian legend in this handbook are extremely generalized with almost no references to specific events, although specific characters such as Merlin and Arthur, and special objects such as the cauldron or grail, are mentioned. More elaborate discussions of the cards and of Steward's overall conception of the Tarot are available in his other books.

Stewart revised the Tarot so that it would be more demonstrative of what he believes are its original sources, particularly the Vita Merlini; thus the entire major arcana of the *Merlin* Tarot shows varying aspects of Merlin's life or some aspect of the *Vita Merlini*'s teachings about the seasons and cyclic change. For example, The Fool card is not associated with Percival and the grail quest, but with the young Merlin as a prophetic child, and the Hermit is associated with Merlin as a wise man. The Magician card, which is somewhat predictably identified with Merlin in the *Arthurian* and *Legend* decks, is here associated with the poet Taliesin, and the Emperor card is associated in the text with the Celtic King Rhydderch rather than the expected Arthur.

Card 12, the Hanged Man, is revised to show the outcome of one of Merlin's early prophecies, in which he foretold that one who came to him in three different disguises would die three different deaths: by falling from a high rock, in a tree, and by drowning. The apparent absurdity of this possibility discredited him until the young man actually died when thrown from his horse over a cliff into a tree, where he was trapped with his head suspended into a river. The Wheel of Fortune card is a diagram showing Merlin's journey around the Wheel of the seasons and is intended as a key image representing Stewart's understanding of the relationship between the *Vita Merlini* and the Tarot as one based on the cycles of nature and time, features which are not emphasized in the other decks. The overall impression of the deck itself is, however, one emphasizing an archetypal approach even more dramatically than does the Matthews' deck, and in marked contrast to the literary and individualized presentation found in decks such as Ferguson's. This impression is further apparent in the treatment of the female figures in the major arcana, which appear, according to what Stewart finds to be their associations in the various texts on Merlin, as follows: 3, The Star, associated with Ariadne; 5, Justice, a Goddess of the land; 12, Death, as one aspect of Ariadne; 15, Innocent, also Ariadne; 18, Strength, as having little mention in the Merlin texts; 19, Empress, associated with Merlin's wife Guendoloena; and 21, Priestess, as Morgen.

These three decks exemplify the modern tendency to revise the Tarot in an "annotative" or simple "discursive" manner with reference to a particular mythological or cultural tradition. They also demonstrate the varying interest Tarot designers have in emphasizing cultural specificity by providing detailed images referencing that myth or in emphasizing the "archetypal" content of both myth and Tarot by invoking the myth but suppressing its details. These approaches are indicative of the ongoing belief in developing "higher" consciousness through a specific cultural tradition and the coinciding belief that higher consciousness involves surpassing such specificity.

Notes

1. Illustrations in this chapter from the Rider-Waite Tarot Deck, also known as the Rider Tarot and the Waite Tarot, are reproduced by permission of U.S. Games Systems, Inc., Stanford, CT 06902 USA. Copyright © 1971 by U.S. Games Systems, Inc. Further reproduction prohibited. The Rider-Waite Tarot Deck is a registered trademark of U.S. Games Systems, Inc.

2. Artwork for *Legend: The Arthurian Tarot* © 1995 Anna-Marie Ferguson. Used by permission of Llewellyn Worldwide.

Works Cited

Auger, Emily. "Authors of the New Age." Presentation, Popular Culture Assn. Conference. San Antonio, TX, March 1997.

Campbell, Joseph. "Symbolism of the Marseilles Deck." In *Tarot Revelations*. San Anselmo, CA: Vernal Equinox Press, 1987. 9–25.

Dummett, Michael. *The Visconti-Sforza Cards*. New York: George Braziller, Inc., 1986.

Ferguson, Anna-Marie (writer and artist). *Legend: The Arthurian Tarot* [deck] and *A Keeper of Words: The Arthurian Tarot* [book accompanying deck]. St. Paul, Minnesota: Llewellyn Publications, 1995.

Jung, Carl. *The Archetypes and the Collective Unconscious*, 2nd edition. Princeton University Press, 1990.

Kaplan, Stuart. *The Encyclopedia of Tarot*. Stamford, CT: U.S. Games Systems, Vol. I, 1978; Vol. II, 1986; Vol. III, 1990.

Loomis, Roger Sherman, and Laura Hibbard Loomis. *Arthurian Legends in Medieval Art*. 1938; Rpt, New York: The Modern Language Association of America, 1975.

Malory, Sir Thomas. *Le Morte D'Arthur. The Winchester Manuscript*. Ed. and Intro. Helen Cooper. New York: Oxford University Press, 1998.

Matthews, Caitlin, and John Matthews (writers), and Miranda Gray (artist). *The Arthurian Tarot* [deck] and *The Arthurian Tarot: A Hallowquest Handbook* [book accompanying deck]. Wellingborough, Northamptonshire, England: The Aquarian Press, 1990.

_____. *Hallowquest: Tarot Magic and Arthurian Mysteries*. San Francisco: The Aquarian Press, 1990.

Monmouth, Geoffrey of. *The History of the Kings of Britain*. Intro. Lewis Thorpe. Markham, Ontario: Penguin, 1978.

_____. *Life of Merlin. Vita Merlini*. Ed. and Intro. Basil Clarke. Cardiff: University of Wales Press, 1973.

Stewart, R.J. *The Complete Merlin Tarot*. London: Harper Collins Publishers, Ltd. 1992.

_____. *The Mystic Life of Merlin*. London: Routledge and Kegan, Ltd., 1986.

Stewart, R.J. (writer), and Miranda Gray (artist). *The Merlin Tarot* [deck with book]. London: Harper Collins Publishers, Ltd. 1992.

Waite, Arthur Edward, and Pamela Smith. *The Holy Grail: The Galahad Quest in the Arthurian Literature*. New York: University Books, n.d.

_____. *The Pictorial Key to the Tarot*. 1910; Rpt. York Beach, Maine: Samuel Weiser, Inc., 1983.

_____. *The Rider-Waite Tarot Deck*. U.S. Games Systems, Inc., 1971.

The Once and
Future Queen:
Guinevere in a New Age

Jacqueline Jenkins

Let all, then, who have heard of Camelot, let them come. Let them
come from the farthest shores, let them come again, let them hear the
call and answer; for I would discipline and I would nourish and I would
train chelas, and I would bestow the gift of knighthood and the flame
of Mother to ladies of the flame. I would return you, then, to the joust-
ing and to the tournament. I will return you to the holy quest.

And then one day we will have our Table Round, ... There, too, you
will be bidden to sit. And we will have our Council of the Round Table,
and that council will be the forum of lightbearers who are born to take
the light of earth and fashion the new order of the ages.

From "The Call of Camelot," Elizabeth Prophet, 1977[1]

Typically, it is not Guinevere but Arthur who is most commonly associated with the "once and future" legend of Camelot. Indeed, it is the very
"once and future-ness" of the King which fuels the final pages of Malory's
fifteenth-century retelling of the Arthurian legends, firmly establishing an
imaginative precedence returned to again and again over the centuries. In
Malory's account, his companions watch while Arthur, mortally wounded,
is "lad away in a shyp wherein were three quenys," but beyond that, the
narrator more than once asserts, nothing more can be known with certainty
("nothir more of the verray sertaynte of hys dethe harde I never rede").[2]
Even the corpse, assumed to be Arthur's, can not *truly* be identified, for
the hermit who had charge of the grave "knew nat in sertayne that he was

veryly the body of kynge Arthur" (717). In fact, the narrator, anxious to create doubt about Arthur's death emphasizes once more:

> Yet som men say in many partys of Inglonde that kynge Arthure ys nat dede, but had by the wyll of oure Lord Jesu into another place; and men say that he shall com agayne, and he shall wynne the Holy Crosse. Yet I woll nat say that hit shall be so, but rather I wolde sey: here in thys worlde he chaunged hys lyff. And many men say that there ys wrytten upon the tumbe thys:
>
> HIC IACET ARTHURUS, REX QUONDAM REXQUE FUTURUS [717]

The effect of the possibility of Arthur's transfiguration, his un-death, in the murky period preceding Malory's own already nostalgic century continues to be felt even in our own present: from the Camelot of 1960s US political life to the end-of-the-century popular culture representations of nationhood and masculinity, the fantasy of Arthur and his court re-embodied supports countless returns to the ever-returning King. But not so Guinevere—at least not typically. Recent reexaminations, or retellings, of the legends from a specifically female (even feminist) point of view usually center on the other female characters in the legend more suitable to contemporary fascinations with woman-oriented spiritualism (goddess worship and Wicca, for instance) or woman-oriented communities (typified, for example, by the three queens, Morgan le Fay and her sister-in-power Nimue).[3] Rarely have these interests extended to the character of Guinevere. Obviously, the feminist movement in North America played a large role in creating a market for narratives about powerful, independent women, especially when their power could be shown to run counter to the dominant patriarchal religion, and their independence could be imagined as in opposition to political notions of compulsory heterosexuality (for instance, choosing to be either sexually active or celibate, living alone or within a community of women, like Morgan or Viviane in these new tellings). Guinevere, typically depicted as both Christian and unrelentingly heterosexual, positioned between Arthur and Lancelot, dumped unceremoniously in a nunnery at the end of the story, could hardly compare—in the context just described—with the other women in the stories.

Until recently, however. Something has changed in the way popular culture imagines Guinevere; perhaps it is simply that as feminism continues to move through and influence all aspects of popular Western society, it becomes ever more possible to reimagine even the most traditionally antifeminist depictions as strong female characters. That certainly seems to be the driving motivation behind productions like Sharan Newman's

Guinevere novels[4] and the character of Guinevere played by Julia Ormond in Jerry Zucker's *First Knight* (1995). At least on the surface, the recent made-for-TV film "Guinevere," which aired on the Lifetime Network (dir. Jud Taylor, 1994) offers a remarkably feminist Guinevere (the character is based loosely on the novels of Persia Woolley), one who demands to join her husband in "equality, shared prosperity and trust," and is chosen by Merlin to rule with Arthur not for her lands or her beauty, but "for her mind." In this spectacularly bad film, Arthur is the brawn, Guinevere the brain behind the peace they strive for. More troubling, though, is the internalized antifeminism familiar in the postfeminist years at the end of the twentieth Century. Guinevere's true enemy seems to be Morgan, an obvious remnant of a 70s icon: this Morgan, who runs a school for youths dedicated to the goddess, and who teaches girls that they can be everything boys can be, and who throughout the film utters invectives against masculine religion, the male court, the men who oppress women, and the women, like Guinevere, who do not do the goddess's commands (as revealed by the decidedly biased Morgan, of course) is little more than a caricature of the reclaimed Arthurian women who came before.[5]

More significantly, however, the figure of Guinevere has taken on a power now in ways not before imagined: specifically, the character has been modified to share in Arthur's "once and future-ness," and has subsequently been put to use in remarkable contexts. Guinevere has in this century, due in large part to the increasing popularization of theories of reincarnation and regression therapy, been claimed as the past-life embodiment of several prominent women.[6] Two very recent occurrences in particular require consideration here: Laurel Phelan and Elizabeth Clare Prophet.

Laurel Phelan, temporarily famous in North America and England, revealed her secret—that she had lived as Guinevere in the fifth century—by publishing her "autobiography" in 1996. The ambitiously titled *Guinevere: The True Story of One Woman's Quest for Her Past Life Identity and the Healing of Her Eternal Soul* grew out of Phelan's recognition that her recurring nightmares (of wooden forts, daggers, bloodied bodies, and women's voices calling "Gwynnefwar!") stemmed from past life trauma which could only be cured through regression and self-healing. Initially incredulous that the "egotistical, angry, and completely self-absorbed" Gwynnefwar of her dreams might be that same Guinevere of Arthurian legend who, she had assumed, "lived in a castle where the men wore armor while the women wore beautiful clothes and jewelry," she eventually started to explore the possibility of her past-life experiences.[7] Phelan admits to not liking her Guinevere-self, choosing to distance herself from the early experiences—

until, that is, 1991 when film producer Terence Hayes convinced her that the time was right for a screenplay of the "real" Guinevere's lifestory (Phelan 7).[8] Six hours and several tapes later, Phelan states, the true story of the previously misrepresented Guinevere and Arthur was hers. She writes:

> I am going to relate events exactly as I experienced them in the regressions. All of the information in this book has been received solely through my past life regressions. I decided before writing this story not to read any books or information on Guinevere and Arthur, as I did not want it to influence my own experience in any way.
>
> I still refuse to read any other material, as I feel it is not the truth but rather passed-on information that has become distorted and greatly embellished over the centuries [8].

Guinevere is a remarkably bad piece of writing, called by one reader a "298-page work of adolescent female fantasy."[9] In answer to an interviewer's question about influences on her writing, Phelan unwittingly explains her utter lack of prose skill by asserting that "Nothing actually influenced my writing.... I nearly failed English composition in school ... so I severely doubted my capability in writing a book or a screenplay. Now I have done both and have also written two more books, which I have yet to publish."[10] The most problematic element in Phelan's narrative style is the improbable omniscience of the first-person narrator: her Guinevere, at times, has insight and knowledge about the other characters' thoughts and responses which seem hard to reconcile with a traditional first-person narrative voice. In other words, how can she *be* Guinevere, remember her earlier life, and also know what the other characters are thinking? Phelan, as if anticipating such criticism, notes that

> To uncover Guinevere, I had to regress fully into her body and mind. By doing this, I was able to feel her emotions and think her thoughts as well as see great details around me. The extra gift of past life regression is that you are not limited to staying in the body and can lift from the body to follow those around you for a small distance [xvii].

Doesn't an omniscient point-of-view argue *against* the first-person subjectivity that past-life regression insists on? Phelan continues, explaining that "you can only follow those in your life whom you have a spiritual connection with, and even then only for a short distance. It was by doing this that I was able to gain information about the other people in Guinevere's life and their attitudes about her" (xvii–xviii).

Phelan's version of Guinevere is unusual in several respects: for instance, she associates most closely with her father, who trains her in the typically masculine accomplishments of riding, fighting, and battle strategies;[11] she uses Arthur, at least initially, as a means for power and shared rule; scorns Arthur's religion in favour of the old (Celtic) ways; is sexually repressed, using her body only to control men and never for her own pleasure; and completely dismisses the beauty-obsessed women around her in favour of her own company (except for Merewyn, her wise-woman) or the company of the soldiers. So it is, therefore, more striking that the resolution reached by the character at the end of the story is so very traditional: Arthur dies in battle and Guinevere attempts to rally his remaining army to defend his fort. Betrayed by Gulwain (he was always jealous of her battle-skill), and left to age idly in a nunnery, she determines at 36 to return to Salisbury, the fort Arthur's death lost. Alone on the ground among the ruins, Guinevere finally faces the love for Arthur she had suppressed.

> "I love you, Arthur ... we are one soul ... one spirit ... please ... come for me...," I plead, looking at the sky. "I just want to be with you again."
> "I'm ready...," I whisper as a sense of calm comes over me. I know he is waiting for me. I feel him here. I feel his love. I am ready now. I want to go home.
> "I am ready to be with you, Arthur, and to be your wife" [291–92].

Phelan's Guinevere comes to the realization at the end of her life that her true place is with Arthur, and that their souls are linked across time. She follows this revelation with her suicide—a warrior's death by her own dagger—and concludes with the vision of her "spirit [floating] higher and higher" (292).

For Phelan, the regression into Guinevere's life effected a profound change in her own current personality, especially in her understanding of her history of troubled relationships: finally acknowledging her love for Arthur, she claims, allowed her to finally know love in this incarnation (and she states in her conclusion that she met her husband just months after visiting Salisbury in this life [298]). She also claims that she, previously Guinevere, reembodied and now aware of her past life, has realized that her "path in this life is to teach people, especially women, about inner power and also about reincarnation" (297).

It is hard, however, not to be suspicious of Phelan's willingness to embrace her past identity and learn from it—at the very least, her motivation to write the initial screenplay seems clear (the film rights). Similarly, in the internet interview, she admitted that her plan to write the book developed after an agent contacted her with a publisher already interested (she notes that, thus encouraged by a book contract, she "began writing and finished the book within one month"). Less obvious, though, is the power over others Phelan has realized with her public identity as a "once and current" Guinevere. Already successful before her "autobiography," Phelan states that she has regressed over 2000 people, taught regression therapy and techniques, and intends to publish two more books, one on Atlantis and one on reincarnation and regression, "Healing Through Time."[12]

There are some unsettling similarities between Phelan and that other late 20th Century North American "Guinevere." The figurehead and spiritual authority for the Church Universal and Triumphant since her husband Mark's death in 1973, Elizabeth Clare Prophet ("Mother" to the community) has laid claim to a plethora of past-life identities, including but not limited to Queen Nefertiti, the Queen of Sheba, Bathsheba, Marie Antoinette, Sts. Clare and Catherine of Siena, as well as the early Christian martyr Hypatia, and Helen of Troy; perhaps it comes as little surprise that she also claims to have lived as Guinevere.[13] Reincarnation provides a central tenet for the quite substantial Western US cult—Prophet's husband and first messenger, Mark Prophet shared an equally impressive, if impossible, list of identities, including Lot, Abraham, Aesop, Origen, Mark the Apostle, Sir Lancelot, and Henry Wadsworth Longfellow.[14] Prophet established the community of Camelot in 1977 (in Southern California), and then in 1986 moved the church headquarters to the Royal Teton Ranch with its Glastonbury chapel (in land-rich Montana). The cult has had its share of run-ins with local authorities, over matters as various as environmental concerns, bomb shelters, and arms-stockpiling.[15] (One ex-member writes that, besides the personal weapons staff members regularly kept, the community's security force owned AR-16 rifles and ammunition, constructed a massive bomb-shelter and purchased two armored personnel carrieres: he writes, "Armageddon was coming and we needed to be able to repel the hungry hordes who would want our stored food and our spiritual light."[16])

Prophet's Camelot, with "Guinevere" as its ruler and no corresponding "Arthur," stood for more than the simple place-name of Summit University and the complex of apartments in California. It stood for the essence of the community:

> The dream of Camelot sustained us. We were re-creating the Mystery School that the Brotherhood had tried to establish in England centuries ago. No matter what the hardships, we would not fail. In our hearts, we carried a sense of destiny and passion for our holy cause [Paolini 36].

In an early publication, Prophet wrote that her desire to "bring again Camelot to America... to establish a community of men and women whose quest is the Holy Grail" had finally become "a reality." In conversation with me, an ex-cult member, who with her husband and family had been in CUT for many years, acknowledged that rather than a dream or vision shared by the believers, the members actually believe they are Camelot *reembodied*: each of the members of the community is imagined as one of the Knights, one of the Ladies, of the Round Table.[17]

This Camelot, based on earlier Theosophical movements including the I AM movement founded by Guy and Edna Ballard and popular in the 1930s,[18] seems a bizarre mix of spiritualism and militant control with a grab-bag of inexplicable regulations and admonitions. These ideas include (but are not limited to) the belief that sugar is a tool of the "dark force"; chocolate and alcohol destroy brain cells; hair holds "records" of past deeds, thoughts and emotions, so short hair is safest, but bangs must be clipped so the third eye is not covered; china dolls contain entities that use their glass eyes; pigs were created out of human genes (by the Fallen Ones) so eating pork is really cannibalism; red, orange, black, brown, chartreuse, fuchsia, silver metal, and opals all focus "dark energies"; garlic scares away angels. Other of the beliefs are much more frighteningly racist and bigoted.[19] All along, however, and again recently, the community has denied its status as a cult, and lobbied for a much more mainstream acceptance by its neighbours and the larger religious world.[20]

What interests me here, in the context of this essay, however, is the role Elizabeth Clare Prophet's self-identification as Guinevere played in the development and maintenance of this community. What kind of Guinevere was she?[21] (And, in a related question, how absurd is it, that we can refer to *two* self-identified re-embodiments of this same queen?) Contemporary accounts (admittedly, only from ex-cult members) reveal that Prophet used her status for personal gain. Kenneth Paolini asks, "Why did I live the way I did, in a dirty garage with nine other men and no privacy, while Mother [Prophet] lived in luxury? I rationalized, and Mother told us, that she had better karma than the staff. She was the messenger. She deserved it; we didn't" (Paolini 65). Another ex-member recalls witnessing Prophet gain directly (in financial terms) from her status as queen of Camelot: a new member arrived and gave to Prophet "a large, extremely rare and precious gem, a Russian Alexandrite, which he had obtained during one of his trips to Europe. He was duly rewarded by being knighted."[22] Members who flocked to the community in Montana were required to pay large sums towards the upkeep of the property, and though the land itself was purchased by the members' donations, when in 1999, two-thirds of the land was sold (for $13,500,000) none of the money was returned (Paolini 299–300).

Both Phelan and Prophet, it seems, have benefited in financial and personal terms from their identification as Guinevere reembodied. Both, similarly, have claimed to only want to work good with the knowledge they have of their past lives, and both have been actively involved in the disseminating of knowledge about past lives to their followers (at 2000 patients, Phelan has had considerably fewer "followers" than Prophet, but still the group is quite remarkable). Phelan offers past identities to her patients like talismans, or cures, for financial gain; Prophet offered identities to her cult members as rewards and inducements for particular behaviours. In other words, both cash in on the power attached to them through their self-identification, and through the dream of Camelot running through late 20th-century America. In Phelan's words, the power of the "once and future-ness" of the queen is clear: "As people read what I had written, they were mesmerized and excited about Guinevere's story. Suddenly I realized that this was only the beginning of something greater" (294).

But perhaps the most disturbing conclusion, considering these women and their separate self-constructions as Guinevere, and the effect of their identities on the communities around them, is how indicative their representations are of our current political climate—how easy, that is, their versions of Guinevere fit into the contemporary anti-feminisms which pervade North America at the turn of the century. On the surface, each *appears* driven by recognizably feminist objectives—Phelan makes her 'historical' Guinevere aggressively non-traditional, equal in every way to a man (in fact, she makes her more misogynist than the men in the story around her). Her Guinevere remains, however, completely unfulfilled as a person until she submits to her role as Arthur's wife—and this is the message she teaches to her followers.[23] As Phelan claims:

> I wrote this story in order to help people understand that emotions should not be repressed and that women especially should feel free to be themselves and to be emotionally expressive. This is a story of a woman's quest to understand her femininity and inner power in a man's world. The message is particularly important for women today [Amazon.com].

Prophet, equally, as a strong, non-traditional, female figure—a social and spiritual leader—appears to embody several basic feminist principles, and certainly her supporters were encouraged to portray her in that way. But the reality of the Church Universal and Triumphant is far different, as reported by the disillusioned who have left her fellowship. Prophet's "Camelot" is based on gender stereotyping, sexual repression and simultaneous exploitation, and social and economic inequality and the resulting class-privilege. In the excerpt from "The Call of Camelot" which began this essay, Prophet names her dream the new "holy quest," and describes her community as "the new order of the ages." For both Prophet and Phelan, the "new order" they imagine their separate Guineveres revealing to their followers is far from new—the problems and the inequalities remain the same, just the figure, this time of Guinevere, is new again.

Notes

1. *Pearls* vol. 20 no. 25. Cited in Kenneth and Talita Paolini, *400 Years of Imaginary Friends: A Journey into the World of Adepts, Masters, Ascended Masters, and Their Messengers,* (Livingston, Montana: Paolini International, LLC, 2000) 259.

2. Eugene Vinaver, ed., *Malory: Works* (London: Oxford University Press, 1971) 717. Further citations are from this edition, noted by page number.

3. Consider, for instance, Marion Zimmer Bradley's very popular trilogy which started with the highly influential *Mists of Avalon* (1984), followed by *The Forest House* (1995) and *Lady of Avalon* (1998); in these books, Guinevere takes a literary backseat to the much more powerful figures of Morgan, Viviane, and even Igraine.

4. *Guinevere* (1996), *The Chessboard Queen* (1997), and *Guinevere Evermore* (1998).

5. The anti-feminism of the late 20th-century depictions of Arthur's court is a topic for another paper, and not one I can really explore here. On a related topic, though, see J. Jenkins, "First Knights and Common Men: Masculinity in American Arthurian Film," *King Arthur on Film: New Essays on Arthurian Cinema,* ed. Kevin J. Harty (McFarland Publishers, 1999) 81–95; and "The Aging of the King: Arthur and America in *First Knight,*" *King Arthur's Modern Return,* ed. D. Mancoff (New York and London: Garland Publishing, 1998) 199–212.

6. Specifically, Dionne Fortune, Elizabeth Clare Prophet, and Laurel Phelan. Because this paper focuses on end-of-the-century representations, I will not be discussing Dione Fortune at this time.

7. Laurel Phelan, *Guinevere* (New York: Pocket Books, 1996) 5–7.

8. In the introduction to the book, as well as in an interview with Amazon (available on Amazon.com), Phelan states that a film is in the works, promising (in the interview) a release date of Christmas 1999. To my knowledge, nothing has appeared, nor can any search for information provide a clue as to the actual status of the film project.

9. C. Austin, Review, taken from http://www.celtic-connection.com/lit/guin ever.html

10. Interview available on Amazon.com.

11. This is an interesting point given Phelan's own obsession with her father, with whom she claims to have shared an intense father-daughter bond in other lives (3).

12. Information provided in the Amazon.com interview. As of yet, these books haven't appeared.

13. John Joseph Pietrangelo, *Lambs to Slaughter: My Fourteen Years with Elizabeth Clare Prophet and Church Universal and Triumphant.* Excerpt posted at http://factsource.com/cut/lambs.html

14. Pietrangelo, http://factsource.com/cut/lambs.html

15. From Sandi Dolbee and Philip J. Lavelle, "New Age Church Wants to go Mainstream," *Union Tribune,* 12 November 1997. Posted at http://www.rickross.com/reference/cut18.html.

16. Kenneth and Talita Paolini, *400 Years of Imaginary Friends,* 63.

17. Phone conversation, December 2000.

18. I will not attempt to explain the complex and, it seems from this remove, constantly changing religious beliefs of the Church Universal and Triumphant.

19. Paolini 239.

20. Cf. the defence of CUT offered by the contributors to *Church Universal and Triumphant : in scholarly perspective* , eds. James R. Lewis and J. Gordon Melton (Stanford, Calif.: Center for Academic Publication, 1994).

21. I use "was" instead of "is" because in March 1999, Elizabeth Clare Prophet was determined by the court to be mentally and financially incompetent, and the control of the CUT community passed through various hands. She has, it is now apparent, suffered for many years with Alzheimer's and epilepsy (Paolini 300).

22. Pietrangelo, http://factsource.com/cut/lambs.html

23. Guinevere's happy submission, and the message Phelan offers through it, is completely consistent with some currently popular relationship theories. See, for instance, Laura Doyle's very recent *The Surrendered Wife : A Practical Guide to Finding Intimacy, Passion, and Peace with Your Man* (Fireside, 2001).

About the Contributors

Emily Auger teaches art history at Malaspina University-College in British Columbia, and has recently published in *Dialogue and Universalism*, the *Inuit Art Quarterly*, and the *Journal of Aesthetic Education*. She specializes in native and modern art history and aesthetics, and in popular culture.

Peter Corless is the founder of Green Knight Publishing, a company dedicated to producing popular entertainment based on the legends of King Arthur. Their product lines include "King Arthur Pendragon" role-playing adventure game products and "Pendragon Fiction."

John J. Doherty, the literature librarian at Northern Arizona University, holds an MA in Arthurian Studies from the University of Wales. He edits the web site "Arthurian Resources on the Internet" and has published articles on librarianship, popular culture, and contemporary Arthuriana.

Peter H. Goodrich has pursued Merlin in his many guises for a quarter century. He is a professor of English at Northern Michigan University, editor of *The Romance of Merlin* (Garland, 1991), and *Merlin: A Casebook* (forthcoming), and author of articles on Merlin, Arthurian legend, and on fantasy literature. His research interests also include pan–Celticism and medievalism in English fiction, and Irish literature.

Kristina Hildebrand holds a doctorate in English from Uppsala University, Sweden, and teaches at the University of Gavle. Her dissertation is entitled *"The Female Reader at the Round Table": Religion and Gender in Three Contemporary Arthurian Texts*.

Donald L. Hoffman is past president of the North American Branch of the International Arthurian Society. He has published widely on a variety of Arthurian texts and themes from the use of Merlin in Joachimite and Ghibelline prophecies in thirteenth-century Sicily to contemporary film versions of *Perceval* and the revisions of the Quest in African American (Ishmael Reed) and Caribbean literature (Sam Selvon).

Zia Isola is a Ph.D. candidate in the Department of English at the University of California, Santa Barbara. Her current research focuses on eucharistic poetics in the chivalric romances and pageant plays of Late Medieval England.

Jacqueline Jenkins teaches medieval literature, popular culture, film and gender studies at the University of Calgary (Alberta, Canada). Recent publications include a series of articles on masculinity in American Arthurian film and women's history on film, as well as articles on lay-women readers and lay-devotion in late medieval England. She is currently working on a book-length study of gendered participation in celebrations of the feast day of St. Katherine in medieval Bath.

Norris J. Lacy is Edwin Erle Sparks Professor of French at Pennsylvania State University. He is past president of the International Arthurian Society and is author or editor of some twenty-five books, the majority of them on Arthurian subjects.

Alan Lupack, current president of the North American Branch of the International Arthurian Society and creator of The Camelot Project at the University of Rochester, is co-author of *King Arthur in America*, author of numerous articles on medieval and modern Arthurian Literature, and editor of *Sir Tristrem* and *Lancelot of the Laik* as well as of several volumes of modern Arthurian literature.

Barbara Tepa Lupack, formerly Fulbright Professor of American Literature in Poland and in France and Academic Dean at SUNY, has written extensively on American literature, film, and culture. Her most recent books include *Insanity as Redemption in Contemporary American Fiction: Inmates Running the Asylum*, named an "Outstanding Scholarly Book" by *Choice* in 1996 and a finalist for MLA's Lowell Award; *Critical Essays on Jerzy Kosinski; Take Two: Adapting the Contemporary American Novel to Film; Vision/Re-Vision: Adapting Contemporary American Fiction to Film; Nineteenth-Century*

Women at the Movies: Adapting Classic Fiction by Women to Film; and, with Alan Lupack, *King Arthur in America* and *Arthurian Literature by Women*. Forthcoming is *Micheaux to Morrison: Adapting Black Literature to Film*.

Dan Nastali is an independent researcher and bibliographer. A former member of the editorial staff and columnist of *Avalon to Camelot*, he is now working with Phillip C. Boardman on *The Arthurian Annals*, a chronological bibliography of all Arthurian works in English since 1400.

James Noble is a professor of English at the University of New Brunswick at Saint John. He has published on a variety of Arthurian texts, medieval and modern, and is currently working on a book provisionally entitled "*Am I Not an Erthely Woman*": *Images of Women in Arthurian Texts*.

Bert Olton is a freelance writer and photographer, a member of the International Arthurian Society/North American Branch and author of *Arthurian Legends on Film and Television* (McFarland, 2000).

Brian R. Price is founder and editor of *Chronique: The Journal of Chivalry and the Knighthood*, Chivalry & Tournaments Resource Library. A frequent contributor of articles concerning modern and medieval chivalry, fighting techniques, and medieval tournament formats, he has written two books, *The Book of the Tournament* (Chivalry Bookshelf, 1995) and *Techniques of Medieval Armour Reproduction* (Paladin Press, 2000). He serves on the board for the International Mediaeval Alliance, is an advisor for Swordplay Symposium International, and is the founder of the Scola Saint George (which teaches medieval fighting techniques) and the Company of Saint George (which sponsors medieval-style tournaments).

Jerome V. Reel, Jr., grew up in New Orleans. His education includes two degrees from Southern Mississippi, where he studied with Charles Moorman. His Ph.D. is from Emory University. A professor of medieval British history, he serves as senior vice provost and dean of undergraduate studies at Clemson University.

Michael N. Salda is associate professor of medieval literature and chair of the Department of English at the University of Southern Mississippi. He is the author of *La Bibliothèque de François I au Château de Blois* (1994) and many studies of medieval and modern literature that have appeared in *Chaucer Review*, *Modern Philology*, *Arthuriana*, and elsewhere, and recently co-edited The *Malory Debate: Essays on the Texts of Le Morte Darthur* (2000). He is currently editing John Donne's *Metempsychosis* for the Donne Variorum Project and writing about women's literacy in thirteenth-century France.

Elizabeth S. Sklar is on the English faculty at Wayne State University, where she teaches Old and Middle English language and literature. She has published on a variety of Arthurian subjects, medieval and modern, and sits on the Executive Advisory Council of the International Arthurian Society North American Branch. She is also area chair for Arthurian Legend in the Popular Culture Association, and has recently completed a term as member of the PCA executive council.

Jason Tondro is a freelance author and graduate student at the University of California, Riverside. His body of work includes academic papers, novels, screenplays, and role playing games. He has presented several papers on Arthurian comics at the Popular Association annual conference.

Index